Praise for *The New Gold Standard*

"No doubt this behind-the-scenes look at The Ritz-Carlton will inspire
you to work toward your own Gold Standard. Michelli's five principles
will help you break through the sea of sameness plaguing most
industries and equip you with what it takes to blow the doors off
business-as-usual—a must for thriving in this economy!"

—DR. JACKIE FREIBERG,
author of BOOM! 7 Choices for Blowing the Doors Off Business-as-Usual,
NUTS! and GUTS!

"As a business leader, there are two vital aspects required of the books I
choose to read—insight and information. Dr. Michelli's new book
provides an exponential measure of both—information on HOW The
Ritz-Carlton creates such a compelling experience for their customers,
and insight on WHY it is so critical to do so! He has provided a
compelling book about The Ritz-Carlton experience."

—SCOTT MCKAIN,
vice chairman of Obsidian Enterprises and author of What Customers Really Want

"The Ritz-Carlton is truly the New Gold Standard, and Dr. Joseph
Michelli has done a great job of capturing the five key leadership
principles which Simon Cooper and the Ritz-Carlton team have
been applying relentlessly, energetically, and with localized creativity.
Anyone interested in excellence in the 21st century would profit
from reading The New Gold Standard."

—NEWT GINGRICH,
founder of Center for Health Transformation and former speaker of the house

"Simon [Cooper] and [The Ritz-Carlton] leadership team understand
the role human nature plays in driving business outcomes better than
any organization in the world."

—JIM CLIFTON,
chairman and CEO of The Gallup Organization, Washington, D.C.

"The Ritz-Carlton Hotel Company has a global reputation for service excellence because their leadership team insists on it— every day, in every business decision and every communication inside and outside the company. We've learned a lot at Bank of America from The Ritz-Carlton team in our own work to build a customer-centered culture. All those lessons are captured here in this book. The New Gold Standard *offers a view inside one of the most successful customer service cultures in the world, and is a valuable addition to business literature on the subject."*

—KENNETH D. LEWIS,
chairman and CEO of Bank of America

"The Ritz-Carlton Hotel Company wrote the book on legendary customer service. And in The New Gold Standard, *Joseph Michelli writes the book on The Ritz-Carlton. Required reading for anyone who wants to learn how to create passionate employees and raving fan customers!"*

—KEN BLANCHARD,
coauthor of The One Minute Manager® and The One Minute Entrepreneur™

"The Ritz-Carlton is the best hotel chain in the world because of the unique experience they offer. This book shows you how to install the same customer-focused attitude toward service that makes a world leader."

—BRIAN TRACY,
author of The Way to Wealth

THE NEW GOLD STANDARD

5 Leadership Principles for Creating
a Legendary Customer Experience Courtesy of
The Ritz-Carlton Hotel Company

JOSEPH A. MICHELLI

New York   Chicago   San Francisco   Lisbon   London
Madrid   Mexico City   Milan   New Delhi   San Juan
Seoul   Singapore   Sydney   Toronto

The **McGraw·Hill** *Companies*

1 2 3 4 5 6 7 8 9 0 DOC/DOC 0 9 8

ISBN 978-0-07-154833-5
MHID   0-07-154833-5

Interior design by Mauna Eichner and Lee Fukui

McGraw-Hill books are available at special quantity discounts to use as
premiums and sales promotions, or for use in corporate training programs. To contact a representative please visit the Contact Us pages at
www.mhprofessional.com.

Except as otherwise described in the background section of Chapter 1,
Ritz-Carlton in the text refers to The Ritz-Carlton Hotel Company, L.L.C.

This book was prepared with the assistance of The Ritz-Carlton Hotel
Company, L.L.C.

This book is printed on acid-free paper.

To Nora Michelli, whose graceful and heroic response to breast cancer inspires and strengthens faith.

Contents

Contents

Foreword

When I took on the job of president of The Ritz-Carlton Hotel Company, my first priority was to visit with, and personally talk to, many of the Ladies and Gentlemen who work at our hotels and resorts around the world. While seeking to encourage hotel managers to be highly effective leaders, the people I most wanted to reach out to—and thank—were those who wash the laundry, deliver the room service, maintain the boilers, and clean the guest rooms. Without them, we would not be the award-winning hotel company that we are—a company that is consistently recognized for service excellence and unmatched quality and that is now the subject of Dr. Joseph A. Michelli's book *The New Gold Standard*. While our guests may never see many of these people who work behind the scenes in what we call "the heart of the house," connecting with them is truly the best part of my job.

Talking and listening to our Ladies and Gentlemen only increases my appreciation for the passion they possess to serve our guests and one another. To me, they and their families are the true unsung heroes of the hospitality industry. This is not a job for people who expect a nine-to-five schedule. When a person chooses to work in a hotel, weekends and holidays off are rare, and while others may stay home during inclement weather, our Ladies and Gentlemen manage to come to work so that they can continue to serve our guests.

When Hurricane Katrina devastated New Orleans, trapping over 1,000 guests in our Canal Street hotel for five days, the conditions were difficult and challenging. Most of our Ladies and Gentlemen chose to stay at the hotel throughout the storm because they understood how much our guests would need them until they could be evacuated to safety. The same was true of Hurricane Wilma, which scored a direct hit on Cancún, Mexico. Our staff stayed with the guests until we could arrange for them to leave the storm-ravaged area. And in Jamaica, every time a tropical storm disrupts people's lives in Montego Bay, the Ladies and Gentlemen at our Rose Hall resort not only stay on site but they bring children from a local orphanage to the hotel to shelter them from the storm. I have scores of letters from grateful guests marveling at the genuine care and comfort they received from hotel staff even as power went out and conditions were frightening during these times of crisis.

I have learned to say a sincere thank-you in many languages as I visit hotels from Dubai to Dallas and from Shanghai to Santiago. In return, I have been touched by stories about how working at Ritz-Carlton has changed and improved the opportunities for our staff members' families to enjoy a better life and a brighter future. What greater satisfaction can I get than knowing we have provided a chance for them to both support their families and take pride in the work they do each and every day?

It was on one of my early visits that I overheard the comment, "The answer is yes; . . . now, what is the question?" I had often been told that offering lateral service was a basic principle at our hotels, but that exchange said it all to me about what makes our Ladies and Gentlemen so exemplary. There is never any such thing as saying "That's not my job." If it means helping out one another or doing something to provide service to the guests, the word *no* is simply not in the vocabulary of those who choose to work at Ritz-Carlton.

This spirit of wanting to serve not only our guests but to lend an extra hand to fellow staffers is how the Ritz-Carlton culture of caring permeates all of our lives. It explains why so many of our employees have stayed with the company for years and why so many of them who began their careers in the 1980s are now key executives at our hotels around the globe. And it explains why their children are now joining our global family. They view providing outstanding service as a career to be proud of, and they strive for the continuous improvement we encourage in all of our Ladies and Gentlemen.

As I look back on the heritage and tradition of César Ritz of more than a century ago, I realize there have been many defining moments that have shaped our brand from a few renowned hotels to a collection of lodging and lifestyle products recognized as the world's best. The Swiss shepherd's son was famous for many thoughts on what makes for a great guest experience, but he did not just talk. He personally intervened to make sure the needs of the guests were surpassed each and every day. Fast-forward many years after César Ritz, and the Ritz-Carlton brand took on a new life and reputation for excellence inspired by the company's first president, Horst Schulze, and the original group of visionary hoteliers who planned for the next generation of this venerable brand. I want to extend my personal gratitude to Horst for the rich legacy I inherited as the result of his innate understanding of the true meaning of luxury.

Perhaps the most significant moment came in the late 1990s when Marriott International purchased The Ritz-Carlton Hotel Company, and it became their premier luxury brand. While some skeptics believed this purchase would diminish Ritz-Carlton's cachet and reputation, the exact opposite happened. Chairman Bill Marriott has continually kept his original commitment to offer the resources necessary for the Ritz-Carlton to expand internationally, while at the same time allowing the brand the independence to grow its legacy to the point where it is today: the world's most recognized and acclaimed luxury name. I am extremely grateful to Bill Marriott and his leadership team for allowing Ritz-Carlton to experience dramatic growth, achieve outstanding financial results, and still retain its unique identity.

As you read *The New Gold Standard*, I hope you will gain a clear understanding of what a privilege it is for our Ladies and Gentlemen at The Ritz-Carlton Hotel Company to provide service as memorable as the beauty of our surroundings. They truly understand the amenity that matters most to our guests is not a fancy chocolate on the pillow but a dedication to service that never wavers. Each of them appreciates that if the service he or she offers does not surpass the expectations of our guests, then all the splendor of the hotel becomes far less meaningful.

As for me, I want to thank Marcelle, my unsung hero and wife of 35 years, for taking this incredible journey with me. When people ask me about my job, I like to tell them, "I have absolutely the best job in the world and am living the dream of my vocation being my vacation.'"

SIMON F. COOPER
President, The Ritz-Carlton Hotel Company

Acknowledgments

I have always found this section of a book the hardest to write. Not because I lack gratitude, but because I can never find the words to fully express my appreciation. Worse yet, invariably there will be countless numbers of people who contributed to this book who will go unrecognized. So let me start broadly by thanking all the Ladies and Gentlemen of the Ritz-Carlton for delivering an experience that cannot be rivaled and for creating a company that had a book living inside of it, waiting for someone to come along and share their story.

One of the greatest moments in the journey to *The New Gold Standard* occurred when a vivacious Vivian Deuschl, vice president of public relations, at the Ritz-Carlton, returned a call I had placed to her. Vivian opened up the possibility of my writing this book, and she has been opening doors for me ever since. There was never a moment that Vivian faltered as my guide into all facets of the Ritz-Carlton. If Vivian did not know an answer, which rarely happened, she knew someone who did, made the referral, and vigilantly followed up. I only regret that all who read this book will not have the opportunity to meet Vivian. She is everything that is right about the business world today: she is bright, passionate about her work, fun to be around, and candid.

Acknowledgments

So many senior leaders, owners, and staff took valuable time to answer my seemingly never-ending questions, and although I can't thank each of them personally here, I have included a list of their names in the Sources. That said, there are a few people who made heroic efforts on behalf of this book. At the corporate level, John Timmerman, Diana Oreck, Katerina Panayiotou, and Sue Stephenson should have regretted giving me their contact information, but instead they consistently responded with the utmost grace and class. Whether it was Sue inviting me to a Corporate Social Responsibility event, Diana allowing me access to a Ritz-Carlton week-long Leadership Center training session, Katerina finding yet another specialized Wow story, or John adding invaluable insights into quality improvement processes and offering his encouragement, each of these individuals will forever have my gratitude. With that gratitude, I must also acknowledge all those, like Paul Westbrook, Brian Gullbrants, and Bruce Himelstein, who encouraged and facilitated the time offered to me by their staff. Additionally, I am grateful for the personal investment in this project offered by Kathy Smith and Bhavana Boggs. Both of these leaders "moved heaven and earth" to lift the quality and accuracy of *The New Gold Standard*.

There have been two presidents of The Ritz-Carlton Hotel Company—Horst Schulze and Simon Cooper. While both men have incredibly demanding schedules, both generously gave me large blocks of their time. Horst is inspiration incarnate and a champion of service professionalism at a level I've never encountered before. Simon is a brilliant hotelier who has taken this iconic brand to new levels. His wit and wisdom serve him well—to not only make Ritz-Carlton successful today but also to position the company for a future generation of leaders.

Ed Mady and Ed Staros were sage counsel and gifted historians of their company. Ed Staros was the strong voice that reminded me to balance history with progress. Ed Mady's graciousness in San Francisco provided a most memorable experi-

Acknowledgments

ence, complete with freshly baked cakes decorated with my *The Starbucks Experience* and *When Fish Fly* book covers. So many other general managers rolled out the red carpet—or in the case of Ritz-Carlton, actually the blue carpet—for me. They include Allan Federer, Timur Senturk, Mark Sherwin, Kate Monahan, and Mark Ferland. A word of warning to the rest of the Ritz-Carlton general managers: be expecting me. Your colleagues and staff have created a truly engaged guest for life.

From a personal perspective, I need to thank my research team of Tiffany Tolmen, Kelly Merkel, Betsie Cole, Jill Merkel, Angell Arnot, Jennie Przbysz, Adam Merkel, and most important, Lisa Christine. Lisa was dogged in her efforts to track down stories, secure releases, and take ownership of this project. I suspect without her, there would have been a lot of blank pages in the book. Martha Jewett, my literary agent, not only possesses the quintessential technical skills (editing, positioning concept, sales, negotiation) expected of an agent but she also has all the interpersonal (nurturing, confronting, scheduling) skills that make a project like this take flight. Also thanks to Lloyd Rich, who always finds a way to get the deal done in a way that respects all concerned.

Donya Dickerson and Herb Schaffner at McGraw-Hill gently kept challenging me to take this book to another level and bring the information "back to the reader." Most important, no matter how unrealistic the timeline seemed, Donya calmly reassured me and swiftly responded to the editorial needs of this project. As always, Heidi Newman, copyeditor extraordinaire, made my writing sound better than it actually is. Anthony Landi, Mark Miller, Tim Meraz, and Terry Moore each shared their creative talents, while so many others helped *The New Gold Standard* show up on bookstore shelves.

Now to the biggest thank-you of all: Anyone who has been involved with this project must know Lynn Stenftenagel. Lynn, my senior vice president of operations, did everything but compose the words to this book. I will never understand how such a valued colleague could happen into my life, but in the revised words of the Gallup CE[11] question, "I don't want to imagine my business or any book project without Lynn."

This book could not have been written without the support and love of my friends and family. They know who they are, so I will forgo printing their names here. That is, with the exception of my immediate family. Fiona and Andrew, I am so grateful that God has given me the privilege to be your father. Nora, this book has been dedicated to you and your ability to use cancer as an opportunity to share the calm and peacefulness of your faith with all of us—with those who know you well and even with absolute strangers. Mom (Marie Michelli), thanks for being the living proof that standards matter.

I am never sure how many people, other than me, actually read acknowledgments to the end. We are probably the same people who are still sitting in the theater long after the credits have finished at the end of the movie. But for those of you who have stayed with me through this personal process, thank you for sharing your precious time with me and with *The New Gold Standard.*

THE NEW
GOLD STANDARD

The Ritz-Carlton Experience

The customer is never wrong!

CÉSAR RITZ

 Over a hundred years ago, a herdsman's son from a family of 13 began working in the hotel industry. While learning his craft, he was fired from various jobs and was even told by one employer that "in the hotel business you need an aptitude, a flair—you haven't a trace of it." From those humble beginnings, the "hotelier of kings and king of hoteliers" César Ritz completely revolutionized the luxury hotel industry. Starting with The Ritz Paris and The Carlton in London, César Ritz emphasized the guest experience, created opulent physical environments, innovated hotel design, produced settings of uncompromising quality, and established what have become the gold standard for luxury and the epitome of service excellence. His marks of distinction have found their way into our lexicon with descriptors like "ritzy" and "putting on the ritz."

Yet, against this backdrop, and with significant attention from the *Harvard Business Review, BusinessWeek,* the *Wall Street Journal,* and other business periodicals, there has never been a book written about The Ritz-Carlton Hotel Company. When I approached its current leadership about providing business readers with a behind-the-scenes look into the company inspired by César Ritz, I was met with the welcoming spirit that has made Ritz-Carlton an icon. I have spent the better part of a year examining the greatness and occasional missteps of the leadership of The Ritz-Carlton Hotel Company. I've met with employees (whom they call "the Ladies and Gentlemen of The Ritz-Carlton") at all levels of the company, and I have traveled to their U.S. properties as well as to dynamic international locations such as Singapore and Dubai.

The New Gold Standard reveals the specific leadership behaviors that produce Ritz-Carlton's exemplary corporate culture, exceptional staff empowerment, and extraordinary commitment to its customers. But before we dive into the leadership mechanics of Ritz-Carlton and what you can learn from its unwavering commitment to excellence, let's look at some of the company's prominent achievements.

⊰ Every Legend Starts ⊱ with a Great Story

While the Ritz-Carlton history has roots in European aristocracy (see the sidebar "The Life of César Ritz" for detailed information on the background of the company), much of the story begins after César Ritz's death in 1918 when his wife Marie permitted use of the Ritz name on acceptable properties in Europe and the United States. Developer Albert Keller later created the Ritz-Carlton Investing Company and franchised the Ritz-Carlton name for hotels he constructed in the United States. In 1927, Keller opened The Ritz-Carlton, Boston, and he later built hotels in New York City, Atlantic City, Boca Raton, Philadelphia, and Pittsburgh.

In many ways, The Ritz-Carlton, Boston, represented the best of the Ritz-Carlton brand in the United States through its attention to detail, practical innovation, and creation of an unrivaled customer experience. Built in response to the mayor of

The Life of César Ritz

César Ritz was born in 1850 in the Swiss village of Niderwald. At age 12 he was sent away by his parents to learn mathematics and French—which he did with limited success. Lacking a clear direction for his life, his peasant farmer father paid 300 francs to an acquaintance in a nearby town to train César to become an apprentice winemaker.

Initially struggling in the hotel industry, César Ritz developed his hotelier skills by working at premier hotels in France, England, and Switzerland, but he aspired to own his own property. Having worked at a poorly run hotel fraught with double-bookings and luggage-handling problems, Ritz stated, "I did what I could to pacify the clients, but ultimately I learned the essential attribute of business: diplomacy."

After a decade of managing the summer season at the luxurious Grand Hotel National in Lucerne, Switzerland, César Ritz became the general manager of the Grand Hotel in Monte Carlo, where he met the master chef Auguste Escoffier.

Together Escoffier and Ritz opened a restaurant in Baden-Baden, which led César Ritz to be selected to manage the newly opened Savoy in London. Customers at the Savoy urged Ritz to open a hotel in Paris. With help from Alexandre-Louis Marnier-Lapostolle (who was indebted to César Ritz for suggesting the name Grand Marnier for the liqueur that Marnier-Lapostolle had invented), Ritz purchased a mansion in Paris and spent two years preparing it to be his 210-room hotel. The Ritz Paris hotel opened in 1898.

By the time of The Ritz Paris opening, César Ritz had a controlling interest in nine other restaurants and hotels including the Carlton in London.

In June 1902, César Ritz suffered an emotional collapse. Although he was involved in planning the London Ritz, which

> opened in 1905, he was not able to return to his business. His eventual successor was his son Charles.
>
> Even though César Ritz's tenure at the helm of his own hotels was relatively short, he is credited with influencing luxury hotel design and service standards that persist to this day.

Boston's call for a world-class hotel, The Ritz-Carlton, Boston, leveraged the reputation of the Ritz properties in Europe and delivered a regal hotel to an emerging high society in Boston, opening with a room rate of $15. Through the years, The Ritz-Carlton, Boston, defined the American luxury hotel experience by providing uniformly clad waitstaff, private baths in all guest rooms, and small lobbies for a personal guest greeting place.

Ritz-Carlton sales revenues have tripled in the past several years, from $1.2 billion in 1998 to nearly $3.0 billion in 2007. Additionally, the company continues to accelerate its global growth plan and focuses on a strategy that includes the reinvestment of more than $1 billion in upgrades and renovations. Despite these financial accomplishments, the Ritz-Carlton brand has not always maintained a steady level of fiscal success.

Following the New York Stock Market crash in 1929, American and European hotels carrying the Ritz-Carlton name faced financial collapse and closure. In fact, with the exception of The Ritz-Carlton, Boston, all Ritz-Carlton hotels in the United States were closed. The market's difficulties derailed the well-crafted strategy that had brought Ritz-Carlton the loyalty of the world's wealthiest and most influential clientele. As the company's traditional customer base experienced a great loss of wealth, the leadership at the hotels had difficulty filling the sumptuous dining halls and elegantly appointed suites. Even hotels that survived through much of the crisis were facing challenges to operate, much less maintain, the standards of luxury that guests had come to expect from Ritz-Carlton.

During these difficult times, Keller went to great lengths to keep the Boston hotel open. In one instance, he tried to mask the low occupancy at his hotel by turning on lights in unoccupied rooms prior to a visit from his wealthy father. Keller hoped that the deception would enable him to convince his father to loan him the money he needed to keep the hotel operational.

The economic challenges of the Ritz-Carlton brand and other hotels in the luxury category continued throughout World War II, as occupancy rates remained low in the face of global uncertainty. In fact, during the war, a number of these hotels' large meeting spaces in Europe and the United States were taken over for military planning and staging.

Post–World War II and the Rise of the Ritz-Carlton Business Traveler

While much of the early success of the Ritz-Carlton brand was linked to the leisure and social lives of the world's most affluent individuals, the post–World War II economy saw the emergence of international business travel. In fact, during a portion of the time that César Ritz's son Charles served as chairman of the board of the Ritz-Carlton Management Company, 70 percent of registered guests at the London hotel his father created were Americans staying on corporate accounts.

With international business expansion, Charles Ritz engaged another round of brand extensions through controlled leasing agreements with properties in locations such as Lisbon, Madrid, and Rome. As evidence of the Ritz family's commitment to excellence, the Ritz-Carlton Management Company sued the Rome hotel owner for failing to live up to exacting company standards. It is even reported that during the week Charles Ritz died in 1976, he was still actively identifying quality improvement needs to the staff at The Ritz, Paris. Passing from the perfectionism of César Ritz, through the dogged efforts of his son Charles, and into the passion for excellence of modern-day leadership, their legacy has continued to inspire the delivery of the highest levels of luxury to customers.

From Atlanta to Marriott

The history of The Ritz-Carlton Hotel Company, as it is now known, follows its leadership from Atlanta, Georgia, to Chevy Chase, Maryland. In 1983, the Atlanta-based real estate developer William B. Johnson, known for his construction of Waffle Houses and Holiday Inns, was working with a group of veteran hoteliers in the development of a network of luxury properties to be called the Monarch Hotels. One of these founders, Ed Staros, notes that the Monarch Hotel Group bought the rights to use the Ritz-Carlton name in the United States and also purchased The Ritz-Carlton, Boston, for an estimated $70 million. According to Ed, "Given the small amount of marketing dollars we had available, our leadership team realized that it would take a long time for us to develop a reputation for luxury excellence, but if we could work within the context of an established and respected brand, we could expedite the timeline."

Johnson soon placed the corporate leadership responsibility in the hands of the inspirational and dynamic president Horst Schulze, whose charismatic leadership style helped The Ritz-Carlton Hotel Company grow from four U.S.-based hotels in 1983 to 40 properties around the world in 2000. However, in spite of Horst's steadfast leadership, an economic downturn from the 1980s cut deeply into the hotel industry with magnified effects on the Ritz-Carlton, given its aggressive expansion (eight new hotels in 1990 alone). At one point, Horst acknowledged that the company was in default on a loan for $70 million and that it would need to restructure other debts.

After a series of similar financial challenges and crises, Marriott International purchased a 49 percent stake in Ritz-Carlton in 1996. Today The Ritz-Carlton Hotel Company is a wholly owned subsidiary of Marriott International, and the parent company has given the brand access to vast economic and support resources. Yet despite this change in ownership—as well as the relocation of the corporate offices to Chevy Chase, Maryland—Ritz-Carlton's leadership and management culture has remained strikingly autonomous and independent.

Even with its early history of financial difficulties, The Ritz-Carlton Hotel Company has grown as of January 2008 to manage 69 hotels worldwide. Approximately half of the Ritz-Carlton properties are in the United States, and the other half are in business and resort locations such as China, Egypt, Indonesia, Russia, and South Korea. By the year 2011, Ritz-Carlton is poised to have 100 properties worldwide. The company is also experiencing additional growth in new product lines including its Residences, Clubs, and other fractional ownership properties, and it is also widening its global footprint in emerging markets such as India.

Names and Faces May Change, but Quality Endures

Facing struggles, stumbles, and transitions, Ritz-Carlton's leadership has been steadfast in its commitment to service and quality. Even during some of the financial challenges of the business's life cycle, Ritz-Carlton continued to be recognized across multiple industries for its consistent excellence. While many leaders would have taken a defensive position during economic threats—allowing cost containment to cut deeply into the level of products and services delivered—the leadership at Ritz-Carlton set out to benchmark its practices against the most quality-driven companies. They did this by measuring and improving quality through the Malcolm Baldrige National Quality Award evaluation process, a program that allows businesses to benchmark against other recognized "world-class" leaders.

Ed Staros, one of the original group in Atlanta that developed The Ritz-Carlton Hotel Company, notes, "I remember in the late eighties there were economic concerns, and other hotels were doing things like cutting out mouthwash and changing the flower arrangements. Horst Schulze was adamant always that we weren't going to cut costs and maintain any lasting success. Just because the economy was bad, it didn't mean the guest didn't want mouthwash. Rather than cutting back, we wanted to become more efficient and even improve our product through total quality management. If you're a widget factory and there are 20 steps to make a widget, and you study your business with a systematic approach to improving quality and you figure out you can make an improved widget in 18 steps, all the better. Essentially, that was our quest, to not cut corners but to become more focused and to get the maximum quality through efficient processes."

Through a willingness to be routinely audited by representatives from world-class businesses and a commitment to continually rework quality processes, Ritz-Carlton became the first company to twice win the prestigious Malcolm Baldrige National Quality Award in the service category. Harry S. Hertz, director of the Baldrige National Quality Program, National Institute of Standards and Technology, puts the significance of the award in context by explaining: "Over the 19-year history of the Baldrige program, there have only been four two-time recipients of the Award. In every case [these companies] created sustainable organizations. Using the Baldrige Criteria, they significantly expanded their businesses from their first Award to the second, they were able to be more prudent in their customer or market selections, and they strengthened their strategic position for the future. They are true role models for the United States."

Additionally, leadership has positioned the company to receive every major award bestowed in the hospitality industry and by the leading consumer organizations. Ritz-Carlton properties have consistently been honored with Mobil Five-Star Awards, AAA Five Diamond Awards, and various forms of Best Hotels of the World status from *Condé Nast Traveler* and *Travel &*

Leisure magazines. Travel industry expert Jim Strong, CTC, ACC, president of Strong Travel Services Inc. in Dallas, Texas, and author of the book *Craving for Travel*, says, "I think the significance of Ritz-Carlton in the overall market is that they have raised the bar. They continually put the competition on notice that they are out there and are going to perform the best they can, above and beyond what the competition is doing and that they are always going to be a leader in the industry."

On top of winning accolades for individual hotel properties, Ritz-Carlton has received countless forms of recognition, including being ranked highest in guest satisfaction for luxury hotels in the J.D. Power and Associates 2007 North America Hotel Guest Satisfaction Study; a *Consumer Reports* designation as the No. 1 luxury hotel company in all areas, including service, upkeep, problem resolution, and value; and the distinction of being the Luxury Institute's Most Prestigious Luxury Brand. Routinely, Ritz-Carlton ranks as one of *Fortune* magazine's Best Service Providers. It has also been ranked highest in customer satisfaction among luxury hotels in the Market Metrix Hospitality Index (MMHI), and, in publications like *Travel Weekly*, it repeatedly wins reader polls as best luxury or upscale hotel. Culinary awards such as the Mobil Five-Star and AAA Five Diamond recognitions for such restaurants as The Dining Room at The Ritz-Carlton, Buckhead, in Atlanta are far too numerous to mention.

What started as a simple commitment to share best practices in developing a "world-class" quality organization (a condition of winning the Malcolm Baldrige Award) has turned into a full-service leadership and corporate training arm of Ritz-Carlton, named the Leadership Center. Approximately 50,000 individuals representing companies throughout the world have participated in leadership training since the inception of the program in 1999. Among notable competition, the Ritz-Carlton Leadership Center was named the best global training company in the February 2007 issue of *Training Magazine*.

Despite the accolades, leadership at Ritz-Carlton faces the same stumbling blocks you encounter daily in your business. As evidenced by examples throughout this book, the greatness of leaders is maximally tested in times when their company is most vulnerable.

·◦〗 What's in It for You 〖◦·

From the modest background yet powerful vision of César Ritz, through economic highs and lows, leadership at Ritz-Carlton has successfully maintained a disciplined focus on respect for staff, quality improvement, brand repositioning, corporate adaptivity, cultural consistency, and unparalleled service excellence. As such, Ritz-Carlton has earned international respect as a benchmark for corporate culture, development of ultimate customer experiences, consistent product excellence, and an empowered workforce.

So what does Ritz-Carlton have to teach you? While many readers will be drawn to this book through their loyal connection to the brand, others may have an awareness of the company only through something Ritz-Carlton leaders refer to as its "mystique." Some may be looking for a book simply to help them position their goods or services in relation to the explosive market of luxury products or the luxury lifestyle. Yet others may have an interest in using the book to help their staff better understand "the art of anticipation" built into the Ritz-Carlton service approach.

The New Gold Standard represents a follow-up to my book *The Starbucks Experience: 5 Principles for Turning Ordinary into Extraordinary.* Where Starbucks leadership took an ordinary product like coffee and significantly added value by staging it in an environment of affordable luxury, Ritz-Carlton has elevated the luxury experience to a true art form.

The New Gold Standard is primarily intended to help managers, owners, and leaders understand the driving principles, processes, and practices that have generated unusual staff loyalty, world-class customer engagement, and significant brand equity for Ritz-Carlton. However, it also provides perspective on those same principles from the viewpoint of frontline workers (both customer facing and non–customer facing), customers, and other stakeholders. Whether you wish to attract, hire, and retain the "right" employees, are interested in producing transformational customer experiences, or are looking for ways to maintain the relevance of your product and service offerings, *The New Gold Standard* shares the wisdom of Ritz-Carlton leadership. Ritz-Carlton leaders are responsible for stewarding an icon in the luxury market, through a constant quest for excellence, to continue its success in a changing global economy and with changing customer needs. Even in areas of international growth, succession planning, finding the best location for your business, or determining meaningful quality enhancements, Ritz-Carlton offers a rich tapestry of leadership successes and breakdowns that can help you shorten your path to greater success.

Of course, one challenge in writing a book about a company like Ritz-Carlton is to avoid the perception that leadership at Ritz-Carlton can do no wrong. I have heard striking examples to the contrary, including one hotel that was designed and constructed such that the swimming pool is located in the shade for much of the day. How does such a thoughtful planning and design team produce that outcome?

Then there are the little things, like the process of introducing a new Ritz-Carlton writing pen. Brian Gullbrants, vice president of operations, explains, "Our company had been using the same pen for a long time, and frankly it did not look as good as some of the ones used by competitors. So senior leadership decided to produce a new pen, and we had people try out a number of them. It didn't take long for us to choose one. We had the pens produced and sent them off to a new hotel opening. While I was at a meeting at that property, the tip of my new pen fell off, and I looked at Ron, our vice president of purchasing, and said, 'We have a problem.' As you might guess, mine was not the only pen with the problem. Now that we had already introduced the new pen, we had to go back to the supplier and the manufacturer; we needed to rethink everything. So we recalled the pens. It was a mess. We made a mistake. We didn't do enough homework. We thought we had; we had all the right intentions of rolling out a new and improved product, but it wasn't tested or piloted and that was one of those quick decisions where we cut a corner on quality by thinking it was just a pen."

Leaders at all levels can learn not just from the company's best practices but from the mistakes and recoveries that have ultimately strengthened the success principles that Ritz-Carlton follows.

The Making of a Legend

So what is at the essence of this iconic company? What is the Ritz-Carlton experience? While the answer reflects some variability based on the source you ask, there is a striking consistency of opinion.

For Robert E. Watson, managing director of Protravel International, Inc., the experience is characterized as "service value. What sets Ritz-Carlton apart is its service. Ritz-Carlton partners with us in the travel industry to get the most for our client. If we don't perform the service together, if we don't get that little extra something for the client, if we don't come up with that nugget, that little bit of something new, what would a client need us for? People are spending a lot of money today. And they don't mind spending it, provided they get value for their dollar. In today's world, however, value doesn't always match price. The experience at Ritz-Carlton is true value for us as travel partners and for our clients."

For community agency partner Colleen T. Brinkmann, chief marketing officer of the North Texas Food Bank, the Ritz-Carlton experience "is like a Lexus—they set the standard in their industry. But through their volunteer efforts with us, I would say the experience is very personal, very real, and colorful, but above all else respectful and gracious, even to the point of their Ladies and Gentlemen thanking us for providing them with the opportunity to participate in volunteer service."

Ritz-Carlton General Manager Tony Mira describes the Ritz-Carlton experience as "a Wow experience, like no other. It's one that you walk in and you know, whether you're a guest or an employee, that you are going to be treated like nowhere else in our industry. It's taking the genuine care and comfort of our guests to the highest level. That, to me, is the Ritz-Carlton experience."

Maybe the best way to demonstrate the unique value proposition achieved by Ritz-Carlton is to offer an example from a family that happened upon empowered Ritz-Carlton staff. Natalie Salazar, age 12, was a champion figure skater who began noticing pain in her legs while preparing for a regional competition as a step toward the Olympics. While originally thinking it was joint inflammation, the condition was ultimately diagnosed as a type of cancer known as *osteosarcoma*. Her chemotherapy treatments were unsuccessful, and at age 13, Natalie was told she was going to die. Her biggest regret was that she would never be able to go to her high school prom. Natalie's eighth grade teacher, Mrs. Lewis, attended the same church as Laura Gutierrez, area director of human resources at The Ritz-Carlton, Dearborn, where Natalie's story was told. Laura and the Ladies and Gentlemen at Ritz-Carlton rushed into action. Laura described Natalie's special night:

"We hosted Natalie's Prom in our ballroom, and it was attended by 18 classmates and 7 of her championship ice skating team members. Our audiovisual technician was the disk jockey, our IT technician was the photographer, our banquet director provided security, and everyone pitched in to make this an extra special event. Our convention service team put pin lights up and laid a dance floor, and our business center put together a PowerPoint presentation with pictures of the kids from kindergarten to eighth grade, complete with some drawings Natalie's former kindergarten teacher had provided."

Laura goes on to add that "our team hosted a grand prom complete with Prince Charming who guided her down the red carpet to Natalie's favorite song 'Sweet Escapes.' There, she danced the night away with Prince Charming. What an emotional night for everyone. The best part was she smiled the entire night, she danced every dance, she ate all of her favorite foods (salami, cheese and vegetables, and lots of ice cream). She limboed, hula hooped, chicken danced, Hustled, and led the train around the room. Parents joined the celebration at 10:30 p.m. just before Prince Charming turned into a frog. The kids had so much fun they didn't want the night to end. After a tearful good-bye, Princess Natalie was led to her waiting chariot for much-needed rest at home. She commented as she drove away, 'Tomorrow I'm off to the hospital for some tests. I can't wait to tell them all about this.' And she did just that."

According to Laura, "The buzz around the hotel was incredible. We were making a difference in a child's life, and in the lives of her parents and teachers who for one full year had worried about Natalie, supported her, and cared for her." Natalie's father said, "We are immigrants to this country and have no family here. When Natalie became ill, we didn't know what we would do. But Natalie's teachers and friends and the staff at Ritz-Carlton became our family." Natalie's mother added, "I've been blessed with many friends, but I didn't know there were such wonderful and caring hearts as we've found with everyone at Ritz-Carlton."

Natalie was only 13 when she lost her battle on Thursday, September 20, 2007. The seamstress at Ritz-Carlton who had made Natalie's prom dress also made the dress in which she was buried. In Natalie's honor, Laura and the staff of Ritz-Carlton commemorated what would have been Natalie's fourteenth birthday on October 22, 2007, complete with the cake Natalie had described to Laura the evening before her death. Laura continues to keep in touch with Natalie's parents. While many other companies support members of their community, the Ritz-Carlton culture of service routinely delivers caring such as that provided to Natalie's family.

From my perspective, the Ritz-Carlton experience is reflected in leadership committed to unrelenting quality, respect for all that the company's staff encounters, and, oddly enough, also a great spirit of candor. As a result of this candor, I have identified five core business principles that I will use to structure your behind-the-scenes examination of the company. This inside look reveals the ideals that fuel the consistency and greatness of this legendary organization. Each principle presented in the following chapters not only offers insight into service, hospitality, and creating a luxury lifestyle experience but also provides opportunities to increase excellence in *all* aspects of business and personal life. Through dedicated adherence to these principles, everyone can elevate his or her business to the Ritz-Carlton gold standard. *The New Gold Standard* reflects both intuitive and counterintuitive aspects of leadership, which may be fairly easy to comprehend, yet far more difficult to master. It is my belief that constant and steadfast focus on these Ritz-Carlton principles will result in your developing and maintaining the new gold standard for your industry.

Specifically, the principles are these:

1. Define and Refine

2. Empower through Trust

3. It's Not about You

4. Deliver Wow!

5. Leave a Lasting Footprint

These guideposts, while inspired by the journey and leadership of Ritz-Carlton, have application across all industries and geographical boundaries. They reflect an opportunity for you to strengthen and touch the lives of your staff, teams, customers, shareholders, community, and the bottom line. In the words of César Ritz, "People like to be served, but invisibly." Whether it's through washing bed linens or creating an international strategic plan, these principles can connect you to your invisible power as you fully serve staff and customers alike. Let's explore each of these principles derived from the Ritz-Carlton *New Gold Standard* to maximize your ability to drive relevance, quality, and, of course, world-class service, throughout your business and personal life.

PRINCIPLE

1

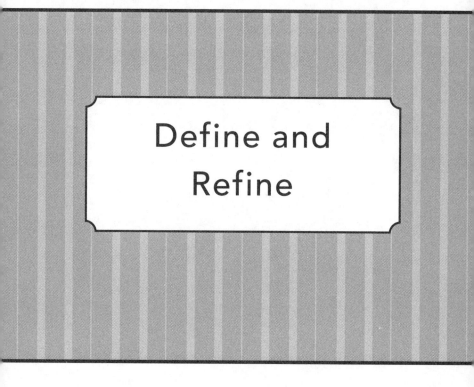

Define and
Refine

Set the Foundation: Communicating Core Identity and Culture

*The loftier the building,
the deeper must the foundation be laid.*

THOMAS KEMPIS

As you study a legendary company such as Ritz-Carlton, it becomes clear that being an industry leader and a standard-bearer for customer service did *not* happen by default or come without risk. In fact, the early founders of the company established a lasting legacy by developing a distinct set of guiding concepts, which they called "Gold Standards." These standards continue to serve as the basis for the ongoing and international success of Ritz-Carlton. As President Simon Cooper notes, "You can't put the veneer of quality on a business that lacks a sound foundation. The Gold Standards, and the disciplined business practices that emerge from them, create the platform for the achievements of our company in areas as wide ranging as our attractiveness to job seekers, our recognition for customer engagement, and our accomplishments in quality excellence throughout the world."

The effect of those core cultural elements means that Ritz-Carlton's name is both its greatest asset and at times its worst liability. Because Ritz-Carlton sets the bar not just in the hotel industry but for many service companies, analysts typically offer copious admiration or harsh criticism when it comes to the company's decisions or any changes it undertakes. Vivian Deuschl, vice president of public relations, shares the feeling of being under closer scrutiny than many of the company's competitors: "While other hotel companies would probably get high marks for an initiative to enhance the service experience, making it more responsive to the needs of their changing guests, when we dared to do it, the publicity we received in both the *Wall Street Journal* and on *ABC Nightline* stressed the criticism of some guests and analysts for the way we had been doing things, such as responses like 'certainly, my pleasure.' The headline in the *Wall Street Journal* was 'Taking Off The Ritz—A Tad' with a cartoon of a doorman hovering over a guest, trying to grab his suitcase. Under the training for our evolved Service Values, we no longer had doormen automatically assuming guests wanted their luggage taken." Sandra Ryder, area director of public relations at the Atlanta Buckhead and downtown Atlanta properties, says, "On the upside, virtually everyone in my community welcomes my call when they hear I am from Ritz-Carlton. On the downside, even minor breakdowns and problems at a Ritz-Carlton property can draw enhanced criticism and media attention."

While the long-standing success of Ritz-Carlton can cause it to be viewed through a distorted lens, the greatest risk facing the company is complacency. President Simon Cooper and Senior Vice President of Sales and Marketing Bruce Himelstein both acknowledge that the outstanding reputation of Ritz-Carlton is most vulnerable to leaders and staff who could fail to be responsive to the needs of a changing customer base, who avoid taking risks, or who allow the brand to become out of step with the times. But with such an impressive track record of accomplishment, it would be equally unwise to initiate poorly thought out change . . . simply for change's sake.

Alexandra Valentin, director of learning at The Ritz-Carlton, Central Park, aptly noted, "For us at Ritz-Carlton and for many other great businesses, it is easier to rise to the top than it is to stay at the top." So how do leaders decide which aspects of their business *can't* change and which components *must* evolve to retain preeminence in their industry and consistently deliver a high-level—and relevant—experience to their customers? In essence, successful leaders like those at Ritz-Carlton *define* the pillars of enduring excellence they believe are fundamental to their original success and longevity. Then, and only then, can those leaders *refine* strategic changes that they believe will fuel growth and evolution.

For Ritz-Carlton leadership, the bedrock of its success lives in well-defined Gold Standards and extraordinary discipline in keeping those Gold Standards alive in the daily lives of the Ladies and Gentlemen of the company. These Gold Standards define the company, differentiate it from the competition, and serve as the beacon for sustainable service excellence.

Cult versus Culture

There is a fine line between being a fan of something and being fanatical about it. When it comes to the Gold Standards, Ritz-Carlton leaders and frontline staff alike can appear, from an outsider's perspective, to be teetering toward the fanatical. Julia Gajcak, vice president of communications and marketing, relates, "When I used to work for a competitor, we would joke about the almost obsessive and cultlike focus on culture at Ritz-Carlton. Behaviors like carrying around a 'Credo Card' delineating the Gold Standards, identifying that card as part of an employee's uniform, and attending daily lineups seemed a bit odd to those of us outside of the company."

Julia added, "I actually brought that issue up to Sue Stephenson, the former senior vice president of human resources, and current vice president of Community Footprints, as I was being interviewed for a leadership position at Ritz-Carlton. I told Sue, 'I probably shouldn't say this as a job candidate, but I don't feel that employees should have to carry a credo card to remind them of what their company is all about.' And Sue responded, in such a gentle and respectful way, 'How funny that you say that. You know, I feel the same way. I don't have to put my beliefs on a piece of paper and remind myself of them every day at lineup. But the fact that my company has actually written them down and communicates what it values means so much to me as a leader in this organization.' Sue went on to say, 'The Gold Standards are there for people who want to be reminded, and maybe haven't memorized them, and if you don't feel like carrying the card, you don't carry it. But, hopefully you have these beliefs in your heart.'" Julia shared that she "got over the hump and embraced the culture because Sue responded with such respect and epitomized the Gold Standards that I've come to value at The Ritz-Carlton Hotel Company."

⋅⊰ The Gold Standards ⊱⋅

While many companies have finely worded statements of vision, purpose, and values, few business leaders can rival Ritz-Carlton when it comes to keeping those roadmaps and cultural anchors at the top-of-mind of their staff. Through a diligent commitment, Ritz-Carlton leaders have found a way to bring the purpose and values of the company into the daily lives of their Ladies and Gentlemen. As noted earlier by Julia Gajcak, one of the most basic strategies for keeping this information front and center for employees is a trifold pocket card that bears the title "Gold Standards" but is referred to as the "Credo Card." This card is not only a part of every staff member's uniform but it is also typically referred to on a daily basis and readily shared with guests. Jonathan G. Foss experienced this firsthand. As he shares, "I was a guest at the Cancún property when Hurricane Wilma battered us. I was so struck by the way the staff operated with a single-minded purpose for guest safety and comfort that I asked what enabled them to be so cohesive. A staff member showed me the Credo Card and gave it to me. I actually had him sign it."

Given the daily reinforcement of the content of the Credo Card, you would be hard-pressed to find a Lady or Gentleman at the Ritz-Carlton who can't immediately articulate the following:

The Credo

The Motto

The Three Steps of Service

The Credo

In its most elegant form, the Ritz-Carlton has defined the "ultimate guest experience" in three easily remembered stanzas:

The Ritz-Carlton is a place where the genuine care and comfort of our guests is our highest mission.

We pledge to provide the finest personal service and facilities for our guests who will always enjoy a warm, relaxed, yet refined ambience.

The Ritz-Carlton experience enlivens the senses, instills well-being, and fulfills even the unexpressed wishes and needs of our guests.

(Copyright © The Ritz-Carlton Hotel Company, L.L.C. All rights reserved. Reprinted with permission.)

One of the founders of The Ritz-Carlton Hotel Company, Ed Staros, who is currently vice president and managing director of The Ritz-Carlton Resorts of Naples, Florida, relates, "We developed the Credo in 1986. We had just opened The Ritz-Carlton, Naples, on December 3, 1985. And after each opening, Horst Schulze, our president at the time, would bring those who helped open the hotels back and say, 'Let's huddle.' He would then ask, 'If we could turn back the hands of time to two months prior to opening, what would we have done differently to create a better opening?' So we kept fine-tuning the opening process."

According to Ed, "The Naples opening involved mobilizing the largest staff we've ever had in one room—probably close to 600 new employees. And I remember the discussion at the postopening debrief about how difficult it had been to have the Naples staff get their arms around our mission statement, which covered a full single-spaced typed page. When we presented that mission statement at Naples, there were a lot of people staring at the chandeliers. Keep in mind, these employees had been with us for only three hours before we tried to get them to embrace our detailed mission.

"During the debriefing session," Ed continues, "we had an open conversation around the table, saying, 'What if we took the essence of the mission statement and condensed it somehow, so that even brand-new employees in their third or fourth hour could fully understand our culture in three or four sentences?' Horst then came up with the word *credo* because the word is a Latin derivative that means 'I believe.' I think that was a brilliant word to utilize because it was almost like the Pledge of Allegiance or the Boy Scout Oath, in that people are being asked to pledge their commitment to three core aspects of our culture."

No matter what the nature of the business, a company's leadership is always tasked with making their vision come alive at the front line. Often this objective is driven by the clarity of language used to paint the picture. Diana Oreck, vice president of global learning and of the Leadership Center, keenly analyzes the Credo, stating that it is "made up of very powerful words that reflect our commitment in the way we treat our guests.

They are words like 'genuine care and comfort,' 'pledge,' and 'finest personal service,' as well as 'enlivens . . . instills, and fulfills unexpressed wishes and needs.' That is our business, and that is what we are here to do. Above all else, and without regard to our technical skills as bellmen, concierges, or Ladies and Gentlemen in our laundry area, the Credo defines who and what we are at Ritz-Carlton, and it is very clear when someone is and when someone isn't living up to what he or she pledges in the Credo."

Maurice Pearson, who started with the company in loss prevention and who has been promoted to an assistant director of housekeeping, reflects, "I got into some trouble when I was young, but I didn't want to keep going down the wrong road. I survived Iraq twice. I got out and made it home. The same day I was supposed to come to Ritz-Carlton and fill out an application, I got in a really bad car accident. But finally, I went through the employment process and through my journey here, I was named Employee of the Year at my hotel location. My goal is to be a hotel general manager one day. The Credo has been so important for me, to provide service to guests and for my growth and development. It sets you up for success. If you take it and embrace it, you can't do anything but excel here. Every word of it is true. Every word."

Maria Thompson, sales administrative assistant at The Ritz-Carlton, Phoenix, puts it a little differently: "I think if the corporate world took our Credo and applied the concepts to whatever industry they were in, and really applied it from the very top to the very bottom of the organization, the world would be a better place, in terms of corporate life. By a 'better place' I mean better retention, happier managers, and greater profitability."

Ultimately the value of the Credo or any other core cultural roadmap is the opportunity it affords those inside the business to realize how the ideal customer and staff experience looks and feels. The true success of such a credo is whether or not it actually produces tangible experiences causing guests to enjoy "enlivened senses, states of well-being, and fulfillment of unstated needs and desires." These outcomes can clearly be validated by guest comments such as, "I walked to the elevators and was charmed by the marble floors, tall mirrors, and beautiful artwork in the elevator lobby. Throughout the lobby and public areas of the hotel was an understated atmosphere of luxury and comfort. I entered my room with aching muscles and a tired mind. The lights were already on, but they were softly lit, casting a dim glow throughout the room. The radio was playing classical music, my bed had been turned down and an oversized terrycloth robe lay on the bed." Or from observations such as, "My stress melted away as I drew myself a bubble bath in the huge marble-filled bathroom. The towels in the room were not the small, rough pieces of linen that are so common in hotels. No, these were large, soft, terrycloth towels." When leadership defines a powerful vision and clearly communicates that vision to all staff, employees can turn that vision (for example, "create an experience that enlivens the senses, instills well-being, and fulfills even the unexpressed wishes and needs of our guests") into reality.

The Motto

At first glance, The Motto of the Ritz-Carlton, "Ladies and Gentlemen serving Ladies and Gentlemen" may appear overly staid and outdated, lacking refinements to make it relevant to a modern workforce. Yet packed into its formal language is a clear understanding of the relationship between, and implicit respect for, both the employee and guest.

Horst Schulze, cofounder and past president of The Ritz-Carlton Hotel Company, shares the origin of the Motto: "I started in the hotel business when I was 14 years old as a busboy. When my mother took me to the hotel to work for the first time, she said, 'We could never go to this hotel. This is only for important people. For important, fine people. So you're lucky. Behave yourself. Wash your hands.' She was a typical mother. I went to the hotel and the general manager talked to my mother and me for 15 minutes and told us we could never be like the guests who came to his hotel. 'So don't ever get jealous. This is for Ladies and Gentlemen—very important people.'

"By the time I started working in the restaurant, I knew the guests were very important. But a few months later I realized that the maître d' I watched every day was just as important because every guest was proud when he talked to them. Why? Because he was a first-class professional. He was somebody special—because of the excellence he created for the guests. So when I went to hotel school about a year and a half later, the teacher asked me to write a story describing what I felt about the business. And I wrote about the maître d' at my hotel. I titled it, 'Ladies and Gentlemen Serving Ladies and Gentlemen.' I wrote we could be excellent like he was…absolute excellence. When you walked into a room, you knew he was there. In any moment all of us who serve can be Ladies and Gentlemen, just like the guests. I think it's a powerful thing that shouldn't be missed by the wonderful people in this industry. They should understand that."

Former Ritz-Carlton President Horst Schulze

As a boy growing up amidst the vineyards of Winningen, Germany, Horst Schulze knew that his future lay in hospitality. At age 11, he informed his parents that he wanted to work in a hotel, though he'd never laid foot in one—or even in a restaurant.

Three years later, Horst quit school to work as a busboy at the Kur Haus more than 100 miles from home. The young Schulze juggled his job with weekly hotel school, where he penned the essay, "Ladies and Gentlemen Serving Ladies and Gentlemen."

Horst's early career took him to Europe's grandest hotels and resorts, from work in the ski resort town of Gamisch to Bern's legendary Bellevue Palace, Paris's Plaza Athénée, London's Barclay Hotel, and Lausanne, Switzerland's Beau Rivage

Palace. By the mid-1960s, Horst was living in the United States, first in Houston, then San Francisco, where he worked evenings at a French restaurant and breakfasts at the Hilton. It was at the University Club in San Francisco that his career turned to management, and a transfer to Chicago's University Club landed him a position as catering/food and beverage manager.

In 1971, Horst became catering manager of the Chicago Hilton. After several years with Hilton Hotels, Horst was the opening food and beverage director for the new Hyatt Regency in Chicago. His career with Hyatt culminated in his promotion to corporate vice president in 1981.

Two years later, Horst took a position as a charter member and vice president of operations for a new hotel company. That company would become The Ritz-Carlton Group, and its first hotel opened in January 1984.

Horst became president and chief operating officer at Ritz-Carlton in 1988. Prior to his leaving in 2002, Ritz-Carlton had grown to 42 hotels with 15 more under development. Under Schulze's leadership, Ritz-Carlton twice received the Malcolm Baldrige National Quality Award. Additionally, Ritz-Carlton was repeatedly voted the best hotel company in the world by meeting and other trade publications.

Horst was recognized as "corporate hotelier of the world" by *Hotels* magazine. He was also awarded the Ishikawa Medal for personal contributions to the quality movement, and Johnson & Wales University granted him an honorary doctor of business administration degree in hospitality management.

Horst left Ritz-Carlton to retire. But within days, he was once again setting up shop with West Paces Hotel Group, through which he has launched a new hospitality brand, Capella Hotels and Resorts.

To see Horst Schulze interviewed about service excellence, please go to www.yournewgoldstandard.com.

From Horst's term paper in hotel school at age 15, the Motto has served not only to elevate the status of "service professional" but it has also communicated the expectation that staff will treat one another as Ladies and Gentlemen and that the leadership of Ritz-Carlton will protect their Ladies and Gentlemen from guests who fail to behave respectfully. Diana Oreck says, "We are serving wealthy people. We are blessed; 99 percent of our guests are lovely people. However, there are a few who equate money with being rude or abusive. The Motto is helpful for our Ladies and Gentlemen when an isolated incident occurs, and they encounter someone who is really difficult. Our staff can then say, 'We are Ladies and Gentlemen serving Ladies and Gentlemen, and I would really appreciate it if you could address me that way.' If the guest fails to modify his or her behavior accordingly, our leadership is glad to invite the guest to stay somewhere else. In fact, we will even secure the reservation for him or her."

While some have argued that the language of the Motto and the Credo needs to be more progressive and is ripe for change, leadership at Ritz-Carlton evaluated the issue and invited the Ladies and Gentlemen to share their input. Through surveys conducted to determine the relevance of all of the Ritz-Carlton Credo Card contents, staff showed a strong preference for the Motto's remaining unchanged, suggesting that its language imbues a timeless sense of pride in the service professions. According to Brian Gullbrants, who started as a server at The Ritz-Carlton, Phoenix and has moved through the ranks to serve as vice president of operations, "The results were clear and resounding that our Ladies and Gentlemen felt the Motto offered them a magnitude of esteem."

Hervé Humler, president of international operations, and one of the founders of the company, notes, "I am always attending the countdown to opening our new international hotels and orienting our new staff to the fiber of this company, and I start with, 'My name is Hervé Humler, and I am the president of Ritz-Carlton International, and I'm a very important person.'

You know, people look at me, and some laugh, but then I say, 'We are all the same: you're as important as I am, if not more so because I don't have a lot of guest interaction. But we are all Ladies and Gentlemen serving Ladies and Gentlemen.' You would be surprised, particularly with staff from socially and economically challenged parts of the world, how many people tell me that they have never been called or treated like a Lady or Gentleman. It is a part of why we receive recognition by Hewitt surveys as an 'employer of choice' in all of Asia, as well as individually in Hong Kong, Shanghai, Singapore, Seoul, Cancún for all of Mexico, and Istanbul for all of Turkey. There is a great deal of honor and respect attached to the seven words of our Motto, and they have resounding application from Beijing to Santiago."

By not confusing title with importance, leadership at Ritz-Carlton understands that creating an environment of respect universally results in a respectful service culture and being viewed as an international employer of choice.

STRIKING GOLD

- Have you distilled your mission statement into a short, memorable, and operational set of phrases?

- How regularly do you discuss the mission with your staff? How do you incorporate their feedback to ensure that the mission is realized?

- If asked, could everyone in your business provide a clear and accurate understanding of your company's mission and purpose?

The Three Steps of Service

The Ritz-Carlton leadership has included space on the Credo Card for listing the "Three Steps of Service" that some may view as too basic to take up space on the card. Where possible, Ritz-Carlton leadership attempts to resist the urge to overcomplicate the fundamentals of service. This keep-it-simple approach is consistent with guidance provided by business expert Ron Ashkenas, managing partner of the consulting firm Robert H. Schaffer & Associates. Ron observes, "A simplification strategy must be treated as a business imperative—not just a nice-to-have virtue but a key element for driving bottom-line success."

In reality, the consistent execution of simple aspects of service is central to distinguishing Ritz-Carlton from its competition. Whether a company is directly serving customers or is serving other businesses, the basics of caring never change. As such, the leadership at Ritz-Carlton weaves these three steps into the core of the culture:

1. A warm and sincere greeting. Use the guest's name.

2. Anticipation and fulfillment of each guest's needs.

3. Fond farewell. Give a warm good-bye, and use the guest's name.

   (Copyright © The Ritz-Carlton Hotel Company, L.L.C. All rights re-served. Reprinted with permission.)

Guests at Ritz-Carlton properties probably are not consciously aware that they are experiencing the Three Steps of Service. However, customers do express the emotional impact that these steps have on them. For example, a guest at The Ritz-Carlton, Palm Beach, remarks, "I had an excellent experience because the door and concierge staffs were very caring. They remembered me and my family by name. Every time our car pulled up, they would actually get the door for us and greet each of us by name." Guest Richard Whitley reports the significance of a fond farewell during the adversity of Hurricane Wilma: "As guests, we were told we would be evacuating the hotel and that the best time to travel to Merida was in the middle of the night. They brought the buses in at 2 a.m. All of the staff of the hotel gathered to say good-bye to us. It was phenomenal. These people had been with us for the last five days . . . hadn't yet been to see their families, but were there, waving to us as we left."

Ritz-Carlton does not just print the Three Steps of Service on a card and then leave staff to follow the guidelines. In fact, senior leadership realizes the importance of modeling these steps of service in the way they care for their direct reports, and in turn they set an expectation for all managers to serve their Ladies and Gentlemen using the same three steps. Vice President Vivian Deuschl explains, "It's as simple as this: If I'm the supervisor and for some reason I woke up in a bad mood and I don't speak to my staff, they immediately feel, 'Oh, I did something wrong, my boss didn't speak to me, didn't smile at me.' They then go out into the hallways and perhaps they're so concerned about what their boss thought about them that they don't interface with the guests."

One staff member relates what it was like to have his wife and children on the receiving end of a warm welcome. "I got the call that no husband or father wants to get . . . your wife crying frantically, kids crying because Mom is crying, and you are on the other side of the country feeling helpless. She was traveling with our two little kids and missed a connection in Los Angeles. She was getting the typical runaround with the airlines, and all I could think to tell her was to get to a Ritz-Carlton and it would be all right. I immediately called The Ritz-Carlton, Marina del Rey, and I explained the situation. I told them that my family was on their way and should arrive shortly. By the time my wife and kids arrived, the manager was waiting outside to personally greet them, he escorted them up to their room, had robes laid out for all three of them, and without even asking . . . sent up miso soup. I didn't request any of this; all I wanted was for them to be safe. My wife and kids are Japanese-American, so miso soup to them is *the* best comfort food they could have received—it was perfect! The next call I got from my wife suggested that all was calm. The girls were in their robes, and all three were sipping soup. That's why I work for Ritz-Carlton!" When leaders welcome and respond to the needs of employees and their families, as did the manager in Marina Del Rey, they role-model the behaviors they want staff to demonstrate toward customers.

The Three Steps of Service are clearly reflected in the way Ritz-Carlton staff takes care of business partners, vendors, and others who come in contact with the company. Brian Sheehan, chairman and chief executive officer of Team One, the advertising agency that handles the Ritz-Carlton account, relates, "From my perspective, our agency was invited into a relationship with the company so graciously. It is as if they said, 'welcome into our family,' and there's only one way they can treat you: total communion. I think *communion* is a good word because it's community. It's a healthy environment in that regard. It's quite amazing."

In the spirit of consistency, Ritz-Carlton also uses the Three Steps of Service to ensure that new employees are warmly welcomed into the company and that staff are given a fond farewell when they retire, transfer, or depart. Further, the steps are reflected in the spirited welcome evidenced by signed banners from employees at Ritz-Carlton properties worldwide to each new property about to open and join the Ritz-Carlton family.

The 20 Basics

While no longer reflected on the Credo Card, Ritz-Carlton established guidelines for providing service the Ritz-Carlton way. These 20 standards created a consistent approach and expectation for service delivery at a level well beyond the foundation of the Three Steps of Service.

While the 20 Basics have been replaced by more flexible alternatives, these core service standards not only underpin leadership's commitment to driving a positive culture but they also acknowledge a variety of other important and unchangeable aspects of Ritz-Carlton's past and future success. (Please see the sidebar "The Ritz-Carlton 20 Basics.")

The Ritz-Carlton 20 Basics

1. The Credo is the principal belief of our Company. It must be known, owned, and energized by all.

2. Our Motto is "We Are Ladies and Gentlemen serving Ladies and Gentlemen." As service professionals, we treat our guests and each other with respect and dignity.

3. The Three Steps of Service are the foundation of Ritz-Carlton hospitality. These steps must be used in every interaction to ensure satisfaction, retention, and loyalty.

4. The Employee Promise is the basis for our Ritz-Carlton work environment. It will be honored by all employees.

5. All employees will successfully complete annual Training Certification for their position.

6. Company objectives are communicated to all employees. It is everyone's responsibility to support them.

7. To create pride and joy in the workplace, all employees have the right to be involved in the planning of the work that affects them.

8. Each employee will continually identify defects (MR. BIV) throughout the Hotel.

9. It is the responsibility of each employee to create a work environment of teamwork and lateral service so that the needs of our guests and each other are met.

10. Each employee is empowered. For example, when a guest has a problem or needs something special, you should break away from your regular duties, address and resolve the issue.

11. Uncompromising levels of cleanliness are the responsibilities of every employee.

12. To provide the finest personal service for our guests, each employee is responsible for identifying and recording individual guest preferences.

13. Never lose a guest. Instant guest pacification is the responsibility of each employee. Whoever receives a complaint will own it, resolve it to the guest's satisfaction, and record it.

14. "Smile—We are on stage." Always maintain positive eye contact. Use the proper vocabulary with our guests and each other. (Use words such as "Good Morning," "Certainly," "I'll be happy to," and "My pleasure." Do not use words such as "OK," "Sure," "Hi/Hello," "Folks," and "No problem.")

15. Be an ambassador of your Hotel in and outside of the workplace. Always speak positively. Communicate any concerns to the appropriate person.

16. Escort guests rather than pointing out directions to another area of the Hotel.

17. Use Ritz-Carlton telephone etiquette. Answer within three rings and with a "smile." Use the guest's name when possible. When necessary, ask the caller, "May I place you on hold?" Do not screen calls. Eliminate call transfers whenever possible. Adhere to voice-mail standards.

18. Take pride in and care of your personal appearance. Everyone is responsible to convey a professional image by adhering to Ritz-Carlton clothing and grooming standards.

19. Think safety first. Each employee is responsible for creating a safe, secure, and accident-free environment for all guests and each other. Be aware of all fire and safety emergency procedures, and report any security risks immediately.

20. Protecting the assets of a Ritz-Carlton Hotel is the responsibility of every employee. Conserve energy, properly maintain our hotels, and protect the environment.

See Chapter 5 for information about the Employee Promise and Chapter 7 for information about MR. BIV.

The 20 Basics provide clear messages in areas such as staff empowerment and personalized guest service, with staff encouraged to break away from their regular duties to address and resolve guest issues and identify and record guest preferences. The guidelines reflect the need for detailed, uncompromising attention to cleanliness and the importance of the personal appearance of staff. The 20 Basics further address standards for complaint management, communication style, etiquette, and even stewardship of corporate assets.

While future chapters will take a deeper look at the importance of these 20 Basics for creating staff autonomy and the production of memorable guest experiences, it should be pointed out that Ritz-Carlton leadership began to realize that the 20 Basics, if adhered to without creativity, could detract from overall guest satisfaction and fall out of step with the changing needs of the modern guest. Founder Ed Staros explains, "We originally created the 20 Basics to ensure operational consistency. The 20 Basics were never meant to become a script for delivering service; however, people gravitated to the guidelines and started using parts of the 20 Basics as if they were scripts, often not varying their choice of the phrase 'my pleasure.' Of course, 'my pleasure' was just an example. Staff needed to use all of the 20 Basics with discretion. But when it came to 'my pleasure,' it certainly became overused, as if it were the official script of our Ladies and Gentlemen."

In addition to the overuse of the term "my pleasure," some staff members apparently felt so compelled to "escort guests rather than pointing out directions to another area of the hotel" that they ignored cues from the guest that such an escort was not desired. Whether it was following a guest to a bathroom or ignoring his or her verbal opposition to be escorted, it became clear that the 20 Basics needed to be refined into something that encouraged staff members to use their judgment as they performed beyond the guidelines. The result of that refinement process was titled "Service Values" (discussed in detail in Chapter 3), and it was created with significant input from the Ladies and Gentlemen. The by-product of this staff input is a set of 12 evolved values that encourage "ways of being" as opposed to "ways of doing." From a customer perspective, the Service Values enable the staff members to focus on the desired outcomes for individual guests as fully as possible rather than applying a one-size-fits-all approach to every guest and every situation.

STRIKING GOLD

☞ What are the most basic aspects of service you wish to consistently see delivered in your business?

☞ How simply, clearly, and consistently have you presented the expectation of your service standards?

☞ There is a Ritz-Carlton way for providing service, which has been communicated in part through defined service standards. How have you defined the unique service approach that reflects the way your company serves others?

The Immutable Process of Alignment to the Gold Standards

While most businesses go through the requisite exercise of defining key values or composing mission statements, few leaders understand the importance of regular and repetitive presentation of these core aspects of their business. Going beyond the creation and dissemination of Credo Cards, the leadership at Ritz-Carlton perfected a powerful process of daily conversation about the Gold Standards referred to as the "lineup."

To truly appreciate the Ritz-Carlton leadership approach to repeated acculturation of the Gold Standards, imagine joining a group of approximately 20 food preparers and chefs in the tight confines of a shiny and immaculately clean commercial kitchen. You take your place standing in a circle of Ladies and Gentlemen donning tall chef hats and white aprons. You observe that the meeting is taking place at the beginning of a shift, and the master chef starts by sharing The Credo and talking about the importance of creating a unique guest experience. A pastry chef then shares a story of exceptional customer service from a Ritz-Carlton hotel in another part of the world. The story comes from an excerpt of a letter sent in by a grateful guest. Collectively the chefs discuss the story and how it reflects on a core value of the Ritz-Carlton. A sous chef then leads a brief discussion of how the customer story connects with what they can do in their department to create memorable experiences for guests on that very day. A few brief announcements are offered, staff employment anniversaries are acknowledged playfully, and a motivational quote is provided by yet another member of the circle. The meeting is adjourned after approximately 20 minutes.

Now you are whisked off to join a group of executives at the Ritz-Carlton corporate office in Chevy Chase, Maryland. The circle you enter there, while lacking the chefs' hats and aprons, is essentially identical to the one you witnessed at the hotel. Senior leadership listens to the same customer service story discussed by the food preparers. Corporate staff engages in the same types of discussions, as well as the presentation of quotes and The Credo. In both locations (and in all locations of Ritz-Carlton, for that matter) attendees at lineup will be carrying their Credo Cards and referring to them much as athletes might refer to their team's playbook.

This highly interactive process does not operate as an actual staff meeting. The more accurate explanation of its ultimate purpose is that it creates substantial inspirational, social, and cultural benefits.

From the perspective of Marguerite Dowd, executive administrative assistant in sales and marketing at The Ritz-Carlton, Laguna Niguel, lineup is "an integral part of every department in every Ritz-Carlton everywhere in the world. In fact, lineup is a fabulous way to start the day. I love that every day I get kick-started by the words of statesmen or former presidents. The quote from today was from an Irish rock musician who said something like 'my heroes are the ones who survived doing it wrong, who made mistakes, but recovered from them.' In addition to the sayings, we talk about something that's going on at one of our locations in the world, whether it's the opening of a new hotel or some employee who did something extraordinary to help a guest or another employee." Marguerite adds, "I truly feel connected to something larger than myself when I realize that the information we were reading at my sales lineup is being read by every employee in every Ritz-Carlton all over the world. It really is my connection to my company, to all of our Ladies and Gentlemen, and to our guests."

Ed Staros states that the practice of lineup at Ritz-Carlton borrows from a tradition in the culinary division of the hospitality industry and it is also an effort to benchmark effective corporate communication strategies. "In the food and beverage business, an informational type of lineup is very common when you own a restaurant. If your doors open at six o'clock for evening service, it's routine that at around five o'clock you have a huddle and get the entire waitstaff together. The sous chef might come out of the kitchen and say, 'Tonight we have fresh mahi-mahi that was just flown in. In fact, I've prepared one,' and there would be 12 forks for the 12 waitstaff to taste it. It's very uncommon to do that at the beginning of each shift in a non-food-and-beverage environment. We took that culinary lineup to the next level."

Ed continues, "Horst wondered why we couldn't take the lineup to all departments, and it just so happened that I had visited FedEx to benchmark them. As I observed their office, I noticed a TV screen that reported information on how the company was doing with delivery accuracy on that day. When I came back to our headquarters, I told Horst how FedEx used their tracking information to share information in a minicorporate TV broadcast. I started looking into a similar internal cable broadcast option, but we did not have that kind of electronic infrastructure, so that option would have been too costly. We opted for a modification of the culinary lineup process."

For some leaders, this process of daily reflection on values and shared storytelling might seem eerily like "thought control," and participants at Ritz-Carlton do acknowledge that there are both limitations to and strengths of the lineup. Cherie Y. Webb, manager of learning, The Ritz-Carlton, Atlanta, reveals that throughout seven years, "I can't say that every lineup has motivated me, but I honestly can say almost all of the time I feel energized when I leave lineup. I guess it might seem repetitive or that sometimes it did not hit the mark, but really each of us is responsible for making the lineup great."

While at times lineup can fail to inspire the participants, it is most often likely to afford a comforting and safe place for information sharing and the creation of a Ritz-Carlton identity. For example, during Hurricane Wilma, when many other businesses with less-practiced daily communication rituals might have experienced communication breakdowns, Ritz-Carlton staff came together as they always had—through the lineup process.

According to guest Jonathan G. Foss, "I noticed the staff doing their daily meetings at the beginning of each shift three times a day during the whole crisis. I thought that was just incredible. They were adhering to their values. While things like lineup are often cancelled during crises in other businesses, lineup actually served as a place for staff to obtain hope, information, and support." Fred Boutouba, manager on duty/guest relations, who was in charge of the staff during Hurricane Wilma, stated, "Once you embrace the Ritz-Carlton philosophy, once you live it on a daily basis and in your daily life, it is really hard to let go. Lineup is a standard. It's the only way to get everybody informed about the situation you are about to face. I think it's a great tool, and we continued it, especially during these circumstances." Similarly, Myra deGersdorff, general manager of The Ritz-Carlton, New Orleans, notes that "in addition to our regularly occurring strategic meetings, we continued to do lineup during Hurricane Katrina. It offered a sense of normalcy in a time when few things were normal."

So what is the magic of lineup? Among other things it clearly involves the following:

- *Repetition of values.* The core belief that values need to be discussed on a daily basis and that values can't be discussed enough

- *Common language.* The inculcation of a common language with terms like "credo," "a fond farewell," and "unexpressed wishes and needs of our guests"

- *Visual symbols.* The integration of the Credo Card into the experience

- *Oral traditions.* Personal, direct, face-to-face communication in a world increasingly dominated by e-mail, text, and voice messaging

- *Positive storytelling.* The ability to capture, share, and inspire through tangible examples of what it means to live the Credo and core corporate values

- *Modeling by leaders.* The active, daily presence of all leaders in the process and the commitment of resources to free up staff time for daily participation

The last point concerning modeling and participation by leaders cannot be emphasized enough as pointed out by Kevin McConville, regional managing partner of Gallup, a Ritz-Carlton consultant who has spent a considerable amount of time observing and experiencing the culture. Kevin discloses, "We see a lot of organizations that come to the Leadership Center of the

Ritz-Carlton say, 'This is great. This is absolutely great. We should do these morning lineups. I'm not going to do them personally because I'm busy, but the people at the front line should really do more lineups.' By contrast, at Ritz-Carlton, the company's president, Simon Cooper, and the executive team are participating in the lineups the same way that the hotel staff are participating in their shift lineups." Kevin adds, "As somebody who watches organizations try and change their culture, that commitment starting at the top is different at Ritz-Carlton from any other organization I walk into. Leadership is really embedding that very clear spirit and mission—very different from most cultures."

STRIKING GOLD

- How can you increase the consistency and frequency of messages of corporate mission and values?

- Are you willing to take the time to regularly define the link between operational and cultural aspects of your business?

- What are the visual symbols, oral traditions, and positive stories in your business? Is senior leadership modeling and prioritizing your company's values and mission?

LIVING THE NEW GOLD STANDARD

- The mission statements of highly effective companies honor the interests of clients and employees and the sustainability of the business.

- Mission statements and core values are often not understood or remembered in a functional way throughout an organization.

- Imitate, Improvise, and Innovate. But make sure to keep your eyes on the leader! The Ritz-Carlton sets the standard for luxury hospitality. Strive to be the benchmark for your industry.

- Conscious attention must be paid to the traditions and core aspects of a business, which require preservation even in the face of negative trends or economic downturns.

- Everyone you come in contact with in business should be considered a valued customer, whether it's the janitors, the chairman of the board, salespeople, or defined clients.

- You can never overcommunicate your values!

- Leadership lives in the actions, not the words, of those entrusted to move an organization forward.

- Well-chosen words have great power to constructively influence the identity of an organization.

Be Relevant

*We must always change,
renew, rejuvenate ourselves;
otherwise we harden.*

JOHANN WOLFGANG VON GOËTHE

 "I expect elegant. But I also expect that I have to enter into their world instead of their coming into mine." Such was the reaction shared by a modern luxury customer during a focus group discussion concerning Ritz-Carlton. Similar guest comments reflected the perception—and consumer perceptions are reality—that Ritz-Carlton needed to refine its approach to product and service offerings in accord with a changing customer base. As important as it is to establish a framework of values to guide an organization's culture, it's equally crucial to reevaluate mission statements to ensure they are relevant to the evolving needs of customers.

Laurie Wooden, vice president of new business development and corporate strategy, reflects on observations she made when joining the company five years ago. "I was struck by the fact that our Credo proclaimed we were to provide for the genuine care and comfort of our guests, but when I went to our hotels, I saw that we were doing a lot of things that were not comfortable for our guests. For example, at a resort in Florida we required a jacket and tie at dinner, when the guests had been in their bathing suits by the pool all day or wearing shorts playing tennis. It was 90-plus degrees and very humid, and of course guests were choosing to leave our hotel to go have dinner."

Laurie goes on to clarify, "Many of us began to wonder if, as a company, we were serving the needs of customers from another time, not the needs of today's customer or the future customer. That line of inquiry gave us direction in trying to understand what was happening when our buildings, services, or service delivery did not seem to meet the needs of our guests." From that desire to first gain an understanding of the relevance of its products, Ritz-Carlton leadership charted a course on how to evolve. Based on anecdotal observation and extensive research concerning the changing wants and needs of the luxury consumer and luxury traveler (approximately the highest-spending 5 or 6 percent of the traveling population), whom the Ritz-Carlton leadership targets as their market, a number of conclusions were drawn.

According to Paul Westbrook, senior vice president of product and brand management, "Several decades ago our guests were very similar. Essentially, they were affluent people who traveled in similar circles and socialized with one another. They were both business leaders and individuals who had amassed significant wealth. Our company was founded on service excellence primarily conforming to their expectations."

Simon Cooper, president of Ritz-Carlton, contrasts "conventional" Ritz-Carlton customers with the reality of those they serve today: "Twenty-five years ago, guests were expecting a very consistent look of a Ritz-Carlton. That's why we built hotels that were rather traditional and put them on the beach in Florida. In those days, consistency of a look and feel was rewarded. Also, 25 years ago if you cast your eye across the lobby of a Ritz-Carlton, you would find primarily a male guest who was older and in a suit. He had clear expectations as to what he would expect from a luxury hotel. When you cast your eye across the lobby of a typical Ritz-Carlton today, it is incredibly diverse. Diverse in race, gender, attire, and the presence of families and diverse in what this group of guests looks for in a hotel experience. We have had to respond to that because our customers are evolving and our hotels are being located worldwide in vibrant locations such as Shanghai, Doha, and Macao. We needed to evolve with our customers and our communities or we would not be relevant." (Please see the sidebar "Ritz-Carlton President Simon F. Cooper" for more information on Simon and his efforts to strategically position the Ritz-Carlton brand.)

Ritz-Carlton President Simon F. Cooper

Simon F. Cooper is president and chief operating officer of The Ritz-Carlton Hotel Company. He oversees the operations, development, and strategic positioning of Ritz-Carlton.

Under his leadership, the company continues to earn the highest accolades, including being ranked first in guest satisfaction for luxury hotels in the J.D. Power and Associates 2007 North America Hotel Guest Satisfaction Study.

Since joining the hotel company in February 2001, Simon has overseen a major expansion of Ritz-Carlton hotels, developed brand extensions, championed relevant hotel design changes, and spearheaded enhancements to Ritz-Carlton's service approach.

Between 2007 and 2011, Simon and his leadership team anticipate opening 33 hotels, 24 Residences, 7 Clubs, and 3 serviced apartments at locations around the world, including Dublin, Beijing, St. Lucia, and Denver.

Simon joined Ritz-Carlton from Marriott International, where he served for three years as president of Marriott Lodging Canada and senior vice president of Marriott Lodging International, responsible for Canada and New England.

Born and educated in England, Simon earned an MBA from the University of Toronto. He began his hospitality career when he immigrated to Canada in 1972 and worked for Canadian Pacific Hotels & Resorts.

In 2005, Simon was elected to the board of directors of First Horizon National Corporation. In 2004, he was appointed to the Woodrow Wilson International Center for Scholars, Canada Institute Advisory Board. In 1999, Simon was appointed as chairman of the board of governors for the University of Guelph for a three-year term (No. 1 Comprehensive University in Canada, *Maclean's* magazine, 1999 and 2002).

In 1996, Simon was awarded the 1995 Commitment to People Award by the Council of Hotel and Restaurant Trainers, recognizing his loyalty to the personal development of his employees. In 1995, he received an honorary fellowship from Ryerson Polytechnical University.

To see Simon Cooper interviewed about brand relevance, please go to www.yournewgoldstandard.com.

In an effort to develop an understanding of consumer changes that go well beyond demographic variables (younger travelers, more female travelers, and families), Ritz-Carlton leadership examined changes in the fundamental wants and values that drive the modern luxury consumer. As it does before making any potentially widespread changes, Ritz-Carlton leadership partnered with outside groups who possessed great expertise gained through either experience or science. Paul Westbrook reveals that as a means of tapping into that experience, "Ritz-Carlton engaged in conversations with other luxury brands. One such conversation came in the form of what was called the Luxury Industry Panel. Participants at the panel included Bulgari, Mercedes-Benz, American Express, La Prairie, and Prada. This setting gave us the opportunity to share views about evolving luxury consumers and how we could better meet their needs. Further, we explored best practices and even talked about a few less-than-successful attempts to address the wants and desires of our target consumer group."

From a scientific perspective, Ritz-Carlton methodically looked for a marketing partner that could help them keep their brand most relevant in a changing marketplace. After careful evaluation, strategists at Ritz-Carlton selected Team One, a division of Saatchi & Saatchi that specializes in the luxury consumer. Mark Miller, director of strategic planning for Team One, observes, "The great thing about working with Ritz-Carlton has been that we've been involved with a very transformative program. It started with the words of Bruce Himelstein, senior vice president of sales and marketing. Bruce said that Ritz-Carlton leadership wanted to capture the best of the company, epitomized by their logo—the lion and crown—and keep it fresh and relevant. In Bruce's words, Ritz-Carlton wanted to 'blow the dust off the lion and crown, but not blow it up.'"

Working together, Team One and Ritz-Carlton identified the segmentation of the luxury consumer market. Their efforts revealed that Ritz-Carlton appeared to principally appeal to a consumer group referred to as "classic status-seekers." The classic status-seeker is the person who buys a Mercedes and when asked why, says, "It's a Mercedes; what else do I need to tell you?" For this group, the Ritz-Carlton emblem of the lion and crown has always been and continues to be a highly valued icon.

An emerging market segment, for which Ritz-Carlton did not have as strong an appeal, was the "discerning affluents." Research on this group suggested that it comprised more than twice the luxury market when compared to the status-seeker (49 compared to 21 percent). Unlike the status-seeker, the discerning affluents have a level of understanding about their purchases. When asked why they buy a Mercedes, the discerning affluent would say, "It's a Mercedes—the safest car in the world. After all, it's the company that patented crash testing of automobiles for safety." While their specific reasons will differ, discerning affluents analyze and substantiate luxury purchases. Research further identified three additional insights related to discerning affluents. First among these is this group's desire to leave its mark in the world and create a legacy, either through business or family. Additionally, this group of customers pursues life with confidence, choosing its own paths and not following others. Finally, discerning affluents seek to lead more interesting lives where they collect stories rich with detail.

With an understanding of this important luxury customer segment, Ritz-Carlton leadership continued to refine their hotel design and services to broadly address the needs of both types of consumer—the more traditional and the new segment. Mark Miller explains, "Leadership sought to retain the excellence of the guest experience while expanding it to meet the needs of discerning affluents, whose basic currency is found in the stories they collect. When you ask these people about their favorite luxury purchase, vacation travel is always No. 1. And when you ask them why they say that, it's because of the memories they garner. It is as if, for these guests, money is less the currency than time. So when they spend it, they want to spend it on something that has meaning, relevance, and value to them. Collecting a story that other people can't buy off the shelf makes the experience rare and exclusive to them, and, as such, the time invested yields worthwhile gains."

Business analysts such as Jennifer Kirby, consulting editor for mycustomer.com, report that companies often cling to their traditional customer segment without demonstrating the courage to evolve with changing customer trends. Jennifer suggests, "Antennae should be trained to register changing market conditions, e.g., customer feedback, sales force intelligence, monitoring word of mouth. And all staff [should be] alerted to [the importance of] customer experience and their own performance in delivering it." In assessing the demise of Levitz, a large U.S.–based furniture retailer, Jerry Epperson, managing director of the investment banking firm Mann, Armistead & Epperson, articulates, "The problem with something like Levitz isn't so much the consumer perception of the name or even the merchandise mix. The problem is that over many, many years, the demographics have moved and their stores haven't."

STRIKING GOLD

- What changes are you noticing between the customer you served five years ago and the customer you are serving today?

- What do you expect your customers will need from you three to five years from today?

- What aspects of your business can you "make relevant" to your evolving customer base without disenfranchising loyal, established customer segments?

Culling the Uniqueness of the Physical Environment

Robert E. Watson, managing director of Protravel International, Inc., sums up the efforts of the visionaries at Ritz-Carlton to energize their physical environment by saying, "It's no longer your grandma's Ritz-Carlton. I'll never forget my first exposure to Ritz-Carlton in Hawaii. I had a client who went to the hotel in Maui over 20 years ago; he came back and said, 'It was great, but the décor was of out of place for a tropical resort.' When I visited the hotel, I thought, 'I bet the president has a brother-in-law who's in the dark wood furniture business because everywhere you go, it's the same Ritz-Carlton.' But you won't find that anymore. Now each and every hotel is different, depending on the atmosphere and location. I think that's important. The management team at Ritz-Carlton has recognized that there is a younger element out there. Ritz-Carlton is never going to be all things to all people. It's going to be a little bit pricey for many people in their twenties, and for some in their thirties."

"But even then," Robert continues, "I have a lot of clients who have done well in the world of investing who are in their thirties, approaching 40, and they stay at Ritz-Carlton. Those are the hotels they have frequented while on business, and they want their families and children to also enjoy the experience. In some ways, the challenge for Ritz-Carlton is similar to that of Cadillac. For a while young people thought of a Cadillac as being the car of a prior generation. Both Cadillac and Ritz-Carlton have had to change in order to appeal to an increasingly younger customer, without losing the traditional guest. Times change, and we must change with the times. Ritz-Carlton recognizes that."

Yet changing markets don't require dramatic departures from current offerings as many business owners fear. Mark Ferland, general manager of The Ritz-Carlton, Orlando, Grande Lakes, says, "A customer once commented to me, 'So this Ritz-Carlton is going away from the traditional and going to the contemporary.' In our business, people often look at things from an either/or mentality. The designs of our hotels today emerge from a 'sense of place.' For example, in Bachelor Gulch, Colorado, you check in and there's a beautiful fire going with a Labrador retriever sitting next to the fire. That is right for Ritz-Carlton in a ski resort area, but it would be wrong at the headwaters of the Everglades. As a company, we have learned to look at each hotel from the point of view of that hotel's customer."

Mark continues, "That's why, if you go to New York City, in Central Park the guest expects a bit more traditional style hotel. But when you go to Battery Park, which is in the financial district with a different clientele, there is a more contemporary look. I think our president, Simon Cooper, says it best. He calls it 'comfortable contemporary.'" The market shift has genuinely afforded Ritz-Carlton the breadth to offer a "comfortable contemporary" feel without compromising its core elegance.

This search for business relevance is on the mind of many senior leaders today. Ed Zore, president and chief executive officer of the Northwestern Mutual Life Insurance Company, notes in a *Harvard Business Review* article, "Stay relevant. That's the name of the game, no matter what industry you're in." Ed goes on to identify ways to determine if a business is evolving in the direction of its customer's needs: "You can see if you're relevant by how you are performing. . . . Another measure is: Are we gaining or losing ground [on the competition]? . . . We also gauge relevance by listening to our customers. . . . To stay relevant, you've got to keep increasing the value you deliver to customers."

STRIKING GOLD

- What are your sales numbers telling you about the relevance of the products and services you offer to your customers?

- Are you gaining or losing market share in relation to those whom you view to be in direct competition for your customers?

- Have you listened to your customers in a way that allows you to innovate changes in your products or services that increase their perceived value?

Setting the Scene

With a customer base that is increasingly diverse and seeking memorable and unique experiences, Ritz-Carlton goes beyond simply creating a sense of place. To fully maximize the memorable and distinct aspects of their properties, management at Ritz-Carlton incorporates a design concept called *scenography*.

In its most literal sense, *scenography* refers to the art of representing objects in perspective, especially as applied in the design and painting of theatrical scenery; however, Ed Mady, vice president and area general manager of The Ritz-Carlton, San Francisco, explains, "Scenography is as simple as understanding that every business has its themes and its scenes. These themes and scenes should be something you sense in our hotels. They should emerge subtly from the way our property presents itself as opposed to our telling you what we are trying to achieve."

Of his San Francisco hotel, Ed comments, "Our scenography is opportunity and the epicurean journey. That opportunity is defined by Northern California's wine country. San Francisco is often recognized as the no. 2 city in the United States behind New York for its food. Through our great chef, Ron Segal, and through many subtle aspects of the hotel, we focus on an epicurean journey of food and taste. That journey is heightened by the little things, like the flowers we have chosen for our lobby or our offering of fortune cookies near the front desk, since they were invented here in San Francisco." While not every business has the opportunity to create a wide variety of scenes, it is important to appreciate how customers are becoming more attuned to perspective, integration of details, and having products and services placed in an appropriate setting.

Standards and Local Flair

The constant struggle faced by companies applying the Define and Refine principle is knowing when something needs to be defined as an unchangeable brand standard (something that guests will look for across visits or locations as a predictable aspect of their experience) and when something can be refined to reflect local relevance.

In essence, leadership must discern when a business's foundation should be modified to best meet the situational needs of the marketplace. Brian Gullbrants addresses this challenge daily in his role as vice president of operations. According to Brian, "When we talk about brand standards at Ritz-Carlton, we break it down into service standards, product standards, and process standards. What we've done with each of these three disciplines is clearly define what the customer is looking for and exactly what this service, process, or product should be at a certain level. We've identified that our customer wants the highest-quality products. Let's say fresh flowers must be in all of our hotels; now, if you're in a tropical setting, you want to use local tropical flowers, and if you are in New York City, you might want to use long-stemmed red roses or orchids. It just depends on the market and the customer."

Brian adds, "It comes down to defining the level of service, and sometimes down to the specifications of the product. Some items, such as the linens or textiles we use, are standard worldwide. For other items, we allow for regional differences; for example, we might have a North American standard and an Asian standard for the type of tea served, because of applicability to those markets. It's a matter of having standards and exploring when to vary them in a sensible manner. Similarly, when it comes to service standards, we have companywide expectations of Club-level service, but some of the specifics of service are adjusted by property. For example, a business hotel like The Portman Ritz-Carlton, Shanghai, might have the Club Lounge open 24 hours a day since many guests arrive on late-night international flights, while The Ritz-Carlton, Orlando, Grande Lakes, may serve peanut butter and jelly sandwiches in the Club Lounge—given the number of guests who are traveling with kids."

Global brand specialist Cindy Dyer, senior manager of consumer strategy and insight at Frito-Lay, Inc., and former marketer for Pizza Hut, Inc., comments, "Most big companies tend to keep their brands the same all over the world . . . . [They think] if it's Pizza Hut here, it's Pizza Hut everywhere." Cindy notes, however, that great businesses tailor their offerings to the local needs of the customer. "If you are Pizza Hut, it has to be pizza for each market. But you can't just export it and have it be that everywhere you go."

Cindy uses this example: If you have a feature like Pizza Hut's stuffed crust, "the concept is that you put something—a treat—in the crust edge. But it's different from place to place. In the United States, the crust edge is stuffed with cheese. In Asia, they put meat in the crust. In Mexico, they stuff it with cream cheese and jalapeño peppers." In all cases, the quality must be consistent while innovations and customization must be attentive to the unique aspects of the market. Additionally, products need to be presented and marketed in a culturally sensitive way.

Cindy continues: "Find out what's culturally acceptable from a marketing perspective, what's motivating to the customer." Ricco de Blank, general manager of The Ritz-Carlton, Tokyo, shares how cultural factors affected the design and positioning of his hotel in Japan. "It was not an easy task for us to open our hotel in Tokyo, but we benefited from wonderful brand recognition in Japan. Because of the unique needs of our marketplace, we decided to position our property as a leisure hotel and therefore focus on the high-end Japanese leisure market. Many Tokyo residents want to get out of their small homes and spend the night at our hotel, use the spa, or have dinner. Also many Japanese have a lifetime of savings at their disposal and now want to enjoy it. Essentially, we took the solid business foundation of Ritz-Carlton and adjusted it to the market needs of Tokyo and communicated a message about pampering oneself that has garnered us huge success with the Japanese customer."

Changing the product or service to meet the wants, needs, and desires of the regional customer is only half of the battle; your message about your product must also reflect those local nuances.

Varied Relevance

Refining your business to be relevant to your target audience takes many forms. At Ritz-Carlton, this relevance includes ensuring that the company focuses on the unique needs of diverse market sectors. As Ed Mady observes, "Everyone sees things differently. A business traveler could arrive here at 11 o'clock at night and leave the next day at 7 a.m., coming here only to sleep. By contrast, the leisure traveler in the summertime is usually here closer to three days, and what he or she wants from a stay is vastly different. Our hotel has to make a connection with each customer from both segments, and all our services have to be keyed in to their respective needs."

Peter Mainguy, general manager of The Ritz-Carlton, Dubai, cites, "Sometimes the needs of our varying customer groups can seem at odds with one another. For example, our lounge on the Club Floor typically attracts business people. By nature the lounge has been a quiet setting, but increasingly, families are bringing young children to the Club." In an effort to meet the needs of both groups—the business travelers and the people traveling with families—Peter's team created a separate family space in the lounge, and, with vigilance, it has refined the offerings and flow of the lounge experiences so that the two groups happily coexist and thrive.

The process of business refinement is continual and often involves management partnering with all of the staff resources to fuel the evolution. Mark Ferland shares, "It's the job of leadership to provide the environment that makes sure the Ladies and Gentlemen know we're not looking for that amazing invention that's going to change this year's profits for our company, but that every staff member is critical to making each guest more excited about his or her stay. Our Ladies and Gentlemen are in the best position to know what will make the stay of our guests most enjoyable." Sometimes that enjoyment may come from adding something to the experience, while other times it might involve taking something away that clutters or just doesn't belong. Often, it's as simple as asking yourself why you have done something the same way for 10 years. You may be surprised that the only answer is "Because that is the way we've always done it."

Mark cites an example of practical innovation by discussing a butterfly garden his team developed in Orlando. "Now it may not sound like the most exciting thing, but we're focused on ecotourism here. So we're constantly trying to find unique benefits for our guests. We're starting children's tours, and we're actually hatching cocoons of butterflies. We just had two cocoons hatch, and the kids came and watched the entire process." Who came up with the idea? The assistant director of grounds. Mark listened to the groundskeeper's ideas and passion and told him to do whatever he needed and wanted with the project. Two weeks later the groundskeeper came in and said the plants were in place and the project was done. Leadership often involves fostering the environment in which everyday creativity emerges in response to the needs of specific customer groups.

A Broadening View

Ritz-Carlton leadership is looking at how hotels can go beyond the changing needs of business and leisure travelers to also meet the needs of the communities in which the hotels are located. Dermod Dwyer, executive chairman of Treasury Holdings, the ownership group for The Ritz-Carlton, Powerscourt, Ireland, shares his views on location-based relevance: "The Ritz-Carlton group, both as a brand and as a company, has a very innovative vision for the future as expressed in its ambitious plans to expand to over 100 properties worldwide over the next few years. To accomplish this they are going to have to grow in a culturally authentic way, one that has a respect for place. I'm very optimistic that the Ritz-Carlton leadership will achieve this. I have stayed at other Ritz-Carlton hotels in Europe and have been impressed by the manner in which they reflect the indelible standard of excellence that is expected of the Ritz-Carlton brand, but yet each is impeccably in harmony with the spirit and the culture of the host country. Likewise with our hotel, The

Ritz-Carlton, Powerscourt; it's not an American hotel type simply planted in a beautiful location in Ireland; it's truly Ritz-Carlton, but authentically Irish in its essence and its ambience. Ultimately it comes down to continuing to ensure that a major corporation can deliver consistent brand excellence while offering enough freedom at the property level to allow each hotel to blend with its environment and adapt itself to the market in which it is placed."

President Simon Cooper acknowledges that at times efforts to balance the competing needs of communities, owners, and guests can lead to conservative approaches at creating otherwise excellent product offerings. He recalls, "Not that long ago, I signed off on a design for the premier restaurant that was to appear in the hotel we opened in Dallas, Texas, in 2007. My team and I authorized a restaurant that looked like a typical Ritz-Carlton dining room—something you would recognize from five years ago. It had the upholstered chairs, the luxurious tablecloths, and all the fine finishes. It was also a nice continuation of the design of the hotel. It was quite traditional, well done, very elegant, sophisticated, and placed in a large physical space. It would have served all the stakeholders well. But then through fortune, Chef Dean Fearing came along and divulged that he was leaving the esteemed restaurant at the Mansion on Turtle Creek. Here we had the best-known chef in town offering to work with us to make that restaurant more relevant to the changing customer and to the community.

"Dean's restaurant turned out to be a huge departure from what my team and I originally approved. It was a departure for all the right reasons. You take an incredible, recognized chef in the community, a genuinely animated individual who has put his heart and soul into designing the restaurant, and you have what I would call a destination restaurant today." That destination includes a menu of elevated American cuisine like chicken-fried Maine lobster or garlic-basted pheasant, an inviting Rattlesnake

Bar, richly appointed with honey onyx, formal and elegant dining areas, or the option to have a relaxed dinner beneath rawhide chandeliers in an area near Dean's kitchen. In essence, Dean Fearing's willingness to reach out to leadership at the Ritz-Carlton allowed both Dean and the hotel company to produce a concept that not only made both brands maximally relevant to their customers but also offered a significant benefit to the Dallas/Fort Worth area.

Simon adds, "I look at that restaurant today with amazement as Dean helped us refine our focus, so much so that we had to have police control the crowds when it opened. The restaurant did a million dollars in business in its first month. Dean's restaurant is the talk of Dallas. The Ladies and Gentlemen of Ritz-Carlton operate it with Dean, and they do so without waiting for the guest in room 605 to make a reservation. They are filling the restaurant every night regardless of the occupancy rate in the hotel. The restaurant makes us a destination in that community."

Dean Fearing acknowledges that he had a perception of Ritz-Carlton that caused him some hesitation in presenting his restaurant concept. "When my business partner and I thought about suggesting our 'no rules and bold flavors' restaurant to Ritz-Carlton, we thought we might find some resistance. We knew they were committed to excellence, but we didn't know if they would go for a restaurant with no dress code and the ability to eat wherever you want, including the bar. Ritz-Carlton worked with us every step of the way, and what we created was something that transcends anything I could have imagined."

Whether a business expands to an adjacent town or to a foreign country, the relevance of the company to the new community is always at issue because customer needs often vary from one location to the next. Given its rapid international expansion, Ritz-Carlton leadership is challenged with refining its products and services to the needs of clientele from Boston to Beijing and from resorts to urban hotel settings. Bob Kharazmi, senior vice president of international operations, states, "As we started to expand internationally, we were very careful and somewhat apprehensive about how our offerings would be received. To our pleasant surprise, we realized that although there were unique challenges in each market, whether it was China, Shanghai, other parts of Asia, Europe, the Middle East, or Latin America, a disciplined and genuine respect for the wants, needs, and desires of the customer resulted in success. No matter what language you speak, you want to be respected. You want to be treated fairly. You want businesses to be built with you in mind. As we grow, and as our hotels go 8,000 miles away from our corporate headquarters, the attentiveness and responsiveness to the customer are even more critical."

President Simon Cooper believes the longevity of the Ritz-Carlton brand and its overall relevance (like that of so many other companies) is largely linked to having its presence in emerging markets so that the brand has sufficient worldwide distribution both today and into the foreseeable future. Simon admits, "I've been dealt a fantastic hand. I work with an outstanding team, an incredibly successful brand that is doing extremely well through superb customer support and exceptional internal support. I've always said my challenge was not to mess up the success, while positioning the company for future growth. The challenge is both about staying the course and placing hotels in places where guests want us to be. That's why we are positioning ourselves in the Dubai Financial Center and throughout China in places like Sanya and Shenzhen.

"It's about taking a jewel of a brand and frankly hoping that when you hand it off to the next leader, it's more relevant to its customer base. There's no doubt we'll hand off a far bigger chain of hotels. There's no doubt we'll hand off a lifestyle brand that has developed into Residences and Clubs. There's no doubt, at the moment, we'll hand off economically superior performance. Hopefully though, we will continue to execute from a strong foundation but also hand off an adaptive, sustainable company with leadership that continues to challenge itself to be the best in every corner of the world."

Not only is the challenge to position business offerings in a relevant way, but staff at all levels of the organization are encouraged to take ownership of building a sustainable company. Simon continues, "I was conducting leadership training with the Ladies and Gentlemen, and I left them with a quote of Sir Edmund Hillary: 'It's not the mountain we challenge; it's ourselves.' We have to challenge ourselves as long as we intend to lead in this field because we will have external challenges. But the whole idea of leadership is that you continually improve yourself first."

STRIKING GOLD

- ▸ What aspects of your product or service are essential to your brand identity? What components can be changed, if needed, to address geographic trends or cultural differences?

- ▸ Have you positioned your product or service in places where your customers expect to find you?

- ▸ From a scenography perspective, how can you leverage the essence of your location or setting to enhance the overall experience of your customer?

- ▸ What do you do to challenge individuals throughout your organization to share ideas that will keep your business relevant and sustainable?

⇥ Transitioning to Service Values ⇤

This spirit of continual improvement for sustainability goes beyond the design and positioning of Ritz-Carlton hotels. In fact, with an evolving guest that is moving away from formal service and a desired sameness of experience, leadership at Ritz-Carlton sought to determine what, if any, service changes might improve the guest experience. Diana Oreck, vice president of global learning and the Leadership Center, says, "Simon Cooper started the journey into flexibility regarding service delivery in November 2005. He went out on a world tour, speaking to approximately half of the Ladies and Gentlemen of the company—at that time approximately 17,000 of 34,000 employees—and conducted approximately 45 focus groups. Through this process it became clear that the 20 Basics [discussed in Chapter 2] focused on tasks like when to answer a phone or how to escort a guest, . . . and they did not focus on outcomes.

"Our Ladies and Gentlemen suggested that the 20 Basics were helpful when they were first learning their jobs, but the more experienced they became, the more they were likely to modify the way they delivered the 20 Basics as they learned how to read a guest. Clearly, as leaders, we were less interested in adherence to the 20 Basics and more interested in the outcome of a happy guest. We wanted our Ladies and Gentlemen to be creative about producing memorable experiences for the guest as long as it was through ethical, moral, and legal means."

Rather than starting with a preconceived notion of how to revise the 20 Basics, leadership at Ritz-Carlton understood that a significant cultural change initiative would require the participation and involvement of all the Ladies and Gentlemen of the company. While listening to staff as they crafted the final outcome of the evolution process, leadership was aware that the desired end state would have to motivate staff to go beyond the 20 Basics to deliver service as the guest wanted to be served. Accomplishing that meant the final product (which is referred to as the "Service Values") had to rely on observation, intuition, talents, and the acquired skills of frontline staff.

To achieve the desired outcome, leadership helped craft a set of guiding principles that focused staff members on what was needed in guest interactions, while ultimately entrusting them to creatively improvise in the context of the guidelines. John Timmerman, vice president of quality and program management, had this perspective: "There is great value in our 20 Basics because any time you can give employees some conceptual responses, scenarios, examples, or templates, especially if they're not masters of their skill set, it is incredibly helpful to them. Those tools continue to be helpful until the employees become calibrated in their positions and they hit a certain level of performance that they can build upon. Our problem was that our 20 Basics were reinforcing rudimentary functioning even as our Ladies and Gentlemen matured in their development."

Approximately eight months after Simon Cooper began the process of discussing the 20 Basics, Ritz-Carlton leadership crafted a new set of service guidelines, focused on the outcomes necessary for producing transformational and memorable service for guests. On July 3, 2006, Ritz-Carlton officially launched the 12 Service Values, which were placed in the context of a declarative "I" statement that emphasized the power of each Lady and Gentleman. (Please see the sidebar "Service Values: I Am Proud to Be Ritz-Carlton.")

Service Values: I Am Proud to Be Ritz-Carlton

1. I build strong relationships and create Ritz-Carlton guests for life.
2. I am always responsive to the expressed and unexpressed wishes and needs of our guests.
3. I am empowered to create unique, memorable, and personal experiences for our guests.
4. I understand my role in achieving the Key Success Factors, embracing Community Footprints, and creating the Ritz-Carlton Mystique.

5. I continuously seek opportunities to innovate and improve the Ritz-Carlton Experience.
6. I own and immediately resolve guest problems.
7. I create a work environment of teamwork and lateral service so that the needs of our guests and each other are met.
8. I have the opportunity to continuously learn and grow.
9. I am involved in the planning of the work that affects me.
10. I am proud of my professional appearance, language, and behavior.
11. I protect the privacy and security of our guests, my fellow employees, and the company's confidential information and assets.
12. I am responsible for uncompromising levels of cleanliness and creating a safe and accident-free environment.

(Copyright © The Ritz-Carlton Hotel Company, L.L.C. All rights reserved. Reprinted with permission.)

See Chapter 5 for information about the Key Success Factors, Chapter 11 for information about Community Footprints, and Chapter 7 for information about Mystique.

In order to distinguish between the 20 Basics and the Service Values, one need only look at the different guidelines the Basics versus Values offer when it comes to communicating with guests. Where the 20 Basics defined specific ways to speak to a guest (for example, "my pleasure"), the Service Values encourage "professional language."

An important aspect of the Service Values is their hierarchical structure. If you start with 10, 11, and 12, you will notice they represent Functional values—things like safety, security, and cleanliness. Unless you first execute on the functional aspects of your business, you will never move up to the next plateau. To reach the next level of excellence, which Ritz-Carlton refers to as Emotional Engagement, Values 4 through 9 come into play. These involve learning and the professional growth of the Ladies and Gentlemen, teamwork, service, problem resolution, innovation, and continuous improvement.

Beyond the Functional needs of the guest and the guest's Emotional Engagement, Ritz-Carlton leadership has defined a level they call "the Ritz-Carlton Mystique." To achieve this outcome, Values 1, 2, and 3 are needed to create unique, memorable, and personal experiences for a guest. This can occur only when people fully deliver on the guests' expressed and unexpressed wishes and needs and when the Ladies and Gentlemen strive to build lifetime guest relationships.

John Timmerman acknowledges that acceptance of the Service Values didn't occur without resistance, and, as might be expected, much of that initial reticence came from leaders. "When we did the test of the first set of changes, management's negative-to-positive ratio was 7:3. Those results reflect the reaction of general managers and leaders in the corporate office. It was quite interesting though—the employee response was 1 negative to 9 positive. Given those preliminary results, we had general managers go to focus groups. They heard what the customers said; they listened to the employees; they saw with their own eyes the affinity those groups had for the changes. Later we brought all of our general managers together at a worldwide conference, and our president, Simon Cooper, presented the rationale, the data, and then the voice of a highly respected general manager, Ed Mady, who said, 'I have become comfortable with being uncomfortable about this change.'"

Acknowledging that resistance to change is often the result of leaders having to restructure the way they lead others, John explains, "Our leaders' resistance fell into two areas. They were understandably concerned that employees would lose focus. But, while they wouldn't say this, the unspoken hesitance was linked to the fact that they had been groomed over decades to develop the 20 Basics into their own personal leadership style. Many of these leaders could offer 50 inspiring stories around what excellence in the 20 Basics looked like, but now they would have to start from scratch on the Service Values and essentially reinvent themselves."

Despite initial resistance to the Service Values, they have become a well-accepted refinement to the 20 Basics. In the words of John Timmerman, "I think the Service Values represent one of the most successful changes we have implemented at Ritz-Carlton. On a companywide survey, the introduction of the Service Values received the highest rating of any management process change in the areas of deployment, effectiveness, and implementation. We received full roll-out in six months, and I've seen some things that we've initiated take three years. I think the difference between the Service Values and other changes is that the senior leadership team was involved in the design and helped craft it. We used the customer, both internal and external, to guide that design change and the process of implementation. It may sound simplistic, but I think all of those steps are necessary and are key ingredients in driving major cultural change."

The success of the Service Values can also be measured by the subjective evaluation of those for whom the change has had the greatest impact. Hotel doorman Marty Premtaj says, "Just as our service was more formal, so were the 20 Basics. To me the Service Values are more about encouraging us to serve the guest exactly as the guest wishes. In some ways that is more challenging, but it is also more rewarding for both the guest and me. It's a great thing to know that I am encouraged to do that and am responsible for those outcomes."

Clearly the Service Values are also being noticed by traditional guests at Ritz-Carlton, as some of the formality has been adjusted. Simon Cooper shares, "I had a guest complain to me that he saw one of our bartenders serve a young guest a bottle of beer without a glass. When I looked into it, I informed the complaining guest that the service was a result of the young guest's having asked for his beer to be served that way a day before. That is the challenge and the joy of the Service Values. It encourages our Ladies and Gentlemen to customize the experience to the guest, ensuring that traditional and new-generation guests are each treated respectfully in accord with their wishes."

·◦[Changing the Company]◦· Image—Externally and Internally

Conversations with Ritz-Carlton leadership indicate clearly that they are committed to "evolution and not revolution." While customer-centric changes had been taking place in the design and service received at Ritz-Carlton, these transformations also had to be effectively communicated to internal and external customers. To this end, Ritz-Carlton leadership and its outside marketing partner sought to create honest images of an evolving company.

The goal of these communications was to gently shift customer perceptions of Ritz-Carlton from that of a staid, Old World, traditional hotel to something more in the middle of a continuum that runs between traditional and contemporary— in essence, neither being on the extremes of iconic or trendy. Because of this objective, marketing images stopped depicting society guests near a grand hotel and instead sought to capture the essence of Ritz-Carlton's service standards. Advertising messages, for example, were designed to show timeless service excellence that is tailored to produce a personal and memorable experience for each guest. Rich marketing images (Figure 3.1) don't focus on the elegance of a hotel property but instead emphasize how service excellence allows for unique and exotic experiences.

Bruce Himelstein, senior vice president of sales and marketing, eloquently sums up the balancing act Ritz-Carlton faces in the ongoing efforts to define and refine. "It's still a primary responsibility for this company to be authentic and relevant. Not to be edgy, cool, and hip. I don't believe the customer would buy that for Ritz-Carlton, and it is not who we are. I think customers and prospective customers will accept that we're going to be in

Figure 3.1

**With a new marketing campaign developed by
Team One, Ritz-Carlton broadly communicated how it
was redefining its brand and evolving luxury.**

*(Advertisement: copyright © The Ritz-Carlton Hotel Company, LLC. All rights
reserved. Reprinted with permission. Photograph: copyright © Christopher Wilson.)*

places they haven't seen us before, and I think they'll embrace
the fact that we are shifting. But if we said for next year's strategy,
we're going to be a sexy brand, the customers would say, 'Who
are you kidding? You're Ritz-Carlton.' There is a lot of white
space between doing nothing and going so far over the edge that
you're not credible. So that's the fine line that we walk all the
time."

"When we err walking that line," Bruce continues, "we err
toward maintaining the historic perception of the brand because
so much equity is sitting there, and one bad move could set back
years of hard work establishing the respect this company carries.
However, along with that, in the past couple of years the edgi-
ness and risk tolerance of this company has gone up, and we're
always pushing."

Whether a company has established brand equity that it
must reposition or is in its early development phase, leadership

must define its culture and "always keep pushing" to refine the business's relevance to a changing marketplace. While there is always a risk of pushing too hard for business refinement, more often the ultimate risk is complacency that emerges from past success. Once-excellent businesses have crumbled before their leadership realized that they had become irrelevant to the changing consumer.

LIVING THE NEW GOLD STANDARD

- Evolving to keep up with current trends doesn't mean overriding all previous successes. Combining the best of the past with the best of the present produces an optimal future.

- Forecast the buying habits of your clientele. Research their styles, habits, and expectations so your offerings are relevant to their changing needs.

- No company can be all things to all people, but it is possible for your organization to be all things to your customers.

- The process of business refinement is ongoing; it keeps the excitement level high and involvement in the organization strong, both on the part of employees and customers.

- Continually improve your organization with a customer-centric view to stay ahead of constant external challenges.

- Transformational, memorable service shouldn't be exclusive to the luxury market. Delivering on customers' expressed and unexpressed wishes creates clients for life.

◦◦⟨ P R I N C I P L E ⟩◦◦

2

Empower
through Trust

Select—Don't Hire

Whatever you are by nature, keep to it;
never desert your line of talent. Be what nature
intended you for and you will succeed.

SYDNEY SMITH

 Displeased customers are more likely than satisfied consumers to take the time to write to corporate leadership. So imagine opening a two-page handwritten letter from a customer who merely wanted to offer gratitude for staff members who deliver subtle but caring service. In such a letter the guest recounts, "One of your employees and I got on an elevator in your building. I pushed the sixth-floor button and he pushed none. Instead of getting off with me on the sixth floor, your employee simply said, 'Have a nice day.' Upon exiting the elevator, I asked, 'Where are you going? Aren't you getting off here?' Your employee replied, 'No, I'm going back down to the fifth floor.'" The guest goes on to write, "I couldn't believe it—how do you find people who are so invested in placing the needs of their guest above their own?" Such was a letter received by Ritz-Carlton President Simon Cooper.

Simon receives a fair share of customer letters, both critical and complimentary; however, he realizes that given his company's steadfast commitment to and passion for selection, training, and empowerment, the Ladies and Gentlemen of the Ritz-Carlton consistently generate extraordinary customer experiences. Simon shares, "Of course we always love to hear the epic tales of Ladies and Gentlemen doing something seemingly on a par with helping a guest by rushing off and stopping an airplane by throwing themselves under it; those types of stories are always amazing. But I like the subtle actions that tell a guest, 'I know what you've gone through,' or 'Here's a little thing to let you know you matter.'"

In order for staff to continually and subtly act in ways that not only satisfy but delight customers, leaders must understand the importance of identifying talent and developing methods for selecting top candidates.

In a world in which human resources conferences typically feature speakers talking about "talent wars," "talent crises," or an emerging workforce that lacks the service ethic of prior generations, how does Ritz-Carlton consistently find men and women who exceed customer expectations?

The obvious, but wrong, answer would be that they attract the best by having an overly generous compensation plan. Simon explains, "When I speak to different groups, one of the things I'm always worried about is that the audience thinks just because we're at the luxury end of the business, we can attract a different kind of employee. So one of the things I always do is remind audiences that our Ladies and Gentlemen come from exactly the same labor force, backgrounds, and quality of life that theirs do. We're not paying a premium; we pay the same as others in our industry. It's really how we select our people and what we do when they join our family."

To truly understand the success of Ritz-Carlton, one must understand leadership's approach to the staff selection process.

·◦] Assessing Candidates [◦·
Takes Patience

Many business leaders have found themselves in the annoying position of having hired someone who turned out to not perform up to expectations. On paper and in interviews, the individual appeared to have the requisite skills and came with glowing recommendations. Behavior-based interview questions suggested that the prospective candidate would exercise good judgment in hypothetical work situations. But in the end, the employee failed to flourish in the position. Leadership at Ritz-Carlton has addressed this key challenge faced by most businesses by espousing a long-standing commitment to assess the strengths of a prospective candidate through a comprehensive process that involves multiple interviews, identifying the right qualities and requirements for each position, and searching for individuals who take pride in providing service.

Consistent with the talent-based approaches championed by experts, Ritz-Carlton leadership believes that excellence occurs by starting with the right raw talent instead of attempting to manage employees to overcome talent deficits. Ed Mady, area general manager of The Ritz-Carlton, San Francisco, illustrates the difference this way: "It's very short, very simple. Luxury is a choice. Luxury is in the eye of the beholder. And if you get your arms around that, then you can say, 'Every single person who walks into the building needs to have individualized, personalized attention.' And how do you create that? Like a factory, there's a conveyor belt, and that conveyor starts in our industry with talent selection and finding people who have innate aptitudes to consistently deliver the luxury service product. We are looking for those with true strengths to deliver luxury service. By that I distinguish between a strength, which is something you do well, and a true strength which is something you do well *and* enjoy." But how does a business leader find people with "true strengths" as customer service professionals?

In developing its selection process, Ritz-Carlton uses its own expertise as well as consultants such as Talent Plus. Melissa Young, pastry chef at The Ritz-Carlton, Washington, D.C., describes her experience with the hiring process that resulted from that leadership effort: "I was in college at the time, and a professor knew that I wanted to work for Ritz-Carlton. That professor contacted the executive sous chef and the rooms manager of Ritz-Carlton and told them about me. After filling out an application, I completed my first interview with the hiring manager and then did a listening interview with the assistant pastry chef. During that interview, he asked me both personality- and pastry-related questions. I had one more interview with the executive pastry chef. Then I flew down to the hotel for a day and prepared pastry items for a tasting by the chefs. Shortly thereafter, I got the call offering me the position. It was exciting making it through the selection process." While the involved nature of selection at Ritz-Carlton may be too slow for some businesses, it demonstrates the importance that leadership places on assessing the strengths, commitment, and skills of the applicant.

Understanding an individual's strengths helps an employer determine whether an applicant possesses the raw talent needed for a particular job. Leadership at Ritz-Carlton invests heavily in the formal assessment of strengths through structured interviews. Each Ritz-Carlton employee has gone through a series of personal meetings before being "selected," rather than "hired," for a job.

This important distinction between hiring and selection is best explained by Hervé Humler, president of international operations: "*Hiring* can be nothing more than finding anyone to fill a job, but *selection*? That is choosing the best person to provide exemplary service."

To increase the chances of finding the right person, interviews conducted in the selection process not only involve Ritz-Carlton departmental managers but also frontline Ladies and Gentlemen who have been certified as interviewers. New hires feel pride knowing they were selected after going through such an involved interviewing process. Tony Mira, a general manager at Ritz-Carlton, comments that despite his 28-year history in the hotel industry with extensive leadership experience, "It took 14 interviews for me to get this job, which is common for a general manager position at Ritz-Carlton. Four of them were with the owners of the hotel. But 10 interviews were with Ritz-Carlton staff, starting with two initial interviews at the corporate office, including the vice president of human resources who is in charge of talent management. You can't help but feel special, whether you are a leader or a frontline employee, when people take so much time to get to know you and afterward deem you acceptable."

That pride in being selected also serves as a motivator to live up to the trust that has been placed in the individual upon being hired. Adam Hassan, boiler operator in the engineering department, explains, "When people take so much time to select you, you really want to prove that they made the right choice. So if I see anything unusual, I take care of it. I don't have my boss telling me to go do it; I go do it on my own because I don't want to let the guests or the other Ladies and Gentlemen down. If I turn my head on a broken lamp, I am not living up to the standard of a service professional. Everybody here does the same thing: They walk in the hallway and if they see a piece of paper, they bend down and pick it up. That comes from the heart; it comes freely, because they have chosen us as if we owned the place."

The hiring process not only serves as an opportunity to find people to perform necessary functions for a business but ultimately also sets the tone for the pride people take in their work. By creating layers of evaluation, new hires feel that leadership has invested in getting to know them. Further, they realize that leadership wants to ensure that those who join the company can meet or exceed the standards of those who have come before them. Ultimately, staff members feel a responsibility to live up to the trust placed in them through their offer of employment . . . and they even become recruiters themselves.

Susan Strayer, director of talent management at Ritz-Carlton and author of *The Right Job Right Now: The Complete Toolkit for Finding Your Perfect Career*, observes, "Our Ladies and Gentlemen are our greatest recruiting force. I was asking a Lady at our Naples property how she got in the organization. She said it was through one of her friends. And she felt special because her friend had referred her."

While many business leaders understand the value of a patient, methodical selection process, they often take shortcuts and compromise their sound business platforms. In essence, they succumb to the "we need bodies now" pressure. Human resource professionals are tasked to prioritize getting open positions filled, even at the expense of prudent selection.

Unfortunately, the same people who clamor for "hiring someone quickly" also tend to be the people who are first to complain when that "someone" turns out to be the wrong "someone" days, weeks, or months later. Ed Mady puts it this way: "You can't microwave Ritz-Carlton. Processes can be slow here, but when we complete a decision, it is likely to be on target. We really do take time to aim before we hire." As observed by Susan Strayer, who is actively involved in recruitment for Ritz-Carlton, "There is a lot of rushing around on hiring in the labor market right now, and at times that can work against us at Ritz-Carlton. For example, I might meet a college graduate at a career fair and find out another hotel company offered that person a job right there on the spot. We can't do that because we have this rigorous selection process. We may end up losing some candidates, but it's never worth sacrificing the thoroughness of our selection process to do that. By choosing the right people in the first place, our turnover is in the 20 percent range in an industry that averages about 60 percent. That payoff alone, not to mention staff morale benefits, is enough to justify our patience."

Patient exploration for talent, coupled with a willingness to pass over people who are not passionate about service, actually helps attract people who *are* right for your company. Francisca

Martinez, vice president of talent management at Ritz-Carlton, understands the value of pragmatic hiring. "There's quite a bit of self-selection. People committed to quality and service are drawn to us because they know they will be working with the best in those areas. They also know that we are going to develop their talent, and in a world in which no one is guaranteed a job for life, we will enhance their value in the workforce."

By investing the time to personally and patiently assess prospective job applicants, you can increase the probability that each new hire will both be a success and add value to the customer experience. Further, you can grow employee engagement and retention well above industry standards. This workforce loyalty and decreased turnover offers competitive service advantages that more than offset the initial costs of selection.

STRIKING GOLD

- Beyond technical skills, what processes do you have in place to study the commitments and strengths of your prospective employees?

- What is your selection process? Does it involve multiple interviews that include frontline workers?

- How often does expediency take priority over patient selection?

Imprinting Culture onto Raw Talent

Once the costly journey of recruitment and selection are completed, many businesses fail to appreciate the critically important opportunity they are provided during the orientation process. In many companies, orientation is seen as a necessary evil, conducted only to fulfill legal requirements and provide an overview of the employee handbook. By contrast, the orientation process at Ritz-Carlton is a benchmark for how businesses can maximize the engagement and satisfaction of their workforce.

In an existing Ritz-Carlton hotel, the process of bringing on new employees has a consistent pattern. Orientation takes place in the hotel meeting rooms and lunch is in the hotel restaurant so that new employees can be received as welcome guests. Senior leadership, starting with the general manager of the hotel, personally greets each newly hired employee. Initiating the Three Steps of Service (discussed in Chapter 2), the new hires are warmly welcomed, and their stated and unstated needs are anticipated and met. Tom Donovan, general manager of The Ritz-Carlton, Kapalua, shares, "Even though each property has its differences, the process of new employee orientation is very much the same. I have been the general manager in Bachelor Gulch, Colorado, and Kapalua, Hawaii, and all new employees at both properties appreciate the personal attention they receive in orientation. We have our highest-ranking people at the hotel level actively welcome our new hires into employment. As a general manager, I am saying 'congratulations,' and 'you are part of our family.' I would not invite family to visit me and have a designee of mine at my house to greet my guests. That's why I am at each orientation."

Prior to covering job-specific information, the Ritz-Carlton orientation consists of two days of discussions about the Credo, Motto, Service Values, and other core cultural components. Michael Clemons, a newly hired bellman at The Ritz-Carlton, Dallas, notes, "I have never worked for a company that has done a better job with orientation. Literally, the senior leadership spent days talking to us about the history, values, and purpose of this business. I couldn't believe that they would spend so much time examining how we can make a difference for guests. I also felt like they were helping me see that I had been chosen because I could create memorable guest experiences. Don't get me wrong, I've worked at places that said their mission was important, but we would spend only a few minutes on the mission during orientation and we hardly ever talked about it after that. Ritz-Carlton orientation is all about fully understanding and committing to the culture of service. They don't rush you through that, and it really is only the beginning of that conversation."

In support of grounding new hires deeply and immediately in mission, vision, and values, new staff members cannot start employment until they have completed the orientation process. Kathy Smith, senior vice president of human resources, indicates, "It's quite a culture shift for managers who come from outside Ritz-Carlton to understand that no one, absolutely no one, begins working for Ritz-Carlton before they go through orientation. We drive this home in our management training. While it may seem like a case of 'what would it hurt if we bring someone on board to help us with a banquet before he or she can be scheduled for orientation?' the reality is that skipping orientation negatively affects the way the new employee comes to know us, and it denies that person his or her deserved welcome into a relationship with the company."

Leadership at Ritz-Carlton also sees employee orientation as essential to global service excellence. Jean Cohen, vice president and general manager of The Ritz-Carlton, Grand Cayman, notes, "Service excellence is quite simply the rock upon which the brand is built. No matter what the location, indigenous design, or specific amenities, a consistent quality of service is what Ritz-Carlton guests can expect to find whether they are visiting a hotel in California, China, or Grand Cayman. While some people are surprised that our newly selected Ladies and Gentlemen are not permitted to start working until they go through their full two-day orientation, Ritz-Carlton feels that it is paramount that these staff members have a full understanding of who we are and the philosophies behind the Gold Standards before they can start learning their specific job tasks. This is merely one example of how Ritz-Carlton consistently places the fundamentals of service excellence above other concerns."

⊰ Training the Talented ⊱

While selection at Ritz-Carlton is a rigorous process of identifying committed service professionals, individuals come to the company with varying levels of technical skill and backgrounds both inside and outside the hospitality industry. New staff members are assigned learning coaches who train and certify them on the core competencies of their jobs.

Mandy Holloway, senior director of global learning at Ritz-Carlton, observes, "We take training and learning very seriously. We focus on the design of learning, measured competency, and whether the skills learned are truly being delivered to the customer. We are on a journey right now where we're evolving from a training organization into a learning environment. We understand very clearly that 70 percent of learning realistically is on the job. This feeds through to operational certification, making sure that within the employees' first 21 days, they are certified within their jobs, in alignment with the Gold Standards for the hotel. We have great tools like online training modules and detailed operational manuals that help facilitate that certification process. Those tools also are in alignment so that we can analyze operational skills acquisition against the results of mystery shopper and customer engagement surveys. In essence, secret shoppers are looking for the exact criteria that staff members are certified to meet. As such, we're not doing training for the sake of training."

By way of example, Mandy adds, "Let's assume that all members of the front desk staff have worked with a learning coach and have achieved certification from that coach on the core competencies of their job by the twenty-first day of their employment. Let's also assume that problems are being detected either by mystery shoppers or from guest surveys that the front desk staff is not consistently confirming the guests' length of stay during the check-in process. Even though the employees were at one time proficient and certified at that skill, the customer feedback affords the opportunity for what we call 'just-in-time learning' to take place to quickly refresh that service delivery standard."

Mark DeCocinis, regional vice president of Asia Pacific, believes that the company's commitment to training and skills certification gives them a competitive advantage in international markets. "For example, Asia Pacific is in a unique position as having won best employer in the region (in all employment categories) in multiple destinations. As such, we are able to attract the very best of talent available in the market. With our sound human resources practices, where every employee joining Ritz-Carlton receives more than 250 hours of training in the first year of operation, we develop and nurture a well-trained and loyal team of Ladies and Gentlemen who are at the very heart of our operations. Therefore, in emerging nations such as China, where there is a chronic shortage of qualified hospitality staff, we are able to appeal to and employ the very best local talent available and fully certify them in our Ritz-Carlton philosophy. This training and being part of the Ritz-Carlton culture engenders a great sense of commitment from all of our Ladies and Gentlemen, and they feel empowered and engaged in their own decision making and in their own career development."

While the 21-day certification process is constantly occurring as new hires are brought into an existing hotel, the task of initially training staff for a new hotel opening is rather daunting. Senior leadership at Ritz-Carlton work together to source the coaching needs of the new hotel by drawing some of the most talented coaches and trainers from throughout the Ritz-Carlton system. Roberto Van Geenen, general manager of The Ritz-Carlton, Dallas, says, "Our process starts about 52 weeks before we open our doors, and every single week we have to meet certain milestones. When I arrived in Dallas a year before the opening, there were only three of us here—the director of sales and marketing, one assistant, and me. But the most intense action occurs in the hotel 10 days before launch, a period we call 'countdown.' During that countdown, we run the hotel like a full-blown operation to make sure everything is ready for our guests."

Roberto adds, "To train a predominantly new group of Ritz-Carlton Ladies and Gentlemen to prepare a hotel for opening, we choose our service champions from around the world. For example, I think we had four or five executive chefs here for our opening. So it's all of our leaders, and they have to be certified; they have to have the global reputation with their technical skills and, most important, with embracing the philosophy. General managers support one another by accommodating the request to have their best people travel and work hard through the 10-day countdown. We start at 6:00 in the morning with the trainers' lineup, and we finish business about 8:00 in the evening. At night, we have what we call 'fun and games.' Those evenings involve all of the trainers, my staff, and me putting things in their right place, stocking minibars, making beds, and doing whatever it takes to make the hotel ready for the next day's staff training and ready for the upcoming needs of guests."

The training and launch efforts at the Dallas hotel earned Roberto and his team official recognition as the best employer in Dallas before the hotel even opened.

Ritz-Carlton has effectively developed structured approaches to help staff members understand and embrace the company's culture during both new hotel openings and the new-hire on-boarding process. In each case, the transfer of corporate knowledge is highly valued both in terms of certifiable operational standards and cultural identity and history.

Bob Kharazmi, senior vice president of international operations, notes that cultural imprinting is essential to the success of Ritz-Carlton hotels internationally. "Our president of international operations, Hervé Humler, and I go to every international hotel opening. We spend 7 to 10 days with our managers. Hervé and I lead the team. No matter what we have going on at our corporate headquarters, we drop everything to make sure the hotel is launched from a solid cultural and operational foundation.

We work with both the front line and leadership, helping them understand our Gold Standards and our approach to business. At our leadership sessions, we define our expectations in regard to our business model, treatment of staff, care of guests, and community involvement. Before we leave the property, we get departments together, and say, 'You know our expectations. You know our culture. What do you want to be? This is your.hotel; this is your department. What do you want to be?' We take all their ideas and before we leave, every single department writes their mission statement. This ensures that the Ritz-Carlton leadership approach is easily adopted and is customized to each international property."

Bob adds, "This transfer of knowledge is catching on internationally, as evidenced by the trainers who were involved in opening our second hotel in Beijing. Of the 80 'best-of-the-best" trainers who came from all over the world to open that hotel, 7 were from the Beijing Financial Street hotel that had only opened 12 months earlier. One can only imagine the very powerful career message that their success gave to would-be leaders."

Over time Ritz-Carlton leadership has developed a very sophisticated process of making training a person-to-person journey that results in the inculcation of corporate values and mission.

Training through Relationship

While formal training programs are in place, more informal and relationship-based development opportunities are also encouraged. A key stage of successfully developing talent in an organization is investing time in the mentoring processes. To that end, personal growth and development discussions are not only built into the employee review process at Ritz-Carlton but they are also required of the management team.

Whether Ritz-Carlton managers or leaders are selected from within the company or transfer into the business, they undergo a manager's orientation. The first two days cover the typical Ritz-Carlton orientation, but day 3 involves the expectations of leadership. Part of the session concerns respecting their Ladies and Gentlemen, a portion is about letting the manager know the importance of facilitating ongoing career discussions, and another significant part is about being a mentor.

From the onset, managers are given the message that if they don't align with these expectations, they may not be a good fit for the position. New managers are essentially told that if they are not driven by and passionate about respect, developing talent, and training, they probably will not be successful at Ritz-Carlton. New-manager orientation addresses a significant problem identified by leadership transition expert Michael Watkins, author of the international business bestseller *The First 90 Days: Critical Success Strategies for New Leaders at All Levels.* "The main reason newly hired outside executives have such an abysmal failure rate (40 percent, according to one study) is poor acculturation," says Michael. "They don't adapt well to the new company's ways of doing things. In fact some three-quarters of 53 senior HR managers I surveyed cited poor cultural fit as the driver for onboarding failures." By clearly communicating cultural standards early on, new leaders at Ritz-Carlton can and do experience more successful transitions.

The benefits of placing expectations on management to develop talent can be found in examples such as the career path of Adam Hassan. "I started at Ritz-Carlton 12 years ago as a banquet houseman, setting up meeting rooms and vacuuming carpets. I worked as a houseman for three years, but my boss knew I wanted to work in the engineering department some day. In fact, my boss at the time encouraged me to pursue my career dreams by letting me work with engineering to repair vacuums and paint hallways. The director of engineering saw that coming from me, so when a job in the engineering department opened up, I was selected. Since then, Ritz-Carlton sent me to school to get my boiler operator license. I just got my certification two weeks ago. Now I'm going to continue to study for certifications in cooling, plumbing, and electrical. It will take me a while because each course takes about six months, but you have to study and prepare yourself. This has been great for me, and it makes me so much better at serving our guests."

While it may be a somewhat unique necessity in the hotel industry, lateral service is strongly encouraged at Ritz-Carlton hotels. In essence, lateral service is the expectation that all Ladies and Gentlemen will pitch in to do what is necessary to get a job done whether or not that task is directly linked to an individual's job description. This type of service occurs daily in the hotels and can be observed in the actions of individuals such as Ed Mady, general manager, and Christoph Moje, hotel manager, of The Ritz-Carlton, San Francisco, and a team of staff members from human resources, the sales office, security, and virtually every area of the hotel. These senior hotel leaders along with housekeepers, desk clerks, and other staff members from throughout the hotel rush to the aid of the culinary staff and banquet servers to plate up (that is, to place items on plates in an assembly-line process overseen with final approval from the chef) and turn a conference room into a dining room.

Ed comments, "This is lateral service—everyone in the hotel making themselves available as best they can to add physical labor. By quickly turning over a room from a meeting space to an eating space, we efficiently manage costs for an important part of our business. At this property, we don't have the luxury of separate large spaces for meeting and feeding." What Ritz-Carlton does have is a staff that has been trained on the importance of lateral service. Ed relates, "Our people understand that they are not just reservation specialists or engineers; they are part of a team that keeps the hotel running. People come from their offices or wherever they are in the hotel and are told that the chef needs them to plate up at 11:45 a.m. or to be present at the room-turn at noon. The food has been prepared shortly beforehand because food has to come right down at service time; you want to keep it fresh and as hot as possible. Service doesn't start until 12:30 p.m., and we have to plate everything up over 45 minutes; the chef has an estimate of how many people he will need. As the food comes down, the servers allow the office people to do all the detail, and they start getting tables set. First we will be stacking chairs, garbage will be picked up, and the dividing walls will either be put up or taken down. The maître d' or director will use a microphone, telling us where the bread and butter goes and the salt and pepper."

When senior leaders pitch in with frontline workers to get a job done, they demonstrate that service must be delivered universally on behalf of coworkers in order for it to maximally occur for customers. Esezi Kolagbodi, doorman at The Ritz-Carlton, Berlin, discusses the impact of leaders sharing the workload: "I appreciate my company because a supervisor is never too important to drive a car down for me, the doorman. And the hotel manager assists me in carrying luggage without my saying a word. In short, it's a place where leaders show you that we are all one, where leadership is not saying it, but doing it. And I mean in all areas of the hotel."

This spirit of leadership through teamwork is reflected also in the comments of Ricco de Blank, general manager of The Ritz-Carlton, Tokyo, who notes, "Service must start with me. Service is what makes us Ritz-Carlton. Others can copy the design of a hotel or make a better design, but great service lasts forever. I eat in the employee dining room. I serve the employees' lunch on Saturday. I paint their locker room. It is the least I can do since they run the hotel." By encouraging lateral service, cross-training organically occurs, departments become less isolated from one another, and staff members gain a greater empathy for the functions of those in other areas of the business.

While some leaders might think customers cannot infer the quality of training offered inside of a business, Robin Sanders of Sanders Travel Centre disagrees. "I think Ritz-Carlton offers the best training at all levels of their business," she remarks. "Other great hotels might train well at the salesperson or concierge level, but not as well below midlevel. Across the board, Ritz-Carlton has the best overall training of staff that I've ever seen." In support of her observations, Robin reflects on an experience she had at The Ritz-Carlton, Dallas: "The hotel had been open only a few weeks, and we went to the ribbon cutting. When I pulled in to valet my car, the staff member didn't give me a ticket. He took my car, remembered me, and brought my car back to me perfectly and amazingly. All of this was done early on in the life of that hotel. The only way you can exceed a customer's expectation is through excellent training, great processes, . . . and like the valet who was parking cars that day, hiring staff members who fully buy into your culture."

Robin's comments summarize the end goal for all training: It is offered to provide the tools necessary so that every staff member believes in the mission and delivers consistent excellence.

Maintaining a Vital and Engaged Workforce

Employees who leave companies typically do so after about a year, but according to recent research, 90 percent make the decision to stay or leave within six months of employment. With a firm understanding of the speed with which employees can become disillusioned and disengaged from their work, Ritz-Carlton leadership has established something called "Day 21." On the twenty-first day on the job, after becoming certified in the operational standards of their positions, staff members are given a forum to freely discuss the positives and negatives they have encountered in their first three weeks. The newly hired Ladies and Gentlemen can talk openly about things such as whether they have been given all the tools they've needed to achieve success, the quality of their job trainer, and whether the culture described to them at orientation is present in the employees' day-to-day experiences. Day 21 becomes an opportunity to listen to the needs of the Ladies and Gentlemen, solve problems, and reenroll staff members before they have an opportunity to disengage or become toxic to the workforce.

Emnet Andu, who moved to the United States from Eritrea, works as a server at the Atlanta Grill in the downtown Ritz-Carlton, Atlanta, and talks about how revitalizing that review was for her. "Day 21 blew me away. Not only did they listen to me—I mean *really* listen to me—talk about how I was feeling at Ritz-Carlton, but they posed important questions about my work." Alexandra Valentin, director of learning, The Ritz-Carlton, Central Park, notes, "It's amazing how open staff are at Day 21. Commonly our Ladies and Gentlemen will talk about problems they had with their training or how they are sharing resources with another department and how those resources are in short supply. We collect all of their issues and concerns and take them to the guidance team at the hotel to get the issues addressed. While we keep the specific comments anonymous, we do make sure that we go back to all of the Ladies and Gentlemen so that they know how their issues were resolved. It is important not only to listen but to make sure they are apprised of the outcome."

Leaders who pay attention to details of concern to their staff members and who take action on those details ultimately model the impact that detailed attention can have on the customers their staff serves.

STRIKING GOLD

- ▶ How effectively do you acculturate leaders into your organization?

- ▶ As a leader, where do you participate in activities to role model the importance of lateral service?

- ▶ What listening processes do you have in place to reengage new hires early in their employment tenure?

·•] Celebrating the Anniversary [•·· and Yearly Recalibration

While most leaders strive to not forget the birthdays of people important to them, many fail to acknowledge the anniversary of their employees' hire dates. Ritz-Carlton has a built-in process to celebrate the hire date of each employee, called "Day 365," an annual acknowledgment of a staff member joining the Ritz-Carlton family. By highlighting that day, leadership can show appreciation for and celebrate the contribution of the individual, just as a birthday celebration validates the significance of an individual in a family. Additionally, Day 365 serves as an opportunity to refresh a staff member's skills against operational certification standards.

Daniel Mangione, assistant pastry chef, describes how Day 365 is handled at The Ritz-Carlton, Half Moon Bay: "Day 365 is your 1-year anniversary. At our hotel, on your yearly anniversary you are given a certificate celebrating your service. You are given a full hot breakfast with coffee and eggs and the like. The general manager is there as well. You talk about the company. You speak about your time at Ritz Carlton. It is not just for people who have been there 1 year; it is anyone who is celebrating a service anniversary that month. I remember that I sat at a table with people who had been there 1 year, 5 years, and 18 years. It is important to be acknowledged and to hear the stories of others who are celebrating a proud tenure."

Julia Gajcak, vice president of communications and marketing, describes the impact of personal recognition. "It's not unusual to feel excited on the first day on any job, but at Ritz-Carlton you may find a handwritten card from your boss and flowers. We know that the exhilarated feeling needs to be nourished in order for it to remain past Day 21 or Day 365. It takes a commitment to your people to honor them spontaneously and in a planned way so that the enthusiasm of their first day matures into something solid and strong. In the end, it's simple for us at Ritz-Carlton: Our people make the company. Our leadership simply selects the right talent, develops that talent, listens to their needs, and celebrates them through good times and bad. Our people do all the rest."

Selection, listening, and celebrating—not a bad menu for leaders!

LIVING THE NEW GOLD STANDARD

- Ritz-Carlton hires from the same labor pool as every other company. It's their dedication to hiring the best service professionals—no matter how long it takes—that helps them obtain and maintain top performers.

- A thoughtful process for finding job candidates who are dedicated to service pays bountiful dividends . . . in employees who produce more, are happier, and stay longer.

- Leaders who focus detailed attention on the wants and needs of their staff ultimately see that same detailed, personalized attention being passed on to customers.

- Competence increases job satisfaction and engagement. Training, along with recognition for a job well done, will enhance the longevity of your staff.

- Lateral service training strengthens the organization and breaks down silos. When leadership works side by side with staff, a "we're all in this together" message is clearly received.

- Rather than a perfunctory exercise in HR regulations, orientation is a chance to invite new employees into your culture, mission, and vision in a welcoming and supportive environment.

- Celebrating milestones like the anniversary of a hire date tells the employee that he or she is valued, respected, and appreciated!

It's a Matter of Trust

Trust each other again and again.
When the trust level gets high enough,
people transcend apparent limits,
discovering new and awesome abilities for
which they were previously unaware.

DAVID ARMISTEAD

When you look at Ritz-Carlton's Service Values, it is clear that leadership has crafted guidelines to ensure that guests' needs will be met. Whether those needs involve basic safety and security, a sense of emotional well-being, or the desire to be offered a unique memorable experience, the Service Values encourage staff to do what it takes to reliably care for the guest.

In order for the Ladies and Gentlemen to meet these fairly lofty objectives, the employees need to know they can trust leadership. Gilbert Fairholm, author of the book *Leadership and the Culture of Trust,* suggests that social factors and self-serving business practices have eroded the confidence employees place in their employers. He explains, "True leadership is a process of building a trust environment within which leaders and followers feel free to participate toward accomplishment of mutually valued goals using agreed-upon processes." At Ritz-Carlton, leaders foster trust by first creating a financially viable business that affords staff members the materials and training they need to be successful. As observed by Allan Federer, general manager of The Ritz-Carlton, Millenia Singapore, "While we have always placed our culture and the needs of our Ladies and Gentlemen as top priorities, in recent years we have become increasingly effective at driving financial success as well, without compromising our culture."

In order for staff to place trust in leadership, corporate executives must make fiscally sound decisions that create sustainable employment. President Simon Cooper is clear: "One of the things we must achieve to do good beyond our walls is to be profitable within them. In our orientation, for example, we make absolutely no bones about our need to be financially sound. We don't want anybody at Ritz-Carlton to think that 'profit' is a bad word. If we don't make a profit, people don't keep jobs. If we don't do well and don't grow the company, then opportunities don't grow in other parts of the world. There is so much that comes from being successful. If our expenses exceed our revenues over time, all that goodwill we are creating in the lives of others will ultimately go to waste. You've got to build a sustainable business, and I don't mean just sustainable in today's environmental terms. I mean sustainable in terms of generating long-term profits over time. To that end, and it may surprise some in the context of delivering a luxury product, I'm a believer in not overresourcing. I've seen enough occasions where resources were added when times were good, and then when times were bad, they had to go."

◄[Stretching and Succeeding]►

So how does Ritz-Carlton stretch human resources and still deliver the consistent, highest-quality experience for the guest? In a word: trust. Staff members trust leadership to make staffing decisions that protect employee interests over the long term. From a financial perspective this trust is fostered, in part, by simplifying and creating transparency around certain economic elements in the business. By making financial goals clear and understandable, staff, in turn, are entrusted to participate in the business's overall success.

Each year senior leadership at Ritz-Carlton evaluates and revises, as necessary, the separate components of the five key factors that are essential to profitability in that 12-month cycle. These five factors are then published on tabletop pyramids along with the Gold Standards (see Figure 5.1). These pyramids are prominently displayed in staff areas throughout Ritz-Carlton

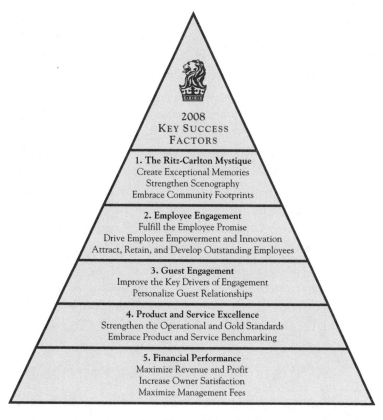

2008
KEY SUCCESS
FACTORS

1. The Ritz-Carlton Mystique
Create Exceptional Memories
Strengthen Scenography
Embrace Community Footprints

2. Employee Engagement
Fulfill the Employee Promise
Drive Employee Empowerment and Innovation
Attract, Retain, and Develop Outstanding Employees

3. Guest Engagement
Improve the Key Drivers of Engagement
Personalize Guest Relationships

4. Product and Service Excellence
Strengthen the Operational and Gold Standards
Embrace Product and Service Benchmarking

5. Financial Performance
Maximize Revenue and Profit
Increase Owner Satisfaction
Maximize Management Fees

Figure 5.1
The Tabletop Pyramid for the 2008 Key Success Factors

properties, but more important, staff discussions are initiated about the Key Success Factors.

Consistent with the Service Value "I understand my role in achieving the Key Success Factors and creating the Ritz-Carlton Mystique," the Ladies and Gentlemen are empowered to participate in department-level discussions of how they can individually impact all of the Key Success Factors—thus building greater staff involvement in the business by drawing a line-of-sight connection between each employee and the overall success of Ritz-Carlton. The 2008 Key Success Factors are indicative of the straightforward and uncluttered nature of these business targets.

While these business factors are fairly stable, staff is made aware of shifts in emphasis from year to year, depending on changing priorities of leadership. For example, the three items that were identified under "guest engagement" in 2007 were reduced to two items in the 2008 Key Success Factors by eliminating "increase guest satisfaction" and modifying "enhance sense of well-being" to read "improve the key drivers of engagement." The shift of focus from "enhance sense of well-being" to "improve the key drivers of engagement" is the result of research that was done on guest behavior. For example, prior to 2007 it was known that if a customer gave Ritz-Carlton the highest rating (5 on a 1-to-5 scale) on a survey question about his or her sense of well-being, that customer was 12 times more likely to be fully engaged with the brand. As a result, "enhance sense of well-being" was determined to be a Key Success Factor in 2008.

More recently, Ritz-Carlton conducted additional analyses on customer engagement and found that four factors account for 85 percent of overall guest engagement results. These four indicators are (1) sense of well-being, (2) anticipation of guests' needs, (3) room condition, and (4) room assignment. Collectively these four predictors are referred to in the 2008 Key Success Factors as "drivers of engagement."

Because leadership forms a mutually respectful partnership with employees, staff members receive training on the new research results, which means that employees can shift focus beyond a guest's sense of well-being to the other three guest engagement drivers as well.

Ritz-Carlton leadership strengthens trust by making its business objectives transparent to frontline workers and encouraging all individuals in the organization to give input on how they can drive business success. Further, leadership aligns those key objectives with the core values of the business and exercises discipline to introduce only those initiatives consistent with those publicly discussed targets.

STRIKING GOLD

- Have you defined a short list of annual key success factors for your business, to help staff trust that you will demonstrate discipline in the initiatives you pursue?

- Do you communicate the salient drivers of success to your frontline employees and solicit their input on how they can affect these factors?

- Are the new initiatives you roll out each year aligned both with your key success factors and your core corporate values?

Explicit Promises

It is generally agreed that trust emerges from saying what you do and doing what you say. While the Motto of Ritz-Carlton—"We are Ladies and Gentlemen serving Ladies and Gentlemen"—says that leaders will respect all Ladies and Gentlemen of the company, it does not drill down on what staff members can reasonably expect in the context of that respectful relationship. As such, Ritz-Carlton leadership believes that even greater trust can be fostered through a formal and explicit set of promises made on behalf of the employees. Sue Stephenson, former senior vice president of human resources and current vice president of the

Community Footprints program, served on the team that created what Ritz-Carlton calls the "Employee Promise."

"At the time," says Sue, "we realized there was nothing on the Credo Card that spoke to what the employee could rely on from the employer. We developed the Employee Promise and along with it the Employee Promise continuum, which identifies all the different processes that are in place from career planning to empowerment philosophy that serve as our commitment to our people. The Ritz-Carlton Employee Promise now appears on the Credo Card." (Please see the sidebar "The Employee Promise" and Figure 5.2, "The Employee Promise Continuum.")

The Employee Promise

- At the Ritz-Carlton, our Ladies and Gentlemen are the most important resource in our service commitment to our guests.
- By applying the principles of trust, honesty, respect, integrity, and commitment, we nurture and maximize talent to the benefit of each individual and the company.
- The Ritz-Carlton fosters a work environment where diversity is valued, quality of life is enhanced, individual aspirations are fulfilled, and the Ritz-Carlton Mystique is strengthened.

(Copyright © The Ritz-Carlton Hotel Company, L.L.C. All rights reserved. Reprinted with permission.)

At the core of the Employee Promise is a stated commitment to nurture talent for the mutual benefit of the individual and the company. Jim Bolt, chairman and founder of Executive Development Associates (EDA), a consulting firm specializing in the strategic use of executive development, advises that employees trust leaders to provide them opportunities for growth and if that trust is not met, the employees are likely to move on.

Career and
Development Planning   Succession Planning

Leadership
Performance
Process   **Selecting, Developing,**   Talent Acquisition
                and Retaining a   Orientation
                World-Class Workforce
    Learning and   Operational
    Development   Certification
         Reward and
         Recognition   Daily Lineup

         Empowerment and   Employee
         Innovation Culture   Agreement

Figure 5.2

The Employee Promise Continuum

According to Jim, staff members "place an increasing premium on the amount and quality of development they receive when deciding to remain in an organization. This is a key fact to remember given how critical it is today to retain top talent."

Consistent with Jim's views, Francisca Martinez, vice president of talent management at Ritz-Carlton, remarks, "In a world where employers can no longer guarantee lifelong employment to anyone in their workforce, we realize that we must nurture people for lifelong employability." By annually offering approximately 250 hours of training for each hourly employee, which includes 15 minutes for lineup each day, Ritz-Carlton not only enhances the ability of its people to deliver unparalleled service excellence but also enhances the marketable value of the staff.

Kathy Smith, senior vice president of human resources, comments, "Ironically, one of the problems with developing talent to the degree we do at Ritz-Carlton is that our people become a target for other employers. If you've worked for Ritz-Carlton, it certainly is a plus for your résumé in the hospitality and service sectors. On the other hand, it also makes our leadership better at developing strategies that engage our Ladies and Gentlemen and attempt to protect the company from being vulnerable if talent were to be lured away." From the perspective of Marsha Barns who works in the food and beverage department at The Ritz-Carlton, Washington, D.C., "Almost everyone in the hospitality business knows the training we receive at Ritz-Carlton. Because of that, we have many choices for our careers both within and outside of the company." While it is less than desirable to train staff members who are then sought by your competitors, most leaders would rather face that challenge than hold onto less-developed talent.

Promises Kept

Given that recruitment can be a challenge for virtually every employer in a global economy, achieving a reputation for respecting and empowering your people goes a long way toward becoming an employer of choice within your industry. According to Ken Rehmann, executive vice president of operations, "At the hotel opening in Dallas, there were over 8,000 applicants for 600 jobs. Despite concerns about the challenge of attracting and retaining workers, I find the values that drive our business are increasingly more relevant to a diverse group of workers, which makes it all the more important for us to stand on a foundation supported by our Employee Promise. That is a footing many businesses don't experience."

Because leadership at Ritz-Carlton is committed to setting the proper foundation for the business in all areas including the treatment of their Ladies and Gentlemen, the attractiveness of the brand is not limited to job seekers in the United States. Ricco de Blank, general manager of The Ritz-Carlton, Tokyo, notes, "In the case of Tokyo, we actually opened without having to do a mass hire. We received 25,000 applications and hand-picked each and every one of our employees well in advance of opening. We are in the luxury business; luxury is translated to people through people. Since our greatest threat is mediocrity, we safeguard our business by being so committed to our existing staff that we will have lines of the best people who want to join us."

Just as Ritz-Carlton seeks to be relevant to changing consumers, it also needs to attract a changing global workforce, which it does through employment-specific Web sites, targeted hiring strategies, and branded employment messages that appeal to workers who have a desire to be a part of an organization that is both respectful to its employees and committed to excellence.

Ken addresses this issue of relevance by noting, "The way our leaders treat people transcends culture or age. We treat them with respect and integrity. It's not just words; it's acted out every day in our interactions. We pride ourselves in providing employees with a value system that is universal. The Employee Promise is so impactful to employees in all parts of the world that they quote passages and truly expect it to live in every interaction that you have with them. I think it's a lot of why we were able to produce the operational excellence we have today. It emerges from our structural foundation." Promising to meet a clearly defined set of expectations that serve the primary needs of all human beings promotes a lasting legacy of caring.

Leadership at Ritz-Carlton essentially commits to developing the talent of its people in a manner consistent with the comments of Ken Rehmann—and more explicitly in the ways stated in the Employee Promise. This involves creating an environment of "trust, honesty, integrity, and commitment." While these terms can sound like platitudes in some work environments, they are viewed as the DNA of interpersonal relationships within Ritz-Carlton, and they set the standard for the actions to be taken by employees at every level. Allan Federer, general manager of The Ritz-Carlton, Millenia Singapore, compares leadership tactics: "In my days growing up in the hotel industry, it was not unusual to have a manager scream and berate staff. While I will grant you that such behavior on the part of leaders is an expedient way to get things done, it is not the Ritz-Carlton way."

Allan gives an example of how behavioral challenges can be approached. "In some locations, we have had difficulties with some of our housekeepers knocking on a door and entering a guest room without giving the guest a chance to permit them entry. While some businesses may try to change this behavior with a heavy hand, this provides only short-term results. At Ritz-Carlton, we realize we need to fix the process and not fix the blame. We best achieve the outcomes we desire by using a quality investigation analysis and involving interdisciplinary teams to assess the breakdown.

"At the end of the day, the respectful approach was to acknowledge that the problem was one of leadership failing to explore cultural differences and to train on the benefit of awaiting permission. Through careful listening to our housekeeping staff, we came to understand some of the challenges that they faced, such as not being able to hear if someone was in the room. That has allowed for technological solutions that give housekeepers indications of whether a room is occupied. While no solution is foolproof, our process was based on the importance of relationships and extending respect. It also required us to listen to the voice of those who needed to ultimately buy into the solution. In the end, respect is always the best way to go."

·◦[Trust and Respect:]◦· They Are More Than Words

With all this talk about how Ritz-Carlton leaders respect staff and develop trust with their employees, there is a risk that Ritz-Carlton management is being portrayed as infallible. John Hawkins, author of the book *Leadership as a Lifestyle,* warns, "At a time when leadership books and seminars are flooding the markets, our country finds itself with confused leadership expectations. The countless number of leadership training resources now available provides great opportunity for us to understand the essential components of long-term, effective leadership. And yet, our newspapers and newscasts remind us daily not of our leaders' effectiveness but rather of their failures. It is important that we expect leaders to be role models and to lead us in producing significant results. The standards and values that they live by set the bar for the others in the organization."

While human failings occur with Ritz-Carlton leadership, the standard has been set to foster trust, and it is producing results that trickle down to the day-to-day experience of frontline workers. Julie Lytle, executive assistant of rooms at The Ritz-Carlton, Laguna Niguel, appreciates the unique attention to employees' needs. "I know this sounds less than objective, but I can't imagine a more respectful environment from the application process, through orientation, and into the daily training. The leadership lives the Employee Promise. They continue to help me feel special and valued. They spend so much time, money, and effort welcoming, nurturing, and putting all of us in the places where we need to be to serve the guest."

Clearly, leadership at Ritz-Carlton understands the importance of creating an environment of respect at all touch points in the employee's journey, but additionally they appreciate the benefits of allowing staff to grow in the direction of their interests. Julie continues, "There's a lot of opportunity to move around within the hotel. Ritz-Carlton routinely promotes or hires from within. The individual hotels and the company itself are very supportive if you want to try new things, and they offer an online process to do that. I started at Ritz-Carlton in 1989 as an on-call banquet server and then became a full-time banquet server. Over the years I've been a telephone operator, front-office agent, front-office team leader, and now executive administrative assistant. The whole philosophy is that we're a team and we don't separate ourselves into different areas, while at the same time we have ample opportunities for movement within our hotel or in hotels throughout the world. I know I could take what I have learned here to just about any company. However, I feel so supported and valuable that it would be difficult imagining being anywhere else."

It is even a better testament to the impact of trust when guests recognize the confidence that frontline workers have in their leadership. A recent guest at the Singapore location explains this best: "I have stayed in a lot of hotels throughout the Pacific Rim, and often it seems that staff members are fearful of management and that they are ill-at-ease. I enjoy the emotional tone of a Ritz-Carlton where staff members seem to be performing in a natural and relaxed way."

Staff Engagement: A Step beyond Satisfaction

In addition to anecdotal reports from guests and employees, Ritz-Carlton systematically analyzes the trust and engagement of their employees through formal surveys conducted by third parties such as Gallup (see Chapter 6 for a more detailed review of this assessment process). Additionally, leadership assesses turnover data, information derived from exit interviews, and monthly surveys conducted with guests.

Across all qualitative and quantitative methods used to assess the engagement levels of their staff, it is clear that respectful and genuine treatment of employees at Ritz-Carlton engenders a trust for leadership that is essential to move their business forward. Unless employees know that they are truly valued, they often don't invest the extra effort needed to exceed customer expectations and arrive at innovative service solutions.

Erwin Schinnerl, general manager of The Ritz-Carlton, Boston Common, emphasizes the importance of authentic and honest interactions with staff. "The Ladies and Gentlemen represent the foundation of everything we do within our brand. It all starts with, 'Do I trust you? Do I trust you to create an environment and a workplace that make me feel that I belong and that I make a difference? Do I trust you to tell the truth and demonstrate a frank leadership style? Will you take the time to get to know me and go beyond preventing my disengagement but instead chase my strengths because the strengths of a team will offset our individual weaknesses?' We can make leadership so complicated, but really it comes down to whether we are earning the trust of our people or are simply asking for their compliance as a result of our ascribed authority." Erwin's point clearly distinguishes between a leadership strategy of influence and one based on control.

Ed Mady, vice president and area general manager of The Ritz-Carlton, San Francisco, shares his perspective that the ability to earn trust is a universally consistent process, whether it is from leader to frontline worker or from frontline worker to customer. "People are trusted more when they let others know that the other person matters. Trust emerges when we are remembered and greeted by name, and when our needs are met in a timely fashion." Ed relates, "I was at a fund-raising function for a job training program for homeless people. The program picked up the homeless from the streets and put them into hospitality courses to learn how to work in hotels such as ours. That evening, a woman who had completed the program was asked to speak to about 150 of us at the reception. In the course of her remarks, she said, 'Being homeless and on the streets is a very, very difficult thing. I'm so grateful to this organization and how I was able to come to have this job working in the kitchen. I'm learning how to cook. But the thing for which I am most grateful is that people now call me by my name. Because when you're homeless, nobody knows your name.'" From Ed's vantage point, trust begins with taking the time to know the names of those who work for and with you and extending your interest to discussions about concerns that are closest to their hearts.

Beyond leaders recognizing and taking an interest in their staff, trust is earned by providing staff members with the tools they need to perform their respective jobs. Maurice Pearson, assistant director of housekeeping, began his career at Ritz-

Carlton in loss prevention. "I worked for a hotel general manager who had a 100 percent open-door policy. I went to him and complained that our security system was from the Stone Age. The images were not sharp, and I could not rely on them. I let him have it wholeheartedly and passionately. In a lot of workplaces that would have been the end of the discussion, if not the end of me. However, my general manager evaluated the situation and spent $144,000 on a new security system because of what I said. I thought to myself, 'You have got to be kidding me.' For him to take me so seriously and listen, I decided I better stay here as my career. I couldn't believe it. He worked with me. Now *that's* leadership and integrity."

Developing trust doesn't have to require significant capital investment as in Maurice's case. Often trust emerges from small gestures that remove barriers interfering with an employee's work performance. When leaders listen and execute on the needs of their staff, they model behaviors that fuel trust among coworkers. Paul A. Boguski, guest services supervisor, shares, "I work with a great group of people, and I think the way my boss supports us sets the tone for how we treat one another. Take Adam, for example—he is the MacGyver of the engineering department. On one occasion a brass ball disappeared from the top of my bell cart, so I called Adam. Given our culture, I knew he would come through for me, and sure enough, he took my bell cart for a little while and brought it back having used a brass doorknob to replace the ball."

When leaders earn the trust placed in them, organizations see trusting behavior and team support migrate throughout their facilities. However, when leaders can't be trusted, coworkers often work against each other in self-protective ways.

·≡[Honesty and Authenticity]≡·

Even with recognition, the provision of tools, or the removal of barriers, trust erodes when communication lacks honesty at the management level or in the front line. Business coach Charrise McCrorey suggests, "What's missing in business today is a commitment to honesty. It seems that much of the time, the truth is inconvenient. Business leaders buy into the notion that their team members should be sheltered from certain business issues. In fact, the most powerful teams are led by leaders with a passion for getting to what's true about a person or a situation, and then acting upon it."

At Ritz-Carlton, honesty is a reciprocal commitment between managers and staff. William P. Perry, Jr., executive assistant manager of rooms at The Ritz-Carlton Lodge, Reynolds Plantation in Georgia, notes, "It is rare to terminate someone at our property; however, when terminations have happened, they have mostly involved attendance issues. In those cases, we will have tried to work with individual employees' schedules to accommodate any temporary lifestyle issues that may be affecting their ability to come to work on time. Nonetheless, sometimes an employee will still not meet amended schedule requirements, and we have been forced to part ways. In each case, however, the conduct expectations are fully laid out in the company's handbook, which is given and explained to each employee during new-hire orientation. There are 26 serious breaches of conduct that can cause immediate termination. These offenses range from willful damage of property to use of profane or abusive language."

While the focus of this discussion on trust thus far has centered on being a trustworthy leader, a significant piece of the Ritz-Carlton trust formula involves "being trusting." In essence, the Ritz-Carlton management philosophy is to select the right people, orient them to desired outcomes, train and certify operational skills, and support staff members as they improvise and create the guest experiences in the moment-by-moment interactions with the guest.

Kathy Smith, senior vice president of human resources, clarifies, "We have empowerment as part of our Service Values because we have a lot of confidence in our Ladies and Gentlemen.

We are confident that they will deliver the experience for which they are trained. That training in turn is ongoing and secures their skill sets. Ultimately, however, we know that we have to let our Ladies and Gentlemen figure out how to take their training and fit it with what is right for the guest. So, as leaders, we create the sandbox and general rules of how our people are expected to play in it, but for them to really generate the unique and memorable, we have to empower them. You just can't micromanage unique and memorable outcomes."

If there is a skill that can be alien to "take-charge" management-type, ego-driven personalities, it is the ability to step back, and in the words of Kathy Smith, "let [staff members] figure out" how to make their training effective in serving their customers.

Gary Weaver, an employee who has worked for The Ritz-Carlton Hotel Company for 19 years and is currently a hotel chauffeur in Atlanta, puts it this way: "The hotel leadership tells me what they expect of me, but they let me create what I need to do for the guest. I am not told what to do; I can figure that out for myself. When I pick up guests at the airport, I facilitate the check-in process and have their room key ready for them so that they don't have to go to the front desk upon arrival at the hotel. Or if a guest comes in late and hasn't eaten, I am quick to offer to call room service to make sure food is waiting for them. No manager told me to do that. In fact, even though I choose to do those things, my managers don't require other drivers to do them as some kind of standard operating procedure. Leadership exercises the patience and respect to step back and let my colleagues find their own ways to offer guests a memorable experience, just as leaders have encouraged me to create my own memorable ways."

Transferring Trust to Empowerment

In distrusting work environments, it is common for frontline workers to say, "I will have to get my manager's approval on that." In the culture of Ritz-Carlton, which emphasizes Service Values like "I am empowered to create unique, memorable, and personal experiences for our guests" and "I own and immediately resolve guest problems," the choice to shift responsibility to someone else is not an option. To further punctuate the autonomy and trust placed in the Ladies and Gentlemen, leadership has created a vehicle that clearly permits staff members to use their own discretion in service delivery or service recovery. The approach involves giving each Lady or Gentleman the ability to exercise judgment in spending up to $2,000 per guest per day if needed to either enhance the guest experience or to afford immediate problem resolution. Think about it: Every person, including a member of housekeeping and an employee working in the laundry, is empowered to use judgment, *without seeking permission from a supervisor,* to spend up to $2,000 on each guest each day!

This financial authority is the living embodiment of trust and power conferred to each staff member at Ritz-Carlton. While some might think that this type of empowerment is both ill advised and financially irresponsible, leadership at Ritz-Carlton has determined the trust they place in their Ladies and Gentlemen is well founded. Rather than being extravagant with the resources entrusted to them, the Ladies and Gentlemen tend to be very cautious with their company's money because leadership has instilled an understanding of the importance of fiscal responsibility to the lasting success of the company. Through training and sharing experiences with one another, Ritz-Carlton employees learn not to trade money for conversation or other solutions. They first talk to the guest and find out what is needed to make a situation right. Employees then may use resources to do the little extra something to exceed the guest's expectation while remedying the situation.

The advantage of the $2,000 staff empowerment is that the Ladies and Gentlemen don't have to delay a service response by taking it up to the next level in the organization, and they can take the initiative (without seeking permission) to enhance guest experiences. Often the staff empowerment allowance is used for such simple things as buying Rice Dream frozen dessert for a guest whose child expressed disappointment the prior evening because the hotel restaurant did not have a lactose-free ice cream option or for purchasing a special amenity item when a guest has not received room service in a timely manner.

Vivian Deuschl, vice president of public relations, says, "I've come to learn that the least costly solution is the one that happens immediately. The longer and higher a customer complaint lives in an organization, the more it grows. By the time a complaint hits senior leadership, what could have been resolved by getting the guest the amenity he or she requested with a slight enhancement turns into resolutions on a par with an upgraded night on the Club Level (an elevated service experience affording access to a lounge serving multiple daily complimentary food offerings and the ready assistance of concierge staff)." Since leaders must trust employees in establishing long-term relationships with the company's customers, it is logical to enlist their judgment to invest in customer retention without having to seek undue oversight.

Service breakdowns will occur in all businesses that are vulnerable to the inevitable shortcomings of humans. But trusting environments encourage staff to quickly circumvent blame and move constructively in the direction of problem resolution. That confidence is observed by Ed Staros, vice president and managing director of The Ritz-Carlton Resorts, Naples, Florida. "I don't want to make it sound like everything's perfect at our hotels. It can't be. We're human beings, and we have the opportunity to make mistakes every single day. I like to think, however, that the structure we put together in hiring, culture, and training makes us less prone to error in the actual delivery of service. What I am sure of is that our business is driven by employees who are here for the purpose of serving our guests. We are service individuals who continuously address thousands of human touch points every day. If you think about a hotel with 300 rooms, no manager can work long enough or hard enough to follow along behind his or her people to make sure everything goes right in every guest interaction. To be successful at our level in this business, it takes everyone on the staff having the skills, training, confidence, and above all else, the faith of their leadership to fully and consistently step into creative-problem-solving mode when things go awry."

STRIKING GOLD

- How does leadership in your organization take a genuine interest in the lives and ideas of your frontline employees?

- What can you do to help your employees automatically respond to the needs of customers without seeking higher-level approval?

The Results of Trust

For those skeptical of the wisdom of entrusting frontline workers so unconditionally, leadership at Ritz-Carlton is convinced that believing in their Ladies and Gentlemen releases greatness, while negativity and distrust shrink morale and service impact. The ultimate test of this leadership approach of "empower through trust" lives in the outcomes the approach affords guests and in the pride it instills in the Ladies and Gentlemen. While Principle 4 in this book will offer a comprehensive examination of the Ritz-Carlton Wow experience, the following examples share what can be created in a work environment of mutual trust and respect.

Subtle benefits of "empower through trust" can be found in the actions of staff members such as Emnet Andu, a server at the downtown Atlanta hotel, who cites an example. "A lady sat at my table and asked for grape jelly. Unfortunately, we had only strawberry and raspberry. I let her know the options that were available, and told her I would do everything in my power to get her the grape jelly she desired. I then went back to my team and let them know I needed to go to the nearby store to purchase grape jelly, and they gladly provided me coverage and support. You should have seen the lady's face when I returned with the jelly. She asked where I got it, and I answered her. In that moment, the lady knew that I viewed her as important to me and that she was not being treated as if her needs and wants did not matter. She did not have to sacrifice her needs based on the jelly we had on hand.

"I know it's a little thing but it always seems to be the little things that build lifetime relationships with guests. For me it is great that my company not only trusts me to leave the building during work but goes out of its way to encourage me to do so. In essence, it is the most important part of my job."

On a somewhat larger scale, Daniel Mangione, then a pastry sous chef at The Ritz-Carlton, Sarasota, exercised his empowerment for a person who wasn't even a hotel guest. "I received a phone call from a lady in our community who wanted a recommendation for a local bakery that would create a birthday cake for her daughter. At first I wasn't sure why she had called Ritz-Carlton, but as we started talking, I found out her daughter was turning eight years old and was allergic to soy products. The woman told me that she wanted to find someone who could bake a cake without using soy, but most bakeries did not want to research the ingredients. So she was asking for a referral.

"I told her, 'Ma'am, I am more than happy to create a birthday cake without using soy products.' She came in the next day. I sat down with her, and we shared a cup of coffee. We reviewed the ingredients of the cake I was going to make for her daughter. Working within the restrictions, I made the cake, decorated it, wrote 'Happy Birthday, Janie' and put a candle in it. The mother came and picked it up."

"The next day, the mother came back to the hotel, and I confess I was a concerned that the daughter had had a bad reaction.' As she tried to talk, the lady dissolved in tears, and I saw things going from bad to worse. At that moment, she thanked me from the bottom of her heart for helping her give her daughter something she had never had: a birthday cake. The birthday went off perfectly. Where else would I be allowed to do something like that?"

In a "glass is half empty" world, leaders warn their staffs not to engage in risky actions such as the ones taken by Daniel; however, in the world of Ritz-Carlton, extraordinary efforts to serve others are a culture norm. Most important, the Ladies and Gentlemen of Ritz-Carlton live up to and often exceed the faith placed in them.

Simon Cooper, president of The Ritz-Carlton Hotel Company, captures the benefits of empowerment best: "What makes me proud is when I'm reading about the service excellence of our people and I think to myself, if I were in the situation, I might have stopped halfway through the process and considered myself to have offered excellent service. It's at a point where the employee has done everything that seems feasible, yet the Lady or Gentleman just keeps right on going. Maybe he or she didn't find the lost ring, but he or she went through the laundry. Good for him or her. But then I learn the Lady or Gentleman perseveres to take the washing machine apart, search for the ring down into the drain, and ultimately locates the ring in the catchment area of the drain."

Simon adds, "The guest would have understood if we had said, 'We went through every robe, we turned the laundry upside down, we had five people searching for it.' But every day, in our world, our Ladies and Gentlemen own problems so passionately that they consistently exceed all the trust I can place in them. As such they often exceed any service standard I could contrive. In gratitude, I say, 'First class!' to them."

Ritz-Carlton's emphasis on frontline empowerment and service recovery is validated not only through the anecdotal reports of guests but also by bottom-line results. Company research shows that a guest who is actively engaged with Ritz-Carlton and its staff spends 23 percent more money than one who is only moderately engaged. When employees produce a 4-percentage-point increase in customer engagement scores companywide, the Ritz-Carlton achieves an extra $40 million in incremental revenue.

Corporate executives often talk about the importance of empowerment. Successful leaders, however, translate that talk by giving their staffs tools to make immediate decisions on behalf of customers. Ultimately, by offering their trust, those leaders produce companies that reap significant financial benefits and increased customer loyalty.

LIVING THE NEW GOLD STANDARD

- Set lofty objectives for your staff members, and then empower your staff members to reach them. That means providing training and tools they need, leaders they trust, and smart fiscal decisions that equate to job security.

- When leaders listen and execute on the needs of their staffs, they model behaviors that fuel mutual respect companywide.

- Entrusting frontline workers with financial responsibilities propels them to make savvy decisions and establishes an environment of greatness, whereas negativity and distrust shrink morale and service impact.

- Trusting employees to make financial decisions doesn't necessarily translate to significant capital investment. To the contrary, when problems are solved quickly instead of being allowed to fester into bigger issues, it can mean savings and client retention.

- "Empowering through trust" instills a sense of pride in employees, leading to service excellence at every level of a company.

- Removing barriers interfering with an employee's work performance can mean the difference between an employee's doing his job . . . and an employee's doing his job *and* enjoying it.

- At Ritz-Carlton, extraordinary efforts to serve others are a culture norm.

PRINCIPLE

It's Not
about You

Build a Business
Focused on Others

The service we render to others is really the rent we pay
for our room on this earth. It is obvious that man is
himself a traveler; that the purpose of this world
is not "to have and to hold" but "to give and serve."
There can be no other meaning.

SIR WILFRED T. GRENFELL

Businesses like Ritz-Carlton that are known for their emphasis on human factors (cultural development, service excellence, and employee empowerment) typically fall short when it comes to process-driven quality improvement. However, Jean Cohen, vice president and area general manager of The Ritz-Carlton, Grand Cayman, observes that consistent quality processes are the reason that Ritz-Carlton enjoys a reputation for employee empowerment and legendary service. "Some people may think it is counterintuitive for a company that is so focused on service excellence and the nurturing of the intangible 'Ritz-Carlton Mystique' to be equally driven to record and analyze data. However, quality processes are what ensure that the fundamentals of top service delivery are consistently maintained worldwide. If we do not deliver flawlessly in fulfilling the basic service expectations, we deprive ourselves of the opportunity to engage our guests with anticipatory service or create enduring guest memories." Rather than taking a top-down approach to quality, in which leaders create processes and impose them on staff, Ritz-Carlton has built their processes largely through inquiry.

To keep its sight on the customer, Ritz-Carlton leadership looks beyond daily operational concerns to garner data that can be used to benefit all customers, employees, managers, business partners, and stockholders. Rather than focusing on incremental improvements in existing internal processes, corporate leaders pay attention to the voice of their customers, the wisdom of world-class businesses, the ideas and feelings of their Ladies and Gentlemen, the input of their business partners, and the wishes of the hotel owners. Wide-ranging and disciplined listening programs help them to avoid building their business from the "inside out" (developing a plan of how they think their hotels should be run and imposing their will on all those the company touches). The leadership of Ritz-Carlton, instead, seeks feedback from many teachers as they go about continually and responsively adapting and improving their customer-reaching processes. In the end, by making Ritz-Carlton not be about the leaders but instead about those the leaders serve, the company has greatly prospered.

⟨ Starting with a Look to the ⟩ Excellence of Others

In the early 1990s, executives at Ritz-Carlton looked outside their business to drive internal process innovation. They did this by seeking input from world-class businesses such as Motorola, Westinghouse, Xerox Corporation, Federal Express, and IBM, and they gathered this information largely through the Malcolm Baldrige National Quality Award evaluation process.

The prestigious Baldrige Award had its genesis in response to a 1980 NBC television documentary titled *If Japan Can, Why*

Can't We? which examined how Japanese automobile manufacturers were surpassing U.S. carmakers across a variety of quality indicators. This exposé led to a U.S. government call to action, spearheaded by then Secretary of Commerce Malcolm Baldrige, who encouraged U.S. businesses to accelerate improvement of quality across all industries.

To facilitate this process, Baldrige gathered a team of thought leaders from academia and a cross section of businesses to determine the criteria for a "world-class," quality-driven company. Subsequently, the Baldrige Award was established not only to help businesses measure themselves against world-class quality standards but also to offer recognition and encourage the transfer of knowledge throughout the American business landscape. Criteria considered in the Baldrige assessment process include visionary leadership, customer-driven excellence, organizational and personal learning, agility, focus on the future, managing for innovation, attention to results and creating value, and social responsibility.

Ritz-Carlton submitted its first application for the Malcolm Baldrige Award in 1991. According to John Timmerman, vice president of quality and program management, "The learning we received from this process was extremely rich, and it identified significant gaps in our business model. We knew that closing those gaps would help ensure our performance excellence and sustainability. In essence, we looked outside ourselves to elevate our quality processes. To our delight, in 1992 we won the award. That victory validated all of the effort we had made to close the gaps that the Baldrige examiners had identified. It also put us in the position to help other companies model our processes and success."

Over the years, the leadership team at Ritz-Carlton has "closed gaps" in their business processes by imitating and innovating from the best practices of other trend-setting organizations. For example, realizing that Ritz-Carlton lacked a well-defined process for designing new products and services, leadership directly implemented the Xerox Corporation's six-step approach to quality improvement, as shown in Figure 6.1. Federal Express was studied to look for systematic ways to deliver products and services at Ritz-Carlton. The $2,000-per-day empowerment of Ritz-Carlton employees evolved from ideas gained through the study of Zytec Corporation (now part of Artesyn Technologies) and Solectron Corporation, an electronics design and manufacturing services firm. Both of these companies had participative management practices that mobilized staff to deliver quality products and services.

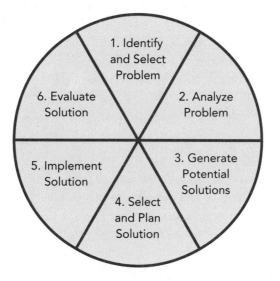

Figure 6.1

Six Steps to Quality Improvement

John Timmerman adds that despite winning the Baldrige Award, Ritz-Carlton leadership continued to look to the Baldrige process as a benchmark for quality excellence. "From 1993 onward, we did our own internal assessment against the Baldrige criteria but did not formally reapply for the award. In 1999 we submitted another application, as our senior management felt that our quality processes were not fully deployed across the organization and they wanted us to go through the process to make sure that we were fully aligned across the organization for the growth we were anticipating." Once again, Ritz-Carlton won the Baldrige Quality Award, making it the only service sector applicant to receive this prestigious award twice.

While Ritz-Carlton has not applied for the award since 1999, leadership continues to bring in external, third-party evaluators to measure the company against the Baldrige criteria. From the Ritz-Carlton leadership perspective, being examined by outside observers leads to a high-performance management system that is designed around systematic processes, a customer focus, reliable data, and continuous improvement. In 2005, the leaders at Ritz-Carlton identified 12 high-leverage opportunities for improvement, including how to provide business continuity in the event of emergency, methods for listening and learning, and long-range projections for action plans. By taking an incremental approach, each year leadership seeks to progressively close gaps and elevate excellence not only in specific business performance areas such as leadership and fiscal metrics but also in the dynamic interface between all the moving parts that are necessary to achieve continual success.

Baldrige examiners identified limitations in Ritz-Carlton's social responsibility efforts. The Baldrige feedback report noted, "Although Ritz-Carlton has a rich set of programs that establish it as a leader in the area of public responsibility and citizenship, there is a gap in their approach to measuring and monitoring effectiveness in this area. For example, the organization has proactive recycling and waste management programs, yet the measures in these areas focus on costs rather than the associated environmental benefits. In addition, the decentralized nature of many community support activities results in some inconsistency in methods for tracking these activities. These gaps in measurement may prevent Ritz-Carlton from fully realizing the level of public recognition that matches its actual contributions toward the environment and the community at large." In response to this feedback, a full-time senior management position was created to oversee the development of a formal social responsibility program. The program began with identification of key environmental and community involvement objectives, uniform criteria to guide the socially responsible actions of hotels throughout the Ritz-Carlton company, and strategies for measuring the impact of these actions. The success of that program, called Community Footprints, is discussed in Chapter 11.

When it comes to benchmarking best organizational practices, John Timmerman emphasizes that it's important to not limit comparisons to firms within your own industry. "When we first started our quality journey, we would see something that we thought our business needed, then implement a solution, and if the customer liked it, we would keep it. We called it 'painting it blue.' Then we received our first feedback report from Baldrige, and it stated that we did a good job at identifying and managing guest complaints, but we didn't necessarily have a method to prevent the problems that led to the occurrence of the complaints. That forced us to go outside Ritz-Carlton and monitor other industries. For example, a lot of our breakthroughs in process management have come from benchmarking manufacturing and aerospace industries."

When Ritz-Carlton studies other businesses, it takes a disciplined and strategic approach, and the most common way it mines for best practices of other companies is through multiday site visits. For example, in 2007 a member of senior leadership at Ritz-Carlton spent three days on site at both Cisco and Corning. These businesses were chosen based on their reputation for driving organizational change and for their expertise concerning innovation (an area identified as one of Ritz-Carlton's Key Success Factors). Those who attended these site visits then brought back their findings and incorporated those results with the observations of others who had done similar innovation benchmarking visits at other companies. As a result, Ritz-Carlton developed a new innovation model that is currently in the process of being deployed across all hotels.

Before implementation, Ritz-Carlton evaluates a process under consideration to ensure that it is

1. Part of a systematic approach for achieving the Key Success Factors

2. Driving employee empowerment and innovation

3. Embracing product and service benchmarking

4. Based on research of proven best practices

5. Transferable to Ritz-Carlton's culture

6. Effective in creating a culture of innovation

The Ritz-Carlton 4-Step Innovation Process (IP), depicted in Figure 6.2, was inspired by business practices in other industries. The 4-Step IP was developed using a research-based approach by analyzing the current body of knowledge from credible sources that include the *Harvard Business Review* and publications of the American Society for Quality. Proven practices were identified from a benchmarking study of external organizations that have a well-established core competency of innovation, such as Disney, Corning Incorporated, and Cisco Systems.

Ritz-Carlton leadership has learned that successful benchmarking involves both a senior leader and a functional lead at the benchmarking site visit. More specifically, a member of the senior team—be it the president, the chief financial officer, or the senior vice president of human resources—has to see the processes of other great businesses from a leadership perspective. While the functional lead at Ritz-Carlton will likely be tasked to implement any desired changes, senior leaders need to create the compelling argument for why the ideas should be executed.

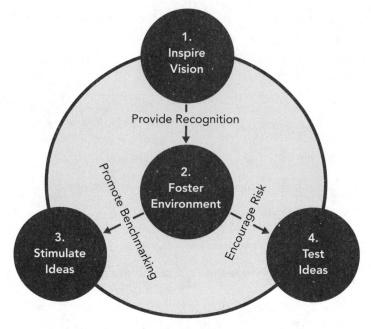

Figure 6.2
The Ritz-Carlton 4-Step Innovation Process

Whether it is Ritz-Carlton executives learning about systems for preventing breakdowns from the manufacturing sector, innovation based on best practices at Cisco or Mattel Corporation, or ideas on how to move service basics to service values from thought architects like Curt Coffman, coauthor of *First, Break All the Rules*, Ritz-Carlton leaders understand the value of seeking out the best of the best to continually take their business to the highest level possible.

·⊰❘ Keeping the Focus on ❘⊱· Those You Lead

As suggested in Chapter 5, the success of Ritz-Carlton is largely dependent on a highly engaged workforce creating a highly engaged customer base. To that end, Ritz-Carlton leadership set out to objectively examine and improve engagement in both these sectors of the business, and they sought Gallup's input to assist them.

To assess the engagement of staff, Ritz-Carlton administers the Gallup Q^{12} tool as shown in the sidebar. This instrument, which has strong empirical validity, asks employees to answer 12 questions to determine whether they fall into the engaged, nonengaged, or actively disengaged categories. Gallup consultants view these three categories as somewhat equivalent to the distinction between owners, renters, and squatters. In essence, engaged employees (the owners) show considerably greater personal investment in the success and growth of the business when compared to their lesser-invested counterparts.

Gallup Q^{12}: Gallup's Employee Engagement Metric

1. I know what is expected of me at work.
2. I have the materials and equipment to do my job right.
3. At work, I have the opportunity to do what I do best every day.
4. In the last seven days, I have received recognition or praise for doing good work.
5. My supervisor, or someone at work, seems to care about me as a person.
6. There is someone at work who encourages my development.
7. At work, my opinions seem to count.
8. The mission/purpose of my company makes me feel my job is important.
9. My coworkers are committed to doing quality work.
10. I have a best friend at work.
11. In the last six months, someone has talked to me about my progress.

12. This last year, I have had opportunities at work to learn and
    grow.

*(Copyright © 1998 Gallup, Inc. All rights reserved. Reprinted with
permission. These items cannot be used without Gallup's involvement
and consent.)*

The items on the Gallup Q^{12} address issues that either
strengthen or weaken the emotional connection between an employee and employer. Some of the areas assessed on this instrument include the degree to which employees have the materials
they need to do their job and whether expectations placed on
them are clear; whether their supervisor takes an interest in them;
whether their opinions matter; and whether they are afforded
opportunities to learn and grow on the job. Kevin McConville,
regional managing partner of Gallup, remembers, "The first assessment we conducted on [Ritz-Carlton employees] placed
them in the top quartile of businesses in our comprehensive
database. While we were impressed, it was not something that
leadership celebrated. They had set much higher standards for
themselves than almost any organization we've encountered."
So, while most companies would have been thrilled with an excellent first score, executives at Ritz-Carlton reacted with disappointment.

At Ritz-Carlton, leadership has an obsession for not only being best in class among luxury hotels but ultimately being the
best in class in all companies. So Kathy Smith, senior vice president of human resources, and Simon Cooper, president of the
company, saw the top-quartile employee engagement results as
table stakes or base expectations. Gallup data led to a renewed
effort to increase the engagement of the professionals and staff.

According to John Timmerman, "Business units that leverage both employee and customer engagement yield over three
times better outcomes than the baseline, be those financial, safety,

or other quality indicators. By asking our Ladies and Gentlemen how they perceive our efforts to create an environment where they can grow and make a purposeful difference, we can make adjustments in the work environment that help our people drive our key business objectives."

Because Ritz-Carlton leaders have executed action plans that were developed at the department level for each of the company's properties (including making employee engagement part of management's performance rewards and prioritizing staff engagement as a key business factor), Gallup Q^{12} scores of engagement have continued to show steady improvement. Kevin McConville of Gallup puts the Ritz-Carlton results in context: "In our overall database we have about 40 percent of people engaged, about 45 percent not engaged, and about 15 percent actively disengaged. At Ritz-Carlton, the numbers are approximately 63 percent engaged, 28 percent not engaged, and 9 percent actively disengaged. In essence, most workplaces have considerably less than half of their people engaged in their work and a larger proportion disengaged to varying degrees. At Ritz-Carlton that ratio is more than reversed, and from a business outlook, the effort of leadership to drive greater employee engagement is showing important financial benefits."

According to Kevin, "In Ritz-Carlton properties where employee engagement improves, the hotel's revPAR (revenue per available room) increases at a rate higher than in hotels that did not show Gallup Q^{12} improvement. If you look at it, their entire business model is really not for the passive employee. At Ritz-Carlton, you need employees to be owners, not renters or squatters. Their fundamental attention to the engagement of their people shows not only in their numbers but in the way we are treated when we visit their hotels."

Kevin shares an experience of a fellow Gallup consultant who was delivering a speech at The Ritz-Carlton Lodge, Reynolds Plantation, in Georgia. "As he was driving to the hotel on that hot day, he drank a blue Gatorade and tossed the empty bottle in the back seat. Two days later when the valet pulled his car around for his drive back to the airport, they had a blue Gatorade sitting in the cup holder. In some companies, the valet would get in trouble for touching personal items and of course wouldn't have removed the old Gatorade or put in a fresh one. At Ritz-Carlton, the goal is to create an environment where blue Gatorade can appear almost magically from an engaged workforce."

Great leaders understand the importance of measuring the engagement of their staff and strategically addressing ways to maximize the motivation and passion of their people. They understand that while engaged staff do not necessarily cause emotionally engaged customers, employee engagement is a necessary condition for sustained customer loyalty. (Please see Figure 6.3 for the demonstrated correlation between employee engagement and guest engagement at Ritz-Carlton.)

STRIKING GOLD

- What outside business experts or process leaders do you invite into your company to evaluate the gaps in the quality of your products, services, or systems?

- Whose processes do you study? Are you conducting site visits to learn world-class best practices? Are the targets of those site visits consistent with your key business objectives? Do they involve both senior leadership and project leads?

- Do you measure the emotional engagement of your employees, either through formal, third-party tools such as the Gallup Q^{12} or more informal means?

- How are you measuring your company's ability to foster an ownership position among your employees? Are you assessing the degree to which employees have the materials and resources they need to do their job?

Build a Business Focused on Others

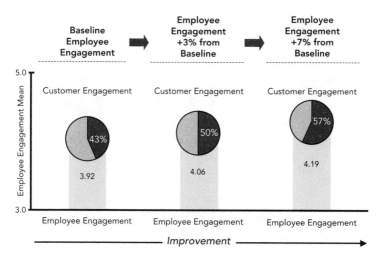

Figure 6.3

The Demonstrated Correlation between Employee Engagement and Customer Engagement at Ritz-Carlton

(Data courtesy of The Gallup Organization)

Focusing on Those You Serve

Like many other businesses, Ritz-Carlton has had a rich tradition of measuring customer satisfaction. Shortly after they began assessing Ritz-Carlton customer satisfaction, Gallup approached executives at Ritz-Carlton about the possibility of shifting their core customer metric to one of engagement. Consistent with their quest for excellence, the leadership of Ritz-Carlton listened to the purported advantages of measuring customer engagement (a better metric of the emotional connection and perceived fit held by a customer toward a business, and overall customer loyalty) as opposed to customer satisfaction (a measure of the thoughts a customer has toward the business's offerings).

Bill Diggins, Ph.D., senior consultant of Gallup, speaks to the inclusive and methodical process that went into Ritz-Carlton's adopting Gallup's customer engagement tool, which they call the Gallup CE[11]. (Please see the sidebar "Gallup CE[11]: Gallup's Customer Engagement Metric.") "Almost immediately upon taking on the account, we started talking to Ritz-Carlton leadership about the concept of customer engagement. Even though it seemed that President Simon Cooper was on board with our vision fairly early on, Ritz-Carlton is a grassroots organization. In order for a change to be made, consensus was needed within the organization. Progress was made steadily, given that the measurement of customer engagement intuitively fit a business that was committed to affecting the guests' emotional experience and long-term loyalty, and by the fall of 2003, Ritz-Carlton agreed to let us do a pilot test."

Gallup CE[11]: Gallup's Customer Engagement Metric

1. How satisfied are you with Ritz-Carlton?
2. How likely are you to continue to choose Ritz-Carlton?
3. How likely are you to recommend Ritz-Carlton to a friend or associate?
4. Ritz-Carlton is a name I can always trust.
5. Ritz-Carlton always delivers on what they promise.
6. Ritz-Carlton always treats me fairly.
7. If a problem arises, I can always count on Ritz-Carlton to reach a fair and satisfactory resolution.
8. I feel proud to be a Ritz-Carlton customer.
9. Ritz-Carlton always treats me with respect.
10. Ritz-Carlton is the perfect hotel for people like me.
11. I can't imagine a world without Ritz-Carlton.

(Copyright © 2000 Gallup, Inc. All rights reserved. Reprinted with permission. These items cannot be used without Gallup's involvement and consent.)

Build a Business Focused on Others

Diana Oreck, vice president of global learning and the Leadership Center, picks up the story from the Ritz-Carlton vantage point, highlighting the respect paid to the customers before even considering whether to place some of the Gallup CE[11] questions before them. "When the Gallup consultants brought in this new set of questions, we thought that some of the items were quite strange. We even did a pilot study to see if the questions would translate to our customers. We were concerned that some of these assertions, like 'I can't imagine a world without Ritz-Carlton,' were very pretentious. We told the consultants, 'No, we are not going to ask our guests to respond to that line of inquiry. We're Ladies and Gentlemen serving Ladies and Gentlemen, and that's an arrogant way to get at the issue of their perception. Customers can imagine a world without hunger, but where did our hotel fit into their imaginations?' Gallup then said, 'We're sorry, but you can't use the questions because unless you have a question like that, you're not going to be able to really quantify guest emotions.'"

Ultimately, Gallup had the science on their side, and guests were comfortable with the survey. Ritz-Carlton implemented all 11 questions of the Gallup CE[11], and now leadership gains regular insights into the emotional engagement of customers. More important, a solid correlation has been established between guest engagement scores on the Gallup CE[11] instrument and important financial outcomes.

While the Gallup CE[11] is well understood and valued by management at Ritz-Carlton, care has been taken to help front-line staff understand what customer engagement means, how it is measured, and the relationship between the results of customer engagement metrics and the overall viability of the business. Where many businesses might establish a single executive at their corporate office as the subject matter expert on customer satisfaction or customer engagement metrics, Ritz-Carlton localizes that expertise to ensure that information is readily available to all employees.

Chris McCarty, Gallup engagement manager, observes, "Ritz-Carlton deploys dedicated quality leaders at the individual hotels. These directors are in charge of consulting about the Gallup CE[11] at the front line and energizing quality programs at the hotel level. They help frontline workers understand how guests are being surveyed, the nature of the survey, and how the results predict future guest behavior and attachment to Ritz-Carlton. The local quality leader's role is really unique. Many of our clients have one centralized person who knows and understands our customer engagement tool. That person then disseminates information about the instrument through marketing or some other less-defined communication channel. But at Ritz-Carlton, the quality leader consistently drives knowledge of customer engagement at the property level, which I believe is a huge communication and resource advantage."

The methodology of the customer engagement survey involves monthly phone interviews with meeting planners and individual guests. In the case of guests, Gallup will secure 33 interviews per property per month, totaling over 19,000 on an annual basis. They will ask the guests the 11 questions of the Gallup CE[11] and also inquire about transactions at the hotel (for example, room cleanliness and the check-in process) as well as emotional factors (the guest's overall sense of well-being and the staff's ability to anticipate needs). Once the data are collected, results are posted monthly, and an 18-month rolling average is used to place each hotel in a green, yellow, or red zone.

Allan Federer, general manager of The Ritz-Carlton, Millenia Singapore, notes, "There isn't a general manager who sleeps the night of the 19th because the results of the customer survey come out the morning of the 20th, and we all want to know. The rewards and incentives for everybody in the company are set up based on the perceptions of the guest; that's how we do it." While managerial bonuses are linked to a variety of factors, they are heavily weighted in the direction of showing improvement on customer engagement scores.

The ongoing nature of the customer engagement assessment allows Ritz-Carlton leadership to monitor and intervene when necessary with specific hotels. John Timmerman explains how variable performance in guest engagement relates to the way hotels are classified: "In our organization, we have hotels that have a lot of fully engaged customers, and we have hotels that have less fully engaged customers. In the past, we would set performance targets by asking individual hotels to set a goal. If the hotel was, let's say, at 50 percent full customer engagement, we would have probably challenged them to show a minimal 10 percent improvement. But what happens if a hotel is at 60 percent full customer engagement? Should we ask them to stay the same or demonstrate a 1 percent or 10 percent improvement in order to be rewarded? The problem with that process was that percentage numbers are relevant only if you can establish at what threshold the numbers reflect that customers are getting the world-class service they deserve from Ritz-Carlton."

Ritz-Carlton proceeded to task Gallup to create a threshold number that reflected the point where each hotel was certain it was delivering on the company's brand promise. To do this, they used Ritz-Carlton's internal performance data, supplemented with external benchmarks taken from companies like Lexus and Tiffany. Ken Rehmann, executive vice president of operations, comments, "When a hotel meets our brand performance marker, it is performing around the 97th percentile in Gallup's global competitive database of hundreds of thousands of business units. That hotel is truly world class, and that puts the hotel in our yellow-zone category. The green-zone hotels are performing around the 98th to the 99th percentile in Gallup's global database. The red zone represents our hotels that are not performing at the level of brand promise. I don't want to scare you and have you think that we've got these hotels that are burning to the ground or that you're going to get a horrible experience. A red-zone hotel is performing around the 94th to the 95th percentile. Some could argue that the 94th percentile is pretty darn good, but from our view it is not world class." Ritz-Carlton uses the monthly customer surveys conducted by Gallup to energize staff and also to highlight hotels in need of additional attention.

Leadership at Ritz-Carlton made the bold decision to clearly place their hotels as red, yellow, and green performers, and in so doing, they manage against the expectations of the customers and not an arbitrary goal. That process created a burning platform within the organization. In the early classifications, about 18 Ritz-Carlton hotels were in the red zone. Calling a hotel "red" was a tremendous motivating force for the staff to find ways to drive guest engagement. Even with increasing numbers of hotels, Ritz-Carlton now averages only four hotels in the red. In some of those cases, the hotels are not making the brand marker because they are going through capital improvement. But even in those cases, the red categorization forces consideration of issues such as the need for capital investment to improve the hotel's performance on the functional aspects of a guest's stay. The general managers at these hotels ensure that their staff members have the training and tools needed and also have participated personally in the improvement process. They challenge the quality improvement teams to identify the root cause rather than fix the symptoms.

The lessons drawn from Ritz-Carlton's journey to customer engagement metrics are many. They include distilling the wisdom of consultant partners, systematically listening to guests, linking performance on customer data to brand-specific standards, and managing to the standards already set. John H. Fleming, Ph.D., chief scientist and principal of Gallup, anchors all of these lessons back to the Ritz-Carlton culture: "Unlike the vast majority of other companies we work with, the Ritz-Carlton has established a foundation that makes this kind of program extremely effective. It generates results because of all the procedures that it built from the day the company was founded to communicate, discuss, and encourage dialogue around both customer and guest issues as well as the issues of the Ladies and Gentlemen. It is enormously effective in identifying quality issues, and its origins lead it to set up structures that many companies would be well off to copy. I think that's what puts Ritz-Carlton in a league of its own."

Building loyal and engaged customers starts with a culture of listening. This culture of listening has resulted in global recognition in customer service excellence through awards like the J.D. Power Asia Pacific 2007 Japan Hotel Guest Satisfaction Index Study. According to J.D. Power, "Ritz-Carlton ranks highest for a second consecutive year. . . . Ritz-Carlton performs particularly well in six of the eight factors: guest room, hotel facilities, staff, food and beverage, check-in/check-out, and hotel services." As it relates to an important factor in customer satisfaction like the ease of the check-in/check-out process, Ricco de Blank, general manager of The Ritz-Carlton, reports on the importance of listening and observing success: "Japan is the country of measurements. A country in which everything is driven by improving quality processes. This helps us to improve every day. Everything is measured. Check-in takes 2 minutes and 50 seconds on the average. We measured it over six months. Now I want to improve that time to 2 minutes and 30 seconds. It's better for the guests and easier for our Ladies and Gentlemen, so I am letting the employees tell me how we can do it."

Simon Cooper emphasizes that successful business practices are not the result of new initiatives or programs but a steadfast commitment to the fundamental processes of listening and measurement. "Leadership has to continually define the platform on which this company's success rests. The planks of our platform include continual listening to our customers and to our Ladies and Gentlemen, as well as living our values and driving quality processes. By doing this, we enjoy success not just in the United States or Japan but also in places like Cancún where we are the only hotel to win Mexico's National Quality Award or in Singapore where we've won the state Quality Award, a huge achievement in a country very focused on quality. By getting the fundamentals right, customers are benefiting on every continent."

As suggested by Ricco and Simon, customer satisfaction or consumer engagement measurement has to go beyond an infrequent exercise in data collection. To truly build life-long customers, receive recognition for service and quality, enhance customer spending patterns, and produce customer evangelism, businesses must place the information they receive from customers directly in the view of leadership and the front line. Further, leaders need to evaluate the performance of business units and their ability to swiftly adjust offerings to enhance their emotional bond with their customers.

⸫] Understanding Changes in [⸪· Your Customer Base

In Chapter 3, we looked at how Ritz-Carlton continues to refine its product and service offerings based on the changing needs of its clients. That chapter discussed how Ritz-Carlton incorporated the subject matter expertise of its advertising agency partner Team One to better understand the discerning affluent. Ritz-Carlton leaders invested over $1 million across three years to further understand changes in the luxury consumer.

Laurie Wooden, vice president of new business development and corporate strategy at Ritz-Carlton, says, "Since customers are always changing, I am surprised to find businesses that are content to do things the way they have always done them. By actively talking to luxury customers, both those who use our hotels and those who don't, we learn a great deal about the changing expectations of our guests. Without that listening, how would we know what best suits their needs? It is exciting to hear the voice of the luxury guest and strategically translate that into products for today and the foreseeable future."

While Laurie references her company's effort to listen to luxury customers who are not currently staying in Ritz-Carlton properties, Simon Cooper readily admits, "Gallup does a great job helping us make sense of our internal metrics and how we are doing with our own guests, but the real challenge is studying people in our market segment who are not staying in our hotels. I find great value in research on my competitors' guests because they have much to teach us about how to further strengthen our business for the future. It's just extremely difficult to get quality data on those who don't choose you."

Focusing on the Needs of Your Business Partners

In addition to listening to and measuring the input of staff, guests, and desired future customers, Ritz-Carlton leadership creates forums to secure the input of their key referral sources in the travel industry (including travel experts who book individual and corporate business with them), joint venture partners (restaurateurs and other retail partners), and the investors and owners of buildings Ritz-Carlton manages.

Nancy Strong, CTC, chief executive officer of Strong Travel Services, shares how Ritz-Carlton has solicited her input: "I attended the very first Travel Industry Advisory Council many years ago at Buckhead in Atlanta. There were a number of travel agents who sat at that table along with many Ritz-Carlton general managers. Our group of travel professionals raised a number of issues, and I remembered thinking I hope the managers are taking notes." Apparently they were. Nancy continues, "Within three to six months every issue we brought up was addressed and handled. You can imagine how we, as travel agencies, their partner clients, felt after that. I mean, you talk about a warm and fuzzy feeling toward a partner! We talked about that for a long time. A large part of the success occurred because they had their decision makers at the table with us. If we had a complaint or a concern about the hotel in Boston, the general manager stood up and said, 'I know what you're talking about; when

I go back I will talk to my team, and we'll get that resolved.' It really got our attention. We were very impressed." In the end, all business is personal. Great leadership involves putting decision makers in a position to listen to the needs of those who understand how to make your business stronger.

Along with travel agent councils, Ritz-Carlton invests considerable amounts of time listening to those with whom they enter into partnerships and with the owners who choose them to manage their properties. Simon Cooper suggests that listening to these relationships ultimately makes Ritz-Carlton a wiser company. "These brands we work with—Spago, Eric Ripert, or BLT—are well-defined and bring tremendous knowledge. They also bring their own following, and we learn something from every project we do with them." Simon adds, "For example, I know we learned to push harder and expect more from working with Chef Eric Ripert when he opened his restaurant with us in Grand Cayman. We expected it to be a difficult place for an opening, and sometimes at Ritz-Carlton, we will allow a slower period in the beginning when we bring on a restaurant. But people like Eric are running hard from day 1, and they expect to be able to fill every seat on the first day. It's almost a different approach than we would take, and we learn from them and hopefully they learn from us as well."

Karim Alibhai is founder and manager of the Gencom Group, which has several properties developed or under development in conjunction with Ritz-Carlton. Karim shares how ownership input is secured and addressed by Ritz-Carlton leadership: "We are involved with a number of hotel chains and are always pleased with the openness of the Ritz-Carlton's leadership to listen for possibilities. Not to just listen out of politeness and then dismiss complex or 'off the beaten path' ideas but to listen for ways to make innovative concepts happen."

Listening does not ensure that situations will always go smoothly, but ultimately it is the path to mutually acceptable solutions in challenging times. Dermod Dwyer, chairman of Trea-

---

STRIKING GOLD

- What efforts do you make to not only measure the satisfaction of your customers but also their emotional engagement with your brand?

- Do employees at all levels of your organization understand your customer feedback metrics? Do they understand the importance of those metrics to the overall success of the business?

- How do you attempt to listen to the needs and opinions of those who choose other providers?

- Would your company be described as a customer-centric business or a more inward-looking business focused on process efficiencies?

- How do you solicit input from business partners, vendors, and other individuals who have a stake in the outcome of your company?

---

sury Holdings, the ownership group for The Ritz-Carlton, Powerscourt, County Wicklow, Ireland, shares, "We've had a very good experience with Ritz-Carlton. From the onset of our negotiations with them we could sense the sincerity of their interest in our ideas and vision. That is not to say that there were no disagreements. It was an intensely challenging but highly creative period of time, bearing in mind that we opened the hotel 972 days after we first broke ground. However, the senior people at Ritz-Carlton were invariably open to other perspectives, particularly from those who knew the country where the hotel aspired to operate. This willingness to listen serves the group well, particularly as one that is growing, adapting and becoming more international in outlook and location. The Ritz-Carlton group has come to understand Ireland well and the marketing tagline for The Ritz-Carlton, Powerscourt, can rightly claim that our hotel is 'authentically Irish and reassuringly The Ritz-Carlton.'" While listening does not avert conflict and tension, it does create a foundation of trust that allows for adaptation and effectiveness.

Soliciting Local Involvement in Business Processes

Ritz-Carlton Service Value 9 states, "I am involved in the planning of the work that affects me." As such, Ritz-Carlton leadership has perfected processes to make the work truly be about their employees. Most hotel decisions are the result of a general manager driving overall top priorities, with departmental leaders' addressing individual improvements within, say, housekeeping or finance.

Brian Gullbrants, vice president of operations, addresses how corporate leadership respectfully incorporates the input of local leadership: "In addition to local priorities, you have brand-level improvement initiatives. So corporate is also saying, 'Guess what? In the rooms division, we need to improve this particular aspect of the customer experience,' and so we're going to create some brand-level enhancement. Here at corporate we include the local hotel leadership to give input formally through councils and in more informal ways as well. Ritz-Carlton won't improve if we drive change from the top."

Similarly, at the hotel level, the priorities driven by general managers and their executive teams emerge from customer data and analyses of process breakdowns. At Ritz-Carlton, these prime target areas are limited to three local objectives, called "the T3." These top three areas of quality improvement receive the attention of cross-functional teams at the hotel level. Ken Rehmann, executive vice president of operations, suggests that this process is well known throughout Ritz-Carlton. "I would say the hotel front line is very knowledgeable about the T3 team process. It's a big initiative. These quality improvement teams tackle important issues and have representatives from every part of the organization."

Alexandra Valentin, director of learning at The Ritz-Carlton, Central Park, describes the quality improvement team process: "We have a diverse group of our Ladies and Gentlemen meeting together to improve our key quality targets. As these teams form, we talk about the purpose of the team, what the data are telling us about the problem, why each of the team members were selected. We also make commitments to the team and discuss the guidelines that we will follow. We then analyze the data more thoroughly and look for trends from guest input over the short and long terms. We look to see if we have faced the problem before and how it was handled previously. We then start mapping out all of our processes that touch the problem area and break down the process into steps to analyze what's not working at each step so we can fix it. All the time we are looking for something out of the norm that we've never done or possibly what other hotels are doing to be successful. We make suggestions that are implemented and track the changes for a period of maybe three months. We usually look for a good pattern of positive change in data like the Gallup CE[11] to see that our solutions are really working." Alexandra's description of the process she has participated in at her hotel is but one example of how leadership seeks solutions from the front line instead of diving into management-driven edicts.

In addition to forming T3 teams, Ritz-Carlton leaders also engage their staffs in annual SWOT (strengths, weaknesses, opportunities, and threats) analyses of the company's annual Key Success Factors, thus producing input and participation from all levels of the business. Jean Cohen, vice president and area general manager of The Ritz-Carlton, Grand Cayman, notes, "Critical to the success of a complex resort in an international location such as Grand Cayman is that the Ladies and Gentlemen embrace and live our service values by being actively involved in the planning of their work. The tools employed by Ritz-Carlton (daily lineups, departmental meetings, SWOT analyses, soliciting employee ideas for innovation) all serve to reinforce the employees' understanding that their opinion counts. These tools provide a forum in which key information can be communicated to the Ladies and Gentlemen, but more important, they provide a structured means for them to employ their empowerment through work planning and processes."

Whether at a Ritz-Carlton in Denver or Doha, employee input is viewed as integral to the company's competitive advantage, Victor Clavell, vice president and area general manager, notes, "The open-communication policies and involvement of the employees in the planning of their work and decision making drive employee engagement and reflect sound business sense."

Put simply, leaders, "It's Not about You." It is always about the customer and the employees. While it may not seem fair at times, making it about those you serve derives the greatest rewards for you and your business.

LIVING THE NEW GOLD STANDARD

- In the end, all business is personal.

- Great leaders take the time to ask; they repeatedly inquire, listen, and then act.

- Monitor internal productivity against your own company's best practices. Then, track other businesses both inside and outside of your industry to see new and significant opportunities for improvement.

- World-class organizations establish unyielding quality standards. Being examined by a third-party evaluator is an effective way to find and fix recurrent problems.

- An engaged workforce personally invests in success and business growth, while creating an engaged clientele.

- Ritz-Carlton has increased revenues through attention to customer engagement—a stronger metric than customer satisfaction.

- Encourage your employees to be involved in the planning of the work and processes that affect them.

Support Frontline Empathy

*They may forget what you said, but they will
never forget how you made them feel.*

CARL W. BUECHNER

 We can conclude our discussion of the science of service of Ritz-Carlton this way: Anticipating the customer's unstated needs is the goal of every employee, and each fulfillment of a need should be as individual as the customer. Consider my experience when attempting to set up an interview with Mark Ferland, general manager of The Ritz-Carlton, Orlando, Grande Lakes. I contacted Mark via e-mail late one afternoon asking if there was any possibility that I could interview him the next day since I was going to be in the Orlando area. Knowing that my request came on short notice, I wanted to give Mark the largest window possible so that he might be able to fit me into his schedule. To that end, I advised him that I had rebooked my flight out of San Francisco, taking the red-eye into Orlando, and that I could meet him any time after 7:00 the next morning.

He could have easily fulfilled my need with an e-mail response like, "I can adjust my schedule; how does 11:30 a.m. sound? I'll meet you at the hotel." But Mark's response to my request is typical of what guests routinely encounter across all levels of the Ritz-Carlton. His e-mail read: "Dr. Michelli, I have made a reservation for you for very early arrival tomorrow morning. Please forward your flight details as soon as possible, and I will have my night manager, Chris Walsh, arrange airport transfer. You will have access to our Club Lounge, which serves breakfast at 7 a.m. Please let Chris know if you need any further assistance upon your arrival. I thought we could have an early lunch at 11:30 a.m. as I am speaking to a group at 1 p.m. Hopefully you can catch a short morning nap before we meet. Please let me know if this will work for you as I will not call you in the morning in the event that you may be resting. Best Regards, Mark Ferland."

Remember, all I asked for was the possibility of a one-hour meeting with Mark. However, his actions embody the spirit of service common to Ritz-Carlton. It is a level of care that transcends attentiveness and embraces genuine empathy. Mark looked beyond my stated needs by placing himself in my position as his guest. What might a person who took an overnight flight need upon landing in Orlando, given a recently changed travel itinerary? Would that person be hungry? Tired? In essence, much of what happens at Ritz-Carlton is an extension of the way people would treat family members and other loved ones, as opposed to the way they might treat complete strangers. The intimacy of interpersonal caring and the art of anticipation are critical aspects of Ritz-Carlton service culture. In fact, they are the secret sauce of the Ritz-Carlton Mystique.

·=[Mystique]=·

In order to create a memorable experience, a service provider has to connect with a guest's individuality and deliver service customized to that guest's preferences. Many businesses do this using customer relationship management software as a way of tracking guest preferences, but few have used this type of technology more effectively than Ritz-Carlton as they support personalized service.

While not every employee in the Ritz-Carlton system has open access to the company's customer relationship management database, aptly named "Mystique," all Ladies and Gentlemen are provided "preference pads" on which they are encouraged and trained to jot down guest preferences. These observations are soon entered into the Mystique system, and that information is readily accessible across properties. Kevin Walsh, senior director of customer relationship management, emphasizes that it is one thing to collect guest information and quite another to make that information useful: "In addition to having the database information available, our property-level guest relations staff disseminates highlights from information about arriving customers through channels such as lineup. The types of information shared hotelwide can include why the guest is coming in, if the guest is having an anniversary or other celebration, the purpose of the guest's visit, what expectations the guest has, and how to make sure the guest's stay is enjoyable. So the information emerges into something we strategically use to better enhance the overall guest experience."

Kevin sees the added value of this shared database, given the growth of the company: "This readily accessible, compiled information is important because our repeat guests are very loyal to Ritz-Carlton, so even if they typically stay at our Central Park hotel, they will likely also stay with us in other cities. We have to make sure when they visit a property that is new to them, we take our knowledge of their preferences to produce a seamless experience so they will feel as much at home with us at the new property as they do in Central Park."

While database information can provide historical details about a customer, it is important to keep that data valid and relevant to the customer's current needs. In order to enliven the information in the Mystique database, Ritz-Carlton guest relations staff members typically call a guest prior to an approaching stay to gain some basic information about the upcoming visit. Maria Thompson, a former trainer in guest relations at the Washington, D.C., Ritz-Carlton, now sales administrative assistant at The Ritz-Carlton, Phoenix, observes the fine distinctions of reading people successfully: "We make a concerted effort to speak to most of our guests. This previsit phase is crucial; it's how we build the profiles of our guests so we can ensure that any special needs are taken care of ahead of time." Maria continues, "If a business person comes in once a week, we don't call each time, but I still try to see the guest during each stay and ask, 'How is your visit? Is your amenity correct? Would you rather have something else? Are you tired of the fruit? How is your family? When are you coming back?' I also make a point to try to be one of the familiar people who are there to greet the guest upon arrival."

Daniel Mangione, assistant pastry chef, reports that a similar process of inquiry takes place for dinner reservations at his hotel. Daniel appreciates the attention to detail. "We have a department solely dedicated to resort reservations. The guest might call and say, 'My wife and I would like to make reservations at your restaurant for 7:30.' That triggers a list of questions from our reservations staff that helps us better anticipate the guest's culinary needs. Our Lady or Gentleman might ask something like, 'Sir, are you celebrating anything special?' to which the response might be, 'Yes, it's actually our anniversary.' Our reservationist's response might be, 'Oh, fantastic, Sir. How many years?' From that, we are able to create a 'Happy Anniversary' plate with a truffle box for the guests upon their dessert course. We also ask questions like, 'By any chance do you or your wife have any food allergies?' Again that information is immediately communicated to the culinary staff.

"The next series of questions ask the guest, 'Do you have any preferences?' They could really like Maine lobster, and if we have a Maine lobster dish on the menu at that time, the server will highlight it. The server can approach the table and strike up a conversation: 'Good afternoon, Mr. and Mrs. Smith. Congratulations on your anniversary. We heard that you enjoy lobster. Let me tell you about our amazing Maine lobster dish that we have on the menu at this time.' If we don't have lobster on the menu that night, we would do everything in our power to get it. If for some reason we can't find it, we will speak with the executive chef and offer an alternative that is close to it or that may suit the palate of that person. The thing is that they are not really requesting Maine lobster; they just prefer it. We go to significantly greater lengths if it is a true request." Daniel's example demonstrates the thoughtful, detailed attention that goes into turning a guest preference into the customized Ritz-Carlton experience.

Marguerite Dowd, executive administrative assistant in sales and marketing at The Ritz Carlton, Laguna Niguel, talks about the impact this attention has when there is execution on those details. Marguerite relates, "A young man who had been married at our hotel called because he wanted to do something really special for his first anniversary. I sell anniversary packages here in the sales department, and we have a very special package for those who have been married on our property. He and I sat and talked, and I heard so much about his wife. It was inspiring to hear how much he loved her. I found out what her favorite flowers were and the types of things she enjoyed. We then decided to reproduce a miniature of their wedding cake. I was able to pull out their original wedding file from a year before. I worked with our pastry chef, and in collaboration with the husband, we, to his wife's surprise, produced a miniature version of their original cake. As I learned more about her original bouquet, I had our florist create a beautiful wedding bouquet and tie it up with satin and pearl pins. The flowers were then placed in a room along with the cake topper prior to her arrival. The gentleman called me the next morning and was on the verge of tears. His wife was swept away by the experience, and he was her hero. It was so much fun working with him and getting to know him. It really made my day to know that I had made a memory for them. I probably got as much, if not more, out of that occasion than they did." To produce the memories, leadership must help staff to both inquire and execute on the details of the information gathered.

One of the greatest risks, however, to asking guests their preferences is that it sets up an expectation that those preferences will be acted upon. President Simon Cooper cites, "That's why we like to pick up as much as we can about a guest from our direct observation, and not draw too much attention to those moments when we specifically seek out preferences." Guest Greg Anderson, director of Crown Council, a prestigious alliance of dental practices, offers resounding evidence for the high cost of asking and then not delivering on a guest's preference.

Greg shares, "We were searching for a location for one of our Crown Council meetings. It had been suggested that the Ritz-Carlton in San Francisco would be a good location. I called the hotel and scheduled a site visit for my entire advance team. I had a most interesting conversation with the sales representative. She asked me if there was anything in particular that would make my stay more enjoyable at the hotel. I said absolutely, yes; my wife loves Caffeine-free Diet Coke. I told the salesperson that if they could stock a few cans of her soda, I would consider it a real treat. She said, 'I can make that happen.' I also happened to mention that the weekend we were going to be in San Francisco was my birthday. She was so excited that she almost came through the phone. I was very impressed with her enthusiasm. She asked me what my favorite dessert was and I told her ice cream, especially any ice cream with cherries in it.

"So we visited the hotel. It was a fabulous property, and it was set up exactly the way we needed it. The location would be perfect for one of our smaller Crown Council gatherings. We stayed about three days, including my birthday, and we never ever saw a can of Caffeine-free Diet Coke or any recognition of my birthday, even though we met with the hotel personnel twice. We elected not to choose this property not because of price or location but because they made a promise and didn't follow through. We figure the cost of two cans of cola and a dish of ice cream was less than $5 . . . and the cost of our lost business, about $500,000." While Greg's focus is on the failure to deliver on the expected amenities, it is obvious that the more the staff of a company highlights their interest in a customer's preference, the greater the expectation that the preference will be acted upon.

Customers implicitly question and test businesses. They privately wonder, "Does this business notice how I am different from other customers? Do they provide the little things that give me a sense of importance and comfort? Is this business more interested in making money than they are in enhancing my life?" Employees at all levels, then, must learn ways to anticipate how various customers will react to avoid such breakdowns and potential loss of business.

Two additional risk factors emerge when considering the use of preferences to personalize service: First, there is the challenge of knowing when something is truly a preference for a customer. Second, the data collected must be appropriate and secure. Ed Mady, vice president and area general manager of The Ritz-Carlton, San Francisco, gives examples: "A lot of preference identification involves paying attention to subtlety. If your name is John Smith but our bellman finds out that you like to be called 'Smitty,' then the name on your amenity card should be 'Smitty' and not 'John' or 'Mr. Smith.' While preferences are difficult targets to execute against, the subtleties of preferences matter." Brian Gullbrants, vice president of operations, offers his guideline for determining when something rises to the level of a preference: "If I order Perrier, it doesn't mean I prefer Perrier; it might be the first time I've ever tried it. If I order Perrier with two lemons without ice, there is a *chance* that might be a preference. But if I order it twice, it *is* a preference. We've got to watch our customers and read them and understand when they truly prefer something versus when they are only experimenting with something. It is not easy."

In support of Brian's comment about the difficulty of parsing distinctions between established preferences and situational choices, Ritz-Carlton has a cache of stories highlighting the hazards of missing subtleties or inaccurately gauging preferences. These examples include situations like that of a housekeeper who noted a guest's preference for mariachi music because he left that music genre blasting in his room in Cancún. The same guest started being greeted consistently with mariachi music in his room in Ritz-Carlton locations like Cleveland or Philadelphia. Turns out, he had it on in the first hotel only because he thought it added to the local flavor, not because he was a fan of the music. Additional stories of failed execution include a bottle of wine that was reportedly sent as an amenity gift to a speaker for an Alcoholics Anonymous event and a gift that was delivered to the head of a major delivery company using the delivery services of his competitor.

While mistakes will be made, Ritz-Carlton leadership works consistently on removing those types of defects both to enhance customer experience and to be efficient from a cost perspective. By focusing on the details of a guest's preferences, the Ladies and Gentlemen of Ritz-Carlton consistently deliver Wow experiences, which are highlighted in upcoming chapters. The ability to "deliver Wow" is buttressed by leadership that offers technology, processes, and training to collect and operationalize knowledge acquired on behalf of guests.

With concerns about personal data, Kevin Walsh says, "We are committed to protecting the guest's privacy. We are careful about the nature of information we have on our guests in our Mystique system, and all elements of customized service are done with the greatest of sensitivity. A lot of times, guests will give us photographs. The guest relations staff will then ask if we can keep the photo on file for the next time they come to visit. If they don't want us to keep it, we delete the picture from their profile."

Kevin adds, "We want to build on the relationship we have with our guest and not detract from that. If we did a Google

STRIKING GOLD

▶ Have you helped your staff understand the distinction between anticipating and fulfilling customer needs?

▶ What processes do you have in place to track customer preferences? Is that data being utilized not only to track customer buying habits but also to personalize customer service?

▶ How do you balance your company's need to track customer preferences with your customer's need for privacy and secure personal data?

search on someone, we might find out that someone's a chief executive officer of this company or a graduate of that college. From the knowledge we capture, we might create a chocolate plate with their business's emblem, or design their school's motto in chocolate. We wouldn't do anything that the guest would not want us to do. It all goes back once again to the culture. Ladies and Gentlemen serving Ladies and Gentlemen. It means for those of us in areas where we seek customer information, that we treat people with the same respect we would desire."

The Mystique system not only records individual preferences but also looks at the customer's history with the company, affords opportunities to offer additional services based on known preferences, and provides a method to track operational problems that the guest has encountered.

Customer relationship management software, like Mystique, represents a double-edged sword for most businesses. On the one hand, these technical solutions create the opportunity to capture and analyze data about customers. On the other, they have the potential to eerily intrude into the choices and habits of valued consumers. While many businesses use these databases to effectively understand buying habits, Ritz-Carlton is a leader at leveraging the information it collects to actually enhance the evolving experiences of its guests. But in a world where not everyone wants their preferences known or recorded, the tracking of preferences is a sensitive and challenging endeavor. Staff must discern the level of disclosure and interaction that individual guests desire while respectfully honoring their privacy.

·≤ MR. BIV: ≥·
Listening When
Things Go Wrong

While it appears inherently enjoyable to look for preferences on the part of guests and to craft customized service that delights them, it is often less pleasant to listen and record the problems experienced by a guest. In a playful spirit, Ritz-Carlton has identified one guest it doesn't want at its hotels: MR. BIV. The Ladies and Gentlemen are urged to immediately track the presence of MR. BIV, an acronym for *mistakes, rework, breakdowns, inefficiencies,* and *variations.* In fact, leadership has provided a physical wooden statue representing MR. BIV created by an engineer in their Marina del Rey hotel.

According to Diana Oreck, vice president of global learning and the Leadership Center: "MR. BIV has brought us to the point where we honor defects. Our approach to MR. BIV is consistent with research that shows if you handle a problem quickly and well, you might get a more loyal guest than if there were no problem at all. While we wish there hadn't been a problem in the first place, we believe there is a need to learn from each imperfection. We want people to report the breakdowns so we can build solutions to remove them from our hotels, not just sweep them under a rug. So MR. BIV has been a real way to take the stigma out of complaints and help us reliably track defects to make the necessary corrections."

In addition to registering these "opportunities," as they are called in the Mystique system, Diana adds, "Incidents of MR. BIV that were registered in the database the night before are typically shared in lineup. Let's say you didn't enjoy your dinner last night at the restaurant, but you're going to be with us for three more days. I want to make sure that when you come in contact with the valet, that Lady or Gentleman can say, 'I understand that you didn't have a positive dining experience last night. Is there anything we can do?' Looking at the breakdowns openly and communicating those findings to the staff allow our Ladies and Gentlemen to go out of their way to make sure that the problem doesn't resurface for that guest, and in the process it helps us regain that guest's confidence."

The additional benefit of maintaining a database of breakdowns is that it affords opportunities to be proactive so that processes can be modified and training can be delivered. According to Simon Cooper, "Accurate collection of breakdowns, swift analysis of trends, and resolution of process problems is fundamental for us to be in a position to give a guest a Wow experience at the Ritz-Carlton." Simon cites specific concerns: "A huge chasm occurs when a guest comes in and does not have a good arrival process . . . or goes to the room and finds the drawer in the dresser wasn't emptied from the last guest . . . or pulls down the sheet and there's a tear . . . or has a cup of coffee served cold . . . or is given a room key that doesn't work. When these breakdowns occur, it is hard to get to a place where we're going to have an engaged guest. The only way across the chasm over the long term is to know what goes wrong and make it right. It is fundamental." Guests expect excellent assessment and eradication of errors as the minimum price of entry in a Ritz-Carlton hotel. It's very hard to get to a positive emotional connection with guests if those fundamentals are not satisfied. Satisfying fundamentals occurs only when staff members own the responsibility for reliably recording incidents.

Much of the focus by Ritz-Carlton on tracking service breakdowns emerged from early leaders who studied defect management processes in the manufacturing sector. By benchmarking companies that made products that experience inevitable manufacturing defects, Ritz-Carlton decided to track service and physical property defects against high-quality standards. This analysis of manufacturers helped leadership at Ritz-Carlton appreciate that the longer defects went undetected, the more expensive the defects were to repair. Additionally, the longer a defect remained in place, the more that defect caused other errors.

Despite having been chosen the recipient of the 2007 ASQ Ishikawa Medal, a highly prestigious individual honor conferred by the American Society for Quality, John Timmerman, vice president of quality and program management, reflects on the need to make quality issues the focus of every individual at Ritz-Carlton. "A gentleman I know and respect in the quality improvement world once said to me, 'John, every time I go someplace, people talk about you and how you're leading quality in your organization.' As I was driving home that night, I realized that he had given me the worst compliment I'd ever received and that I never wanted to get that compliment again. It should not be the role of a senior leader to 'lead quality' in an organization. Instead, my role for the hotel should be to help influence a 'quality culture.' Everyone in this organization is responsible for quality."

Often senior-level leaders are far removed from the customer and how work really gets done. To be effective, leaders have to collect quality data from their people, analyze the data for trends, and have the front line help remedy broken processes. Senior managers are most effective when they perform "the 3C's": *collecting, compiling,* and *communicating* quality performance data. By destigmatizing breakdowns, thereby encouraging employees to forthrightly track shortcomings and take responsibility for product quality, leadership receives data that can readily be used to improve processes and rescue the customer experience— freeing staff time for meeting the true stated and unstated needs of the guests.

STRIKING GOLD

- How safe is it for staff to share operational problems and mistakes, without the fear of consequences?

- What processes do you have in place to track breakdowns and defects? Is it clear how defect monitoring cuts costs, improves customer engagement, and saves staff time and frustration involved in reworking regularly occurring breakdowns?

- How effectively does your leadership collect, compile, and communicate quality performance data?

Radar On/Antenna Up

The Leadership Center at Ritz-Carlton has provided a course titled "Radar On/Antenna Up" both to their Ladies and Gentlemen and to outside business leaders. Aspects of the course involve vigilant use of all five senses to infer the needs and wants of a customer. In some cases a person's needs become clear through listening, in other cases clarity emerges from casual inquiry, and in yet others it comes from watching the actions of guests. In all cases, attention is heightened when the observations are made in the context of service professionals setting aside many of their needs and instead placing themselves in the circumstance of the person they are serving.

Mark Ferland, general manager of The Ritz-Carlton, Orlando, Grande Lakes, understands: "This is not rocket science. It is observation. You can't minimize or overlook the importance of observation because you can find out only so much about the guests before they arrive. One of the keys to great service is to find a way to not be obtrusive but be observant. It's seeing what type of chocolates a person's kids enjoy, or making sure you have a cold bottle of water in hand for a guest who is returning from a run, or noticing that guests are asking for an unusual wake-up call and may need something to take with them for breakfast. We're constantly observing. For instance, we might have a group of three hundred people staying for three nights, and that first morning we have two hundred wake-up calls between 7:00 and 7:15. If we believe we can complete those calls faster, we will proactively change our staffing for the next morning, having observed an opportunity to meet the group's needs better, and turning that observation into action."

Betty Lewis, lobby attendant at Ritz-Carlton, knows the power of keeping your eyes open and observing needs that go well beyond what a guest verbally acknowledges. "I saw a guest who looked pale and was trying to find some cold medicine in the gift shop. As she left the shop empty-handed, I asked if I could be of some service. 'Is there anything I can get for you?' She responded no thanks, but I could tell that she didn't want to be a bother. She then went up to her room. Given that she just didn't look well and had a cold, I thought she would benefit from a cup of my special hot tea. So I made her a cup of tea and took it to her along with a rose, some cold tablets, and a small bottle of water. I put them on a silver tray and knocked on her door. She said, 'Yes?' and I answered, 'I'm Betty, the Lady you met near the gift shop. You look like the cold is about to get you down.' She said, 'I'm so sick.' I handed her the tray and once again asked if there was anything else she needed. As she was lying on the bed, I fluffed up her pillows. She needed that because she was coughing. I said, 'I have some honey and lemon in the tea, and I made sure the water is extra hot. I guarantee you'll feel better within the hour.' The next day the guest, who I later found out was the chief executive officer of her company, wrote a nice letter. What I liked most about the letter was that she said she never thought she could get this kind of care away from home. 'It was a mother's care,' and she said she appreciated it very much."

The art of anticipating unmet and even unstated needs is central to the memorable and unique Ritz-Carlton experience. Vivian Deuschl, vice president of public relations, says it really comes down to taking the focus off your needs and stepping into the shoes of the guest. "If I see a problem, I own it. My title is irrelevant. We all put ourselves in the guests' place. If I walk into the ladies' room and notice a paper towel on the floor, I just instinctively reach down and pick it up, so the next guest will see nothing awry. We all do the same. I know that's what makes our Ladies and Gentlemen great, because they put themselves in the mind of the guest."

Vivian confirms that it is not just frontline workers who are paying attention to the needs of others. "I have a bad back, and some days it's worse than others. One day I happened to be in the office, and Simon Cooper, our president, noticed I was walking rather gingerly, and he asked, 'What's wrong with your back?' I said, 'I need to get a new mattress; the one I have just doesn't have enough support.' I didn't think anything else about it until three days later when the delivery man came to the house and brought a box spring, a mattress, all of the bedding—the entire Ritz-Carlton sleep package. I hadn't heard a word from Simon telling me that it was coming, but what it meant to me was beyond description. At first I was amused, and then I thought, *'How many people work for a company where the president really listens and cares enough to make that special effort?'"*

From President Simon Cooper to Lobby Attendant Betty Lewis, creating the unique and memorable guest experience begins by taking the needs of the person offering the service out of the equation. It continues through a focus on the needs of the person you wish to serve. Leadership creates the environment for this service excellence by assisting staff members to fully attend to others, use all their senses, and ultimately place themselves in the situations of those they serve.

LIVING THE NEW GOLD STANDARD

▶ Maximize the importance of being observant. Great observation is not intrusive but intuitive and attentive.

▶ The highest level of customer care is attained when service transcends attention to detail and embraces genuine empathy.

▶ Customer engagement is measurable. So are the steps to gaining it. Extraordinary service providers connect with each customer's individuality and deliver service that is customized to every person's preferences.

▶ Personalizing service means paying attention to subtlety and nuance in client behaviors and executing to deliver on those client inclinations.

▶ Asking questions and showing concern for your customers is valuable only if you act on those needs.

▶ Collect and track client-interaction data to constantly build on successes and repair breakdowns.

▶ Avoiding faultfinding while tracking service and/or product defects enriches the quality of data that leadership can utilize in the quality improvement process.

PRINCIPLE

4

Deliver
Wow!

Wow: The Ultimate Guest Experience

What you leave behind is not what is engraved in stone monuments, but what is woven into the lives of others.

PERICLES

 As suggested in Chapter 6, customer satisfaction is not enough to ensure business success. Recent research has shown that customers who are only "satisfied" with a company's service are far less likely than customers who are "extremely satisfied" to remain loyal to that business. Specifically, this literature found that customers who reported they were "extremely satisfied" with a business were two and one-half times more likely to make future purchases from that company when compared to customers who rated their overall satisfaction as "average." But what does it take to move customers from the satisfied to highly satisfied range?

Like many other business consultants, Jeanette McMurtry, chief strategy officer for The Hanson Group, believes that extremely satisfied customers emerge through memorable and emotional connections forged between them and a business. Jeanette points out, "This is pretty scary news for businesses in all arenas. Even if you have a perfect track record of accuracy, meeting delivery deadlines, product quality, and service with a smile, your customers won't be loyal to you. Apparently, we've moved beyond the era of 'delighting' customers and are now in an era where much more is expected. Beyond adequate service, consumers today want to be thrilled, to feel a rush of extraordinary satisfaction by getting much more value, attention, or enjoyment than they expected."

Operating from this understanding that customer engagement is linked to the consumers' wanting "to feel a rush," Ritz-Carlton leadership calls this desired memorable and emotional connection a "Wow experience" and encourages staff to personally affect guests to achieve this level of emotional intensity. While terms like *Wow, thrilled,* or *rush of energy* sound more like qualities of an amusement ride than something that could be produced during a luxury hotel stay or a visit to the corner dry cleaner, the idea of a Wow experience or a thrilling customer interaction hinges less on the inherent exhilaration of the product and more on delivering service that appeals to both the thinking and feeling aspects of the consumer.

Although the bulk of customer contact at Ritz-Carlton and most businesses comes from those outside of corporate offices, senior leadership sets the tone for customer care. Leaders help staff see the endless opportunities they have to wow guests across all touch points of the guest's interaction. Ritz-Carlton uses lineup and formal training to show staff how a guest can not only be satisfied but also wowed from their initial phone reservation to well beyond the guest's departure.

There Is Only One First Impression

Service can be memorable either because it delights a customer or because it leaves the customer sorely disappointed. The importance of delivering a Wow moment at a guest's first point of contact is, therefore, a primary goal emphasized by leadership because of the impact on the customers. A guest at The Ritz-Carlton, St. Thomas, comments, "Our Ritz-Carlton trip actually started about one week before we left home. I received a call from Kenya at the resort, as she wanted to confirm our travel plans and ask if we were celebrating any special occasion. It was our five-year wedding anniversary. She also asked if we had any requests, like extra blankets. I did explain that I was pregnant with our first child and I would love a few extra pillows to support my back. She gave me several options such as firm, feather, down, and polyfill. I didn't know there were so many! Kenya also gave me the option of a full-sized body pillow. For those who have never been pregnant, it is hard to describe how wonderful body pillows are. Clearly, if I could've found any way to transport mine from home, I would have. I was already impressed, and I hadn't left home yet." Not only did Kenya confirm that the body pillow was in the room at the time of their arrival but she also extended the warmth of the guests' welcome beyond that telephone call.

The guest goes on to share, "On our first night, we returned to our room to find chocolate-covered strawberries, an ice bucket with a bottle of champagne, and a congratulatory note from the hotel manager. Our bed had roses on it, and it was sprinkled with rose petals. We thought, 'What a nice touch.' Then my husband removed the bottle of 'champagne' from the ice, and it turned out to be sparkling cider. Obviously, they noted my pregnancy and made adjustments to their anniversary gift for us. We were very impressed with that attention to detail."

Taking the time to make a strong first impression, genuinely inquiring about a guest's needs, delivering on those needs, and mastering subtle details, all play a role in differentiating between acceptable and memorable service. From the outset, these actions stand out to guests by communicating that they are appreciated and valued.

Given that people are accustomed to not being acknowledged and not having their names used during service, situations

PRINCIPLE 4: DELIVER WOW!

in which those elements are consistently present draw the attention and delight of the recipient. Additionally, these little things can be the difference between a positively or an unpleasantly memorable guest experience. For example, a guest who checked into a Ritz-Carlton hotel during a very busy event noted, "Our visit to the Ritz-Carlton was at best, horrible. After speaking to the front desk prior to my arrival both the day before and the morning of our expected check-in, one would think our arrival experience would be smooth as silk. It was the furthest thing from it, even though we were booked in a Club Level room. When we arrived, a line was formed through the lobby with only one person attending the desk. Much to our surprise we were greeted in a welcoming way and were told we could not check into our room (it was 4:45 p.m.) for another hour or so because the hotel was having computer problems. We were offered to go up to the Club Level and wait until our room was ready. When we got to the Club Lounge, without our keys, the place was mobbed with other guests in the same situation, not even staying on that floor. It was completely absurd, and we had to be at a concert within an hour and a half and hadn't had dinner or showered. After begging the concierge, Emily, she was able to get our keys."

While unforgettable customer experiences come in all varieties, the initial impression formed by the customer, be that of delight or disappointment, sets the stage for trust or distrust that will color the remainder of the business relationship.

·◌⟨ Taking It to the Memorable ⟩◌·

By sharing information about guests at lineup (including pictures of the guests that are kept in the Mystique system or found on Google) and by utilizing shared communication such as earpiece radios, staff at Ritz-Carlton can typically use the names of guests they have never personally met. Imagine having a limousine driver from Ritz-Carlton radio ahead that you will be arriving at the property in 15 minutes. Upon entering the hotel, the valet, front door staff, front desk personnel, and manager-on-duty all greet you by name, which was possible because they were monitoring that radio communication.

Some people view this level of attention as intrusive or suffocating. In these cases, staff at Ritz-Carlton take note of the customer's objection and modify the practice. However, most people are surprised and pleased when a series of individuals they have never met both know and use their name in a warm greeting. In essence, communication of a customer's name among staff (saving the customer from having to repeat his or her name or other background information) elevates the service experience of ordinary people to the level of that commonly encountered by well-known celebrities and dignitaries. On a smaller scale, it is the difference between having your name taken by a restaurant reservationist but then never being called by your name during the meal versus the waiter who secures your name from the reservationist and starts your meal by saying, "Mr. and Mrs. Smith, thank you for dining with us this evening."

To this end, leadership at Ritz-Carlton emphasizes that every single individual can do what is necessary to create a Wow experience in the recognition of a customer. In many situations at Ritz-Carlton, the Wow literally emerges from the fact that two or more staff members view the guest's needs as important enough to take the initiative to communicate about them. A guest at The Ritz-Carlton, Cancún, explains, "I had a bad headache, so when the maid came to our room to turn down the bed, I answered the door and told her that I would just take a bottle of water because I wasn't feeling well. Not much later, the concierge called to check on me and wanted to know if I needed a doctor. There aren't many businesses where someone like a maid would talk to another person in order to see if there is anything else that could be done for a customer." While it may seem inconsequential or trivial, developing strategies to help staff remember a customer's name and needs makes a business memorable to that customer.

·◦| Creating Belonging |◦·

While acknowledging people by name or offering them a warm greeting sets the stage for a memorable experience, it frequently can be overshadowed by service breakdowns that follow. Although customers may initially feel welcomed by a business or that their needs matter, they can quickly begin to feel that the welcome wears off or that they would be better suited working with a different business. In essence, customers not only ask themselves *"Did the staff warmly and authentically welcome me into an experience with this business?"* but also *"Do I belong here?"*

A guest who stayed at The Ritz-Carlton, Atlanta, in town for an NCAA basketball game, was wowed at how she and her husband were made to feel they "belonged" at that particular hotel. "I had always stayed at the other Ritz-Carlton hotels in the area, and I was wondering if this location would be as grand. From the minute I walked in the door, I was greeted by at least five hotel staff members. The desk clerks went above and beyond the call of duty to make sure I was taken care of—and royally. Keep in mind that I was an average person traveling among a humongous crowd during this special event, and yet I felt like I received special attention amidst the throngs."

A guest at the San Francisco property similarly shares how personal service helped him not only stand out from the crowd but also offered him an extended sense of belonging and comfort. "I travel for business and have stayed all over the world. When I was sent to San Francisco for a work assignment, I was happy but not excited to be away from the East Coast for 30 days. In essence, the Ritz-Carlton was going to be my home for a month. I had a car pick me up at the airport, and when I walked in, two employees welcomed me by name and said they were excited to have me here. How did they know me?" The guest was particularly affected by the genuine concern demonstrated by employees, including one who met him at the door and handed him his room key and took him directly to his room without a stop at the front desk. The guest went on to note that advanced consideration of his needs gave him the assurance he would be well cared for. "When I entered my room, I found they had stocked everything I would ever need. Since I was staying a month, they did research and found out my favorite snacks, magazines, movies, and music. Everything was there for me. I had a bowl of fruit (a favorite snack of mine) and a box of chocolates with my name spelled out on the pieces. They even created business cards for me using the Ritz-Carlton address, which I needed to pass out during my extended stay."

To create that level of true personalization, systems have to be in place to ensure seamless communication and continuity of care for customers. These systems at Ritz-Carlton include interdepartmental training, mock drills for preparedness, situational cross-training, quality improvement teams, and the use of various communication technology aids like earpiece radios. Increasingly businesses are appreciating the importance of cross-functional team communication in delivering Wow service. Whether it is through training, communication, or the development of collaboration metrics that hold departmental leaders accountable for effecting results on collaborative objectives, leaders seek to dissolve departmental distinctions by providing a common frame of reference that best serves the needs of the consumer. Operational Dynamics, an engineering consultancy group headquartered in Sydney, Australia, emphasizes the importance of the need for interdepartmental communication by stating, "Human nature being what it is, organizations often run into trouble at the boundary between business units or between departments. The trouble is that most tasks which need to get done in order to actually service the customer or produce a product require communication to happen across these boundaries."

- In what ways have you designed service delivery that appeals to both the thinking and feeling aspects of the consumer?

- How does staff gain an awareness of the opportunities they have to wow or make emotional connections with customers at every touch point of the customer interaction?

- What processes and technologies do you employ to maximize cross-departmental service?

⚜ Not a Home Away from Home ⚜

In order to have staff deliver the emotional Wow experience, a very clear picture of the customer's desired emotional state must be painted. Past President Horst Schulze points out that originally the message shared with staff at Ritz-Carlton was that guests wanted to "have a home-away-from-home experience. But what we learned when we did a careful analysis of what guests were telling us is that they didn't go to a hotel to replicate what they experienced at their home. They went to a hotel to experience *more* than what they experienced at home. Believe it or not, they wanted a hotel environment to emulate what a child might feel in the home of a loving mother."

Horst adds, "Guests wanted things to be done without their having to worry whatsoever. Think about it. When children open the refrigerator in their mother's home, they find what they like without having to play a role in how it got there. The light bulbs in their home are changed, and they never have to think about who changes them." By sharing this kind of simple example, Horst and others have created a culture in which the Ladies and Gentlemen of Ritz-Carlton understand that service is not only about fulfilling requests but also about noticing and anticipating underlying needs of their guests.

While some may feel that Horst's characterization essentially relegates luxury consumers to the level of spoiled children who wish to be pampered, a closer scrutiny leads to quite a different conclusion. Luxury consumers frequently are very successful people who manage significant stressors in their day-to-day lives. While they could purchase nonluxury alternatives, they seek hassle-free, high-quality products and services, and they are willing to pay a premium for them. Joel Widzer, travel industry analyst and author of *The Penny Pincher's Passport to Luxury Travel: The Art of Cultivating Preferred Customer Status,* puts it best: "Our everyday lives are typically involved with serving others. If you are an employee, you are most likely serving your supervisor and customers. If you are a homemaker, you are probably serving the needs of your family. If you are a business traveler, your journeys are strenuous enough with long daily meetings in a new city each day, as well as being away from the comforts of family and home. We all work hard in whatever field of endeavor we have chosen, and so it is vital to reward ourselves whenever we have the opportunity. I have found luxury travel to be a well-deserved reward for hard work."

By allowing staff to tailor luxury experiences to the specific needs of a guests (for example, the Service Values as opposed to the 20 Basics), guests are served in a manner that is unobtrusive and consistent with their comfort level. In the words of Joel Widzer, "Service employees who are sensitive to a customer's needs know not only when to offer services but when not to. Exceptional service also involves a perceptive attention to detail and the knowledge that often it is the small things that matter most."

Just as a parent is attentive to subtle signs given by a child, the staff of Ritz-Carlton is vigilant in tracking the unique patterns of guest behavior. In fact, Bjoern Hartmann, assistant manager of guest recognition, The Ritz-Carlton, Berlin, believes that attentiveness is the core of his work. "I pay attention to details, and whenever somebody asks me about my job description, I proudly admit that I am getting paid to get the details right so I can make a Ritz-Carlton stay memorable and unique!"

To get the details right, staff must be encouraged to put themselves in the situation of others, paying attention to their practical needs. They must empathize with the guest's emotional perspective by utilizing all of their senses—especially sight and sound—to pick up on guest preferences. Micah Dean, who works as an attendant/server and departmental trainer at The Ritz-Carlton, Atlanta, admits, "I try to actively listen when I'm not being spoken to. Sometimes I hear people talk to each other just in passing, while I am doing something for another guest. For example, I could be taking something to one guest and overhear another guest say, 'Oh, that looks good.' In that case I wouldn't wait for the person who made the comment to ask for the item. The next time the person would see me, I would have that item just for him or her. Or you may know, for instance, that somebody loves our chocolate-covered strawberries, but he or she is going to dinner at 8:00 and won't be back until after the lounge closes at 10:00. So I would put some of those strawberries in that guest's room along with the type of wine he or she was drinking earlier that night."

Micah's comments reflect the importance of looking for opportunities to serve others, even when you are not in direct interaction with those needing service. Rather than defining the customer as the person directly in view, service professionals scan the environment for opportunities to cater to those on the periphery or those not necessarily asking for service. Micah notes, "Anticipating your guests' needs is a simple, almost artistic, skill—one in which you listen and observe the guests' habits while taking a genuine interest in their well-being, whether that interest is directed to their family, their life, or what they did when they were at this property or even off-property."

·⊰¶ Attention Is a ¶⊱· Multisensory Activity

Micah's example of artful attentiveness demonstrates that emotional connections are forged not only through heroic efforts of staff members but through subtle attentiveness. Research conducted by professors Laurette Dubé and Leo Renaghan, published in the *Cornell Hotel and Restaurant Administration Quarterly,* validates the universal importance of "attentiveness" among hotel staff. Of all the service characteristics they studied, "friendliness" and "attentiveness" were the most valued by hotel guests across all traveler groups (leisure, business). The impact of attentiveness is underscored in the comments of a Ritz-Carlton, St. Thomas, guest who writes, "Somehow the staff must have overheard that my son's birthday would be happening during our stay at the hotel. We awoke to a basket delivery of chocolate-chip pancakes, complete with candle and matches and birthday wishes written in chocolate. Trudy, the gift store cashier, sent a bag of goodies: a puzzle and map. They couldn't have made a nicer impression for an eight-year-old who didn't get a party with his best buddies on the big day."

A guest at The Ritz-Carlton, Central Park, offers a similar example of how focused attentiveness fuels customer loyalty and the desire to continue a relationship with a business: "When we entered the hotel for the first time, it was quite impressive because they called us by our names. We happened to mention we were in the city to see the musical *Mary Poppins*. When we came back to our room, the same concierge had the *Mary Poppins* soundtrack playing and told us to take it home with us, as a memento of our stay. My stay there in New York City made me feel like a queen!"

Derek Flint, general manager of The Ritz-Carlton, Beijing, Financial Street, suggests that staff members are able to attentively connect with customers when leadership helps them distinguish between their purpose and their function. "For example, the purpose of a front desk person is not to check someone in. The purpose is to create an exceptional experience for our guests during that check-in. The front desk staff member needs to be more than just proficient in the job function. We can teach functional aspects of a job; what we can't teach is how to fulfill a larger purpose."

Artful attentiveness fits the purpose of delivering Wow experiences—and so does focused vision. One guest commented that he and his wife were wowed by a staff member who observed a subtle choice that his wife had made when she "was eating a peanut butter cookie in the Club Lounge but left it because she had hoped it was chocolate chip. When the waitperson cleared the plate, she noticed the leftover cookie and asked if we liked it. I informed her that my wife was actually in the mood for a chocolate-chip cookie. The waitperson apologized, and only moments later a freshly baked chocolate-chip cookie was handed to my wife without her even asking for it. That is service—reading a customer's desires. While the resort is expensive, things as simple as a magically appearing chocolate-chip cookie gave us our money's worth." Hearing clues about birthdays or special activities and watching for uneaten cookies allow for unstated wishes to be creatively fulfilled.

Communicate, Communicate, and Communicate More

Much of the surprise element in customer service at Ritz-Carlton comes from the constant sharing of information among staff members. However, Melody Treece Vargas, a retail professional and guide to About.com's retail industry site, warns, "Consumers are becoming more privacy and security savvy. They are increasingly reluctant to share personal information. Most will only share once they see a clear benefit, and then many still only share reluctantly."

In essence, customers seem to be most concerned about the intention of the information sharing; if the sharing does not serve the customer's direct need (for example, internally inefficient process requirements, employee gossip, or cross-departmental marketing), it can raise privacy concerns and the possible perception of intrusiveness. However, if handled with discretion and in the service of the wants, needs, and desires of the customer, most individuals are delighted to know that thoughtfulness and communication are occurring on their behalf. A guest at The Ritz-Carlton, Amelia Island, comments, "We were sitting in the lounge having a couple of drinks. One of my peers commented about how nice it would be to have a cigar. A few minutes later, a security guard approached him and asked if he would like to check out the selection of cigars in the gift shop, which had been closed for the evening. The guard then escorted this gentleman to the shop, opened it up, and waited while he picked out a few cigars. Apparently our waitress had overheard us talking about cigars and asked the security guard to take care of us." The commitment to look for ways to share information that will enhance a guest's experience is central to Ritz-Carlton service philosophy and ultimately produces customer memories and stories that are often exchanged and retold by loyal guests.

·⊰ I'm Here for You ⊱·

Some of the greatest opportunities for wowing customers occur when breakdowns happen. From the standpoint of service recovery, Horst Schulze continues his comparison of guests wanting more than a home-away-from-home experience. Horst believes that emotional connections with customers occur by also looking at how a loving parent would handle a problem: "When something went wrong at your home as a young child and you told your mother about it, she would say, 'I'm here for you,' and she fixed the problem. Mom didn't say she'd check with someone else to see if they would take care of it, and she wouldn't start arguing with you or blaming you for the problem. But how do most hotels, and most businesses, for that matter, handle such things? If you complain to a server that the remote control in your room isn't working, the server doesn't say 'I'm here to help.' At best, he or she says, 'Let me call the manager.' We have to give everyone who works for the company a chance to offer genuine care and to say, 'I'm here for you.'"

By affording the frontline staff the power to offer responsive care and to improvise solutions, guests frequently report substantial Wow experiences. One guest relates how a less-than-relaxed dining experience was remedied: "One night we dined in the Mexican beachfront restaurant at The Ritz-Carlton, Key Biscayne. We had an 8:30 p.m. reservation, and the restaurant was rather quiet. However, at 9 p.m. we noticed that the staff was starting to clear tables and blow out candles before we had completed our meal. We mentioned this to the restaurant manager upon leaving, and he apologized and explained that they had a function at that location the next day and they had inappropriately started the setup during our dinner. We left and went back to our room. Ten minutes later, a bottle of champagne together with chocolate-covered strawberries arrived with a handwritten letter from the manager, apologizing again. Now *that* is style."

·❧ Delivering Well-Being ❧·

Not only are such actions viewed as stylish by guests but they also reflect sincere and timely concern for the guests' well-being. A customer at the Kapalua resort notes, "We arrived at the hotel very early, around 8 a.m., on the day we checked in, and the room wasn't ready. Rather than being reminded that the check-in time wasn't until 3 p.m., we were met with fresh orchid leis and an apology by the manager, who came out to greet us. He invited us to leave our bags at the bell desk, and he took my cell phone number to call me when the room was ready. We went to the spa/fitness center to change into our bathing suits; the front desk had called ahead to tell them we were coming. When we got there, we were greeted by name. I was called promptly at 11:30 a.m., exactly when they told us the room would be ready. A staff member met us at the pool with our room keys and escorted us to the room where our bags had already been taken. They couldn't have made our early arrival at the hotel any easier, and they couldn't have cared more about the value of our time. That is what service looks like."

In most cases, smoothing over customer issues occurs only when a business is convinced they have made a mistake during a transaction. At Ritz-Carlton, that spirit of "I am here for you" occurs even when situations are outside of the staff's control. A guest at The Ritz-Carlton, Palm-Beach, describes her unusual experience. "We didn't expect that the hotel would be so kid friendly. They showed a movie outside by the pool nightly. Unfortunately, the night we chose to relax poolside and watch, it started to rain toward the end of the movie so they had to take down the screen. The staff insisted on setting up a VCR and the tape in our room so our daughter could watch the ending."

·⊲[When It Matters Most]⊳·

On a much larger scale, staff members make extra efforts to wow guests in the most difficult of times. As guests in Cancún went to bed on a Tuesday night hearing that Tropical Storm Wilma was going to pass by them only producing choppy waves, they awoke the next day to hear that the largest hurricane ever recorded was approaching Cancún. News reports encouraged visitors to leave the island immediately.

One guest of The Ritz-Carlton, Cancún, reports, "After a mass exodus to the airport, there were no available flights left, and we were stranded. The Ritz-Carlton staff accompanied us to a hotel further inland in downtown Cancún where we stayed as the hurricane hovered over Cancún for three days. While at the other property, the Ritz-Carlton staff provided food, water, and amazingly enough, constant streams of mouthwash and towels, while providing excellent service and smiles during the horrific ordeal. After the storm passed, we found out the Cancún airport was closed indefinitely." Amazed, the guest adds, "At its own cost, Ritz-Carlton chartered a tour bus that took us to the closest airport, in La Mirada, where they made arrangements to charter a plane that took us to Mexico City. While I would never wish such a horrible experience on anyone, I will say that I am now a Ritz-Carlton customer for life."

Whereas many businesses go out of their way to deny responsibility for guest problems, the staff of Ritz-Carlton typically acts responsibly, without ascribing blame, through targeted corrective action. One guest tells of an experience of his daughter at the Ritz Kids program at South Beach where staff jumped in and did the unexpected. "My daughter spilled something on her pants soon after arriving there for the day. Our baggage was lost by the airline, and so she didn't have a change of clothes. Not only did the camp counselors have her clothes dry cleaned but they also went to Macy's and bought her a new outfit. I was floored. This is obviously above and beyond anything I would have expected."

Customers are all too often surprised when businesses accept responsibility for breakdowns, thus providing a strategic advantage for those businesses that admit their faults. John Fleming, Ph.D., principal and chief scientist for Gallup and coauthor of the book *Human Sigma: Managing the Employee-Customer Encounter,* says, "Taking responsibility for customer problems is a huge area of opportunity because most companies don't do a good job of it. It's a low-hanging fruit in building strong relationships."

Consistent with John's perspective and given Ritz-Carlton's stated objective of producing guests for life, problem resolution is a mission-critical skill set. The relationship-strengthening benefits of mastering these skills are demonstrated in the comments of a guest in Maui who writes: "My wife accidentally broke a bottle of makeup that she had brought along and left it in pieces on the counter in the bathroom because she still wanted to use as much of it as possible. We came back to the room one day to find a note sitting beside the broken makeup bottle from housekeeping offering to replace the broken bottle and they didn't even break it."

Demonstrating the Ability to Respond: Responsible Behavior

People are genuinely wowed when others make a concerted effort to take care of their needs, particularly when the situations that produced the needs are not directly the responsibility of the person offering assistance. A guest at The Ritz-Carlton, Kapalua, retells one incident. "We booked two plane tickets to fly over the volcanoes. Despite the claims of the tour operator, which we double-checked by having Ritz-Carlton call them to confirm, there was no air-conditioning on the plane, most sights were only visible on the right side of the plane, and the engine noise was deafening even with headsets on. At $400 a ticket, it was a huge disappointment and basically ruined our day. Because of the constant dipping and steep turning of the plane, both my wife and I got sick during the flight. Everyone was sweating, and the pilot, Captain Bill, had the audacity to play his own band's music through the headsets and ask for tips at the end of the flight! But credit goes to Ritz-Carlton and front office manager JoAnne. We told her of our experience the next day, and after the tour operator refused to grant any concession, JoAnne promptly removed the operator from the hotel's list of activities and credited us for one of the tickets since the hotel had booked the tour for us. It's simply amazing and memorable that they would make right on the inconsideration of someone else."

The steps involved in salvaging a bad experience (whether it is caused by your business or not) are fairly simple; yet all too often these steps are not followed:

1. Share a genuine and compassionate reaction to the person's distress.

2. Offer appropriate apologies.

3. Assure the person you will take care of the issue.

4. Individually, and through the resources of your team, see that the problem is taken care of in a way that meets the satisfaction of the customer and does not recur.

5. Go one step further to demonstrate that you want to try to compensate for the person's loss or frustration.

Bad News Lingers

Although the Ritz-Carlton staff is acculturated to wow customers even when faced with service and product breakdowns, the process of service recovery does not always go flawlessly. When problems are not resolved satisfactorily, they not only create customer churn (for the engaged Ritz-Carlton customer, this lifetime value can be in excess of $1 million) but they also produce people who are vocally negative about the brand. Even if the problem area is rectified at a later time, the initial negative impact can be lasting. For example, during a stay at The Ritz-Carlton, Moscow, shortly after the hotel's opening, Brayno S. Braynov was upset about several problems. One of the two televisions in his suite did not work, and he had difficulties with the lock mechanism on one of the doors. Also, prior to his arrival, a concierge had promised him tickets for a local attraction, but no tickets were presented to him.

While Brayno understood that there could be communication and technical issues with the opening of a new hotel, he was unable to get a satisfactory resolution of his complaints during his stay. Given the nature of his disappointment, he wrote a negative trip review on a popular travel site. But that wasn't all. "In addition to writing my review," Brayno explains, "I e-mailed the Ritz-Carlton corporate office with my complaint, and I also e-mailed the regional vice president who was in charge of hotels in Europe. Although the regional vice president was at a conference in New York, I received an immediate reply from his assistant. About two hours later, I got a phone call from the regional vice president, whom they had woken up in the middle of the night (given our time differences) so he could talk to me. That conversation was a very positive one, and we worked out a resolution to my issues. In fact, I will actually be going back in a couple of months to that same Ritz-Carlton in Moscow."

While there was personal attention given to Brayno after his appeal to regional and corporate leaders, Debi Howard, manager of corporate guest relations, acknowledges, "Failure to resolve problems on site and at the time they actually occur can have a lasting negative impact." Prospective customers who visit the travel Web site where Brayno left his review would not know that his concerns were resolved to his satisfaction since his original post is the only information provided about his visit.

In a world where customer opinions are archived on the Internet and where people are more likely to share a negative experience, the lasting impact of delayed service recovery can negatively affect prospective customers. With the ease of instant worldwide communication and the popularity of social networking and customer reviews, companies can't just practice service recovery but must instead execute *immediate* service recovery. The sooner customers are satisfied, the less likely they are to share a negative review that may have damaging consequences.

STRIKING GOLD

- Does your training communicate the importance of paying attention to the customer's practical needs, empathizing with the guest's emotional perspective, and utilizing all sensory data to pick up on guest preferences?

- Can staff members distinguish between the purpose and function of their job?

- How readily do you and your staff wow customers through immediate service recovery?

Wowing with a Broad Stroke to Leave an Impression That Lasts

Obviously, the easiest and most cost-effective Wow experiences emerge when staff members find customer needs that routinely go unserved at competing businesses. For example, many hotel guests prefer outdoor exercise to using gym facilities on the property. While many other hotels don't anticipate the needs of this group of exercisers, Ritz-Carlton typically provides cold bottled water at the entrance of the hotel for guests returning from a run. Although such considerations are not a personalized offering, they do reflect a thoughtfulness that gets the attention of guests. For example, a customer at The Ritz-Carlton, San Francisco, recalls, "Upon departure, we were given water for the car ride. They knew we were driving to Pebble Beach so they wanted us to be comfortable. Oh, yeah . . . for all you joggers: when you go out running in the morning and come back sweaty, they have towels and vitamin water for you. How nice is that? I bet if you asked, they would run for you too!"

While there are no reports of Ritz-Carlton staff exercising on behalf of guests, leadership has clearly communicated the importance of creating Wow experiences during the guest's stay. Additionally, leadership stresses the value of seizing the opportunity to make a memorable connection through a fond farewell. A guest at The Ritz-Carlton, Half Moon Bay, California, shows how simply, elegantly, and genuinely people can be wowed even as they leave a hotel. "When we retrieved our car from the valet to go home, they had a little note in the car thanking us for staying, another card listing the local radio stations and directions to the freeway, plus two bottles of water for us." Ritz-Carlton staff members understand that memorable and caring service requires nothing more than a handwritten note that says "thank you" or "I look forward to seeing you again."

In some cases, superb service requires no words at all, just the passion to hold the needs of the customer as paramount. A striking example is evidenced by a guest at The Ritz-Carlton, Amelia Island, Florida: "One of our executives had an important teleconference but was expecting a fax from one of the participants. He called the front desk, told them he was going to be on the phone, and asked if a staff member could bring up the fax as quickly as possible when it arrived. The Ritz-Carlton staff member assured our executive that it would be taken care of. He began his conference call, and a short time into the call he heard the soft sound of paper sliding beneath his door. However, it was only the first page of his fax. Thinking they had made a mistake, he returned to his call. A moment later he heard the sound again, and another page appeared from beneath the door. The hotel had someone running his fax up one page at a time, as each page came off of the fax machine! They understood that the fax was important, and rather than wait for the whole thing to transmit, they sent it up as quickly as it came in. Because of these types of experiences, I believe Ritz-Carlton is THE standard by which all other service providers should be measured."

Ritz-Carlton has created the expectation that its business will be the standard-bearer for customer service and memorable customer experiences. Well-selected and trained staff makes it happen at all touch points of a customer interaction . . . one guest at a time.

LIVING THE NEW GOLD STANDARD

- Something as simple as a bottle of water can provide a long-lasting memory . . . if it's handed to a thirsty person who isn't expecting it.

- Wow starts with a commitment to a culture of extraordinary service. Ingenuity brings it to life.

- While it is easy to deliver, a warm welcome is rare enough to stand out in the minds of customers.

- Continuity of care, active team communication, and personalized attention drive life-long repeat business from devoted clients.

- Artful attentiveness, without intrusion, will allow you to infer the needs of your clients the way devoted parents can pick up on preferences that surprise and delight their children.

- The more expediently a problem is resolved, the more quickly it is forgotten.

- Whether or not a business is *responsible* for issues and mistakes, a customer is most likely to remember who took the initiative to fix them!

- Breakdowns will occur despite the best intentions to provide flawless service. Empathy, quick attention, and a willingness to go beyond the resolution will salvage a bad situation and turn it into a winning outcome.

9

Turn Wow into Action

*The world is moved along, not only by the
mighty shoves of its heroes, but also by the aggregate
of the tiny pushes of each honest worker.*

HELEN KELLER

There are Wow moments happening in every
workplace. In some cases, they are the result of
a service culture while in others they are simply the individual acts of high-performing staff members. In many businesses, outstanding work is tracked
and recognized. Ritz-Carlton takes this one step further.
Leadership has designed ways for their "Wow stories"—
remarkable examples of extraordinary service exhibited
by their Ladies and Gentlemen—to be used to reinforce
existing service excellence and to propel future extraordinary acts. In fact, Wow stories are one of the most important vehicles that the leadership at Ritz-Carlton uses
for communicating the values they see as critical to the
success of the company.

Previous chapters have shared the importance of the
daily act of lineup, where employees at all levels—from
cleaning staff to president—meet to hear updates about
the company and learn "Do You Know" trivia tidbits,
which are fun facts about the company or individual
hotels. A crucial component to this assembly is the

sharing of Wow stories. Katerina Panayiotou, manager of internal communication at Ritz-Carlton, is responsible for collecting Wow stories submitted from hotels in all locales and incorporating them into the company's *Commitment to Quality* (the guide sheet used to ensure consistent presentation of information during the lineup process). *The Commitment to Quality* focuses on key corporate themes, such as the Service Values and the Credo or even upgrades to the Mystique database or guest recognition program.

Wow stories are constants in *The Commitment to Quality* and as such are presented at every Monday and Friday lineup. Given the sizable language diversity across the staff at Ritz-Carlton properties, these lessons are translated into 12 languages, including Arabic, Mandarin, Cantonese, and Spanish. For the Ladies and Gentlemen of Ritz-Carlton, these stories, explains Katerina, are "not about the staff members just doing their jobs; it's what they can do to enliven our success factors or to enliven one of our Gold Standards."

Katerina reports that she is inundated with Wow stories, "so much so, that I feel pressure to make sure all the properties have some of their stories featured. We've even developed a database with online links to help streamline the submission and tracking process." If an employee's actions result in a Wow story that appears in *The Commitment to Quality,* the Lady or Gentleman receives $100. While this financial acknowledgment is valued, Katerina reports, "it's more about the recognition and just having done a great job. Our Ladies and Gentlemen take pride in what they do. It's about the joy in being able to serve." In addition to the specific stories selected and presented through the corporatewide daily lineup at each location, there is also a portion reserved for appreciation and recognition of staff at that hotel who have delivered both large and small Wow service moments to guests.

In addition, shares Katerina, keeping track of the stories "helps the hotels provide examples of customer service excellence that match important corporate themes and business targets for the year. We also set objectives on how many stories each hotel will submit each year—holding leadership accountable for constantly catching people doing things well." Wow stories have also helped hotels innovate or improve existing processes. Myra de Gersdorff, general manager of The Ritz-Carlton, New Orleans, reports, "Our staff might hear a Wow story about someone in a hotel halfway around the world expediting a guest's check-in process, and before you know it, they will have found a similar way to make the check-in process easier at our hotel." Similarly, at The Ritz-Carlton, Pentagon City, management noticed that many Wow stories worldwide involved staff accessing items for guests from other departments in the hotel; for instance, a housekeeper offering a complimentary item for a guest that was secured from the hotel's gift shop. This assessment gave leadership insights into how to reduce the paperwork and bureaucratic hurdles involved in these cross-departmental guest service efforts.

Staff members are also encouraged to share praise with one another. In support of this encouragement, leadership has created a series of programs ranging from "First Class" recognition cards to quarterly and annual "Five Star" staff awards for remarkable service. Staff actively participate in identifying coworkers worthy of recognition and participate in the events that honor stellar performers. Employees are made aware of these programs during orientation. In the case of First Class cards, human resources personnel at each property provide note cards for employees to commend one another. While First Class cards are shared in a fairly self-directed fashion, the human resources department is tasked to monitor and encourage card utilization.

The Five Star recognition program occurs on a quarterly basis at each property. Employees are nominated by their peer group, and the criteria used for the nominations are based on the Gold Standards (Service Values, Credo, Employee Promise, and so on). Peer nominations are directed to the guidance team, composed of hotel leadership who select five recipients each quarter. These award winners are recognized at a banquet or a luncheon hosted in their honor. The winners are also publicly acknowledged during the hotel's lineup. These recipients receive special pins, which designate them as Five Star winners. The Five Star recipients from each quarter become ambassadors for the hotel and frequently are called upon to meet with clients or share their stories with customers or business meeting planners. They also frequently participate in the orientation process for new employees in the organization. Each year, 5 of the 20 quarterly recipients are selected as the annual Five Star recipients at the hotel. Those annual winners receive a financial award of approximately a thousand dollars, round-trip airfare for two within their geographic area, and a week's stay at a Ritz-Carlton property.

⋅≼ Aligning the Wow ≽⋅

Most businesses have mechanisms for acknowledging exceptional performance, yet so many rely completely on an annual awards banquet honoring the accomplishments of a select few. In contrast, through daily and weekly presentations of service recognition, leadership at Ritz-Carlton links Wow stories back to the core values of the business as a way of demonstrating how extraordinary service lives in their culture. Specifically, Wow stories are presented to Ladies and Gentlemen in the context of the Gold Standard that is specifically exhibited in the service delivery.

The strategic selection and presentation of Wow stories fits recommendations for increased corporate storytelling from business consultants such as Stephen Denning. The author of *The Leader's Guide to Storytelling: Mastering the Art and Discipline of Business Narrative,* Denning suggests that "although good business cases are developed through the use of numbers, they are typically approved on the basis of a story—that is, a narrative that links a set of events in some kind of causal sequence. Story-telling can translate those dry and abstract numbers into compelling pictures of a leader's goals." Similarly, Noel M. Tichy indicates in *The Leadership Engine: How Winning Companies Build Leaders at Every Level* that "the best way to get humans to venture into unknown terrain is to make that terrain familiar and desirable by taking them there first in their imaginations." At Ritz-Carlton, Wow stories bring to life a compelling vision of leadership's goals while helping staff venture into the often-vague terrain of memorable customer experiences.

STRIKING GOLD

▶ What methods do you have in place to capture positive stories of service excellence or other highly valued employee behaviors?

▶ What forum do you have in which to routinely share these stories?

▶ Do you tell stories that reinforce core cultural values and paint compelling pictures of your goals?

◃ Functional ▹

Beyond the basic benefits of corporate storytelling, leadership at Ritz-Carlton understands the power of defining excellence through example. President Simon Cooper notes, "It's not just that a story is being told but that it is being told to 40,000 people and the story reflects what we as leaders want our Ladies and Gentlemen to consistently deliver." The strategic nature of Wow story selection is best demonstrated by how such stories reflect all levels of employee behavior that are valued by leadership. As you recall from Chapter 3, the 12 Service Values at Ritz-Carlton are divided into three categories (Functional, Emotional

Engagement, and Mystique), organized by how each value affects the guest experience. Given these three levels of guest experience, leadership shares Wow stories as a way to demonstrate how each category of value can be and is enlivened for the guest.

The key to the Functional category is taking care of the basic guest needs such as safety and security. To illustrate the importance of addressing the safety concerns of guests, Ritz-Carlton leadership acknowledges the actions of staff members such as Nicolas Dousson, head doorman at The Ritz-Carlton, Naples. When a guest called the hotel to advise that she had run out of gas, Nicolas did not relegate her rescue to an outside roadside emergency service but instead filled several five-gallon gasoline containers and drove the 40 miles to assist the stranded woman and her children. While rescuing motorists is not in Nicolas's job description, his actions embody service values that relate to guest safety.

Additionally, leadership shares letters and guest comments in order to communicate to staff members the impact they have on customers by making Ritz-Carlton a safe and secure environment. During lineup the following words of a guest were shared with employees throughout the world: "I would like to take this opportunity to express my sincere appreciation and thanks to Andy Sun, Club concierge at The Portman Ritz Carlton, Shanghai. I will always remember his personal attention upon seeing my discomfort and chest pain and insisting on going with me to World Link Clinic. He stayed with me throughout; accompanied me to a hospital as I was diagnosed with a heart attack; stayed with me at the hospital as I underwent an operation; and supported me beyond the call of his duty in my time of need. During my hospital stay, he visited regularly and provided me support until my wife reached Shanghai. Upon my release from the hospital, he was a constant source of support and took any and all steps that were needed to make us comfortable. He is not just a hard-working individual but a caring and compassionate person and an asset to any team." Andy Sun's behavior, which could be viewed as lacking boundaries in some workplaces, is held up as "The New Gold Standard" of concern for the physical well-being of the guest and represents a template of what is not only excellent but what is exemplary at the Ritz-Carlton.

·≡| Emotional Engagement |≡·

Most staff members intuitively understand that business relationships must occur in a safe and trusting environment. The greater challenge is to have them appreciate how much interpersonal power they have individually and collectively to positively affect the lives of their customers and ultimately drive the economic success of the business.

Highlighting Wow stories of innovation and problem solving demonstrates how staff ingenuity translates directly into emotionally engaged customers. One such Wow story occurred at The Ritz-Carlton, Kapalua, as Maria Alvarez, who was then the weddings manager, had been working for an extended period of time with a bride-to-be to ensure that her wedding would be the celebration she desired. The event involved thousands of dollars in flowers, stringed quartets, limousines, and sumptuous food presentations. On the day of the wedding ceremony, an accident closed the only highway that connects Central and West Maui. Because of the accident, the minister and all the vendors, including the entertainers, the florist and flowers, and the sound and light technicians and equipment, were stranded with no way to get to the Ritz-Carlton. The ceremony looked as if it would need to be cancelled.

Scott Doran, a meetings and special events manager, contacted the vendors and began reviewing options. Scott told all of the vendors to get out of the traffic immediately and head back to Central Maui. He called a local helicopter company to fly the vendors to the hotel, only to realize that a helicopter would not be big enough to transport them all. Because the event was scheduled to take place in two and a half hours, Scott secured two airplanes and had all of the vendors, equipment, florists, and flowers picked up at Kahului Airport in Central Maui. One hour before the event, both planes landed at the private airstrip in Kapalua, where they were met by Scott, Maria, and the wedding team who assisted them in loading everything onto resort shuttles and other hotel and personal vehicles. The wedding was not only a success, but given the continued traffic snarls, the hotel took the extra step of providing the entertainers, minister, and florist rooms for the evening and ground transportation the next morning.

Similar Wow story examples demonstrate how innovative problem solving can take less-than-satisfied guests and convert them into emotionally engaged customers. In one such incident, guest Sandy Turner was having dinner at the Grill Restaurant in The Ritz-Carlton, Philadelphia, but she didn't like the way the asparagus was cooked. Chef de Cuisine Kevin Sbraga went to Sandy's table to inquire how she would like the dish prepared, but he was not content with simply satisfying her immediate need. During the conversation, Sandy mentioned that it was her personal dream to open her own café in a small town in Pennsylvania. She told Kevin that she had always wanted to go to culinary school to become a chef, but her professional path in marketing and sales made that challenging. Kevin took that opportunity to invite Sandy to cook with him for a day in his kitchen. According to Sandy, "It was incredibly cool of Kevin to extend that kind of an offer," and "I was jumping for joy with excitement" at the idea.

Shortly thereafter, the once-displeased guest became an official "Guest Chef for the Day." On her day, Sandy cooked veal cheeks, prepped the nightly special, and assisted two other chefs with their work. Her ultimate reward came during the dinner service when she was offered the chance to be the expeditor, an important position that ensures every plate of food is organized before it leaves the kitchen. Later in the evening, her sister and friend came to the property to have dinner especially prepared by her.

By taking the time to learn what customers value and desire, you can create Wow moments not only for them but for their family and friends. This ripple effect of extraordinary service moves broadly and swiftly through social networks, as individuals tell their version of Wow stories to individuals in their peer group, and those individuals retell them to others they know.

Mystique

Beyond guest engagement, Ritz-Carlton challenges the Ladies and Gentlemen to build strong memories and create Ritz-Carlton guests for life. Diverse, sometimes epic, Wow stories are presented to demonstrate unique ways to dazzle and amaze. At The Ritz-Carlton, Dubai, for example, Saad Khatib, assistant manager of the Arabic restaurant Amaseena, was conversing with guests at the general manager's resort cocktail reception. He noticed a gentleman's attention turned toward the champagne on the roaming tray. Saad took the opportunity to pour two glasses for the gentleman and his guest and introduced himself. He learned that the couple planned to dine in Ritz-Carlton's Italian restaurant Splendido the following evening. As the reception came to an end, he wished them an exceptional stay and promised to go down to Splendido to see how their dining experience was going. The next evening, Saad passed by Splendido and found out that the guests had been unable to go all the way down to the sandy beach to enjoy the sunset because the wife's wheelchair made the descent inaccessible.

Empathizing with and anticipating the guest's wishes and needs, Saad came to work early the next day and teamed with Raveendran Thundil, the carpenter supervisor from the engineering division, to organize wooden boards, which they extended from the end of the paved pathway down to the shore. So that the couple could experience a true Arabic evening, Saad placed an Arabic carpet on the sand, with low Arabic seating on top and surrounded the area with tiki torches. When the setup was complete, Saad went up to the pool and told the couple he would meet them at an appointed hour to escort them down to the beach.

Philip Fingerle, the food and beverage promotions coordinator, was waiting on the pathway to capture the experience with his camera. After a complimentary serving of tuxedo strawberries and champagne, Saad and Philip discreetly retreated and let the couple enjoy a very private and intimate sunset on the shore of the Arabian Gulf. In the meantime, Philip prepared a collage with the photographs he had taken of them a little earlier, and he placed everything in their room before they returned. He also compiled a CD with all the pictures, personalized it with a photo label, and handed it to them the next morning. The husband exclaimed, "We haven't smiled so much since our wedding day!" As the closing line of the submitted Wow story acknowledges, "First Class to Saad, Raveendran, and Philip for enlivening the Ritz-Carlton Mystique by creating such a unique, memorable, and personal experience for the couple!"

By sharing stories about staff members such as Saad, Raveendran, and Philip, Ritz-Carlton leadership sends a clear message that every staff member has the full authority to use his or her discretion to produce grand experiences for guests. Some companies might not want to have such a story shared widely throughout their organization, particularly if they believe that the guest's loyalty could have been achieved with far less cost or effort.

⊸] From Extreme Examples [⊱·· to Inspirational Ideas

One is hard-pressed to read a series of Ritz-Carlton Wow stories without thinking, "This all sounds too good to be true." Would a staff member really come in early to collaborate with a peer to build a ramp or create a customized dining experience for a person who hadn't asked for such service? Not only does it happen at Ritz-Carlton, but countless similar examples create momentum that motivates employees to look for ways to have a large impact even in more routine situations.

Yet not all Wow stories are over the top; Ritz-Carlton leadership selects stories that are less heroic in nature. Leadership realizes that in the end, every individual must be able to make the line-of-sight connection between what he or she does and how what he or she does can wow guests and advance the business. In an effort to balance the size and scope of notable service, leadership also shares everyday examples of a single individual doing the small acts of kindness necessary to make a guest's stay memorable.

One example that was selected as a companywide Wow story involved the actions of Mark D. Nadonza, concierge agent on duty at The Ritz-Carlton, Bahrain Hotel and Spa. A guest was getting ready for an early morning meeting that was to happen in a matter of hours when the guest realized he had forgotten his formal dress shoes. The man asked Mark if there was any place that he could get a pair of shoes at that hour. Mark advised that no stores were open prior to the start of the guest's meeting. As Mark searched for a solution, he found out that the man's shoe size matched his own. Mark offered to bring the guest a pair of formal shoes that he had worn only at his wedding. When the guest accepted the offer, Mark raced home and brought the shoes back to the hotel.

Leaders are most effective when they can remove themselves from the day-to-day management of their people and instead offer an inspirational vision of how their staff can enliven corporate values in the service of others. The power of service is magnified when leadership acknowledges teamwork and efforts that break down traditional departmental-based or location-based "stove pipes," as we'll see in the next section.

·≋| Inspiring Teamwork |≋·

As suggested in the previous chapter, most business leaders want people throughout the organization to work with one another to serve customers and strengthen the business. Ritz-Carlton leadership does this specifically by building the importance of collaboration into Service Value 7: "I create a work environment of teamwork and lateral service so that the needs of our guests and each other are met." By sharing stories that highlight effective partnerships, perceived psychological boundaries between departments are torn down. Often these stories demonstrate how two or more people working together have been able to deliver a greater Wow for the guest than each person's working independently.

An example is reflected by the efforts of Cleria Ferreira, Mildred Sjostrand, and William Gilbreath of The Ritz-Carlton, Orlando, Grande Lakes, in-room dining department. Cleria delivered lunch to the room of a meeting planner who was busily rolling up messages and placing them in bottles as part of an amenity that would be delivered to 400 meeting attendees. Cleria observed that the scale of the task would likely cause the guest to stay up the entire night. She contacted her manager to ensure that she would not leave the rest of her team short-staffed if she offered to assist the guest with the project. Even working together, Cleria realized that the project was going very slowly, so she asked the guest to excuse her for a moment. Minutes later Cleria returned to the room with a table and two colleagues, Mildred and William. At that time, in-room dining calls were slow, so the three of them worked around requested deliveries to expedite the process of stuffing messages in bottles. While managers can tell their staff that they want to see teamwork, there aren't many better ways to communicate that message than sharing moments of exceptional team participation as demonstrated by Cleria, Mildred, and William.

Teamwork can occur among a handful of individuals or in a hotelwide effort. Such was the case in Miami during the 2007 Super Bowl held at Dolphin Stadium, when guests of The Ritz-Carlton, South Beach, boarded five motor coaches bound for the game. By the end of the first quarter, a light rain began to fall. Shortly thereafter, the rain became a steady shower with no clear end in sight. According to the Wow story about the event that was shared worldwide at lineup, "Back at The Ritz-Carlton, South Beach, the Ladies and Gentlemen were concerned for the comfort of their guests at Dolphin Stadium. An emergency lineup was held to brainstorm what they could do to take care of their wet guests. The laundry team got set to prepare 300 towels; the meetings and special events team contacted the meeting planners at the stadium and advised them of their rescue plans; the front office team contacted the drivers of the buses to determine their exact location among the 400 buses that were parked at the stadium; the guest services team loaded up the hotel cars with freshly folded warm towels; and Miguel Saldivia and Rubén Paredes from the food and beverage team drove to the stadium with the surprise."

After the game ended, guests found warm folded towels with the familiar Ritz-Carlton logo waiting for them on their bus seats. Back at the hotel, members of the guest relations, guest services, and banquet teams were there to greet the buses with a blue canopy of Ritz-Carlton umbrellas that led guests into the hotel where smiling faces welcomed them back to the warm, relaxed, and dry ambiance with hot chocolate and coffee. Imagine hearing this story as a staff member at a property on the other side of the globe! Would it not inspire you to raise your game to have a comparable story shared about you and your hotel team? The example of the entire team effort at the South Beach property serves as a catalyst to constructive competition between properties in the area of extraordinary customer experiences.

At the same time, leadership looks for ways to show staff how lateral service and collaboration can extend beyond the walls of any specific hotel property. To reinforce this message, examples of how customer service occurs through the seamless efforts of Ladies and Gentlemen of multiple hotel locations are presented. A guest at The Ritz-Carlton, Washington, D.C., experienced this spirit of collaboration when he did not receive the tickets he expected for air travel for a flight from New York City to Jordan the following evening. The guest went ahead to The Ritz-Carlton, New York Central Park, and was dependent on the staff at the Washington, D.C., hotel and the New York Central Park hotel to coordinate efforts to make sure the package containing his paper tickets was forwarded to New York City in a way that secured his international travel.

Charles J. Gilbert, front office agent in Washington, D.C., took charge of arranging transportation and orchestrating the delivery of the tickets to New York. After he was in possession of the package with the tickets, he contacted the concierge to inquire about transportation options such as the price of a limo to New York City, as well as the Acela train. He also contacted the director of transient sales to inquire about shuttle prices from Reagan National Airport to New York City. Charles determined that the fastest, most economical method of travel would be by plane. Charles narrowly made travel connections with just enough time to get to the New York Central Park hotel, and he personally handed the tickets to the guest, as well as a gift from The Ritz-Carlton, Washington, D.C.

Whether multiple hotels participate in securing and forwarding lost articles, concierge staff members work together to make reservations for guests traveling in other Ritz-Carlton cities, or hotels partner with one another to overcome visa problems for guests, the collective resources of Ritz-Carlton can be leveraged for maximum customer benefit. Additionally, leadership captures naturally occurring moments of service excellence and teamwork to demonstrate that department, hotel, and even regional boundaries can be transcended when the "genuine care and comfort" of the guest is truly the first priority of each staff member.

While Wow stories are a powerful way to capture, acknowledge, and communicate examples of service excellence at Ritz-

Carlton, Simon Cooper is quick to caution, "Wow stories are but one tool for communicating with staff. Ultimately, this tool has to be understood in the context of the objective it achieves—namely, helping leadership identify and communicate desired guest outcomes. In order for Wow stories to be maximally successful, they can't stand alone. They must be supported by open communication from leadership to staff and staff to leadership. They must be part of a constant dialogue about service, quality, values, and excellence." Leaders like Simon understand that effective communication occurs when managers define the outcomes they want their staff to achieve, catch their staff as they achieve them, strategically communicate examples of those successes, and encourage staff to spot and share examples as well.

STRIKING GOLD

⯈ Do the corporate stories you share reflect both over-the-top and routine Wow moments?

⯈ Have you created an environment in which all employees can exchange positive service stories?

⯈ How do you capture and share stories of collaboration and teamwork?

⫷ Everyone Is Your Customer ⫸

Ritz-Carlton leadership celebrates service excellence on the part of their Ladies and Gentlemen even when those efforts are directed toward people who are not part of the identified customer base. For example, a selected Wow story praised the efforts of Ajith De Silva from the engineering department of The Ritz-Carlton, Dubai, who was driving the hotel pickup truck to the beach carrying materials for the Ramadan tent. On his way back, he noticed a van stuck in the sand. Ajith stopped the hotel vehicle to help the stranded motorist. After breaking two tow ropes, on the third try Ajith was able to free the motorist. The motorist turned out to be Jason Brown, the publishing director of ITP Publishing Group, a company that produces over 60 magazines, including *Harper's Bazaar*, *TimeOut*, and *Grazia Middle East*. Brown offered to give Ajith a tip for his service, and Ajith politely declined, informing him that at Ritz-Carlton "everyone is treated as a guest—both in and out of the hotel." Rather than receiving the wrath of a boss who might have challenged his judgment, Ajith was held up as an example of Wow service.

Similarly, a letter was received in the corporate headquarters that became a Wow story at the worldwide lineup. The letter read, "Two weeks ago, I went to Georgetown University Hospital in Washington, D.C., for breast cancer surgery. As you can imagine, it was a challenging day, but due to your company's generous and thoughtful donation to patients undergoing breast surgery, I was greeted with a beautiful Ritz-Carlton robe to start my day. The volunteer informed me that it was to help me feel as if I was having a Spa Day at Ritz-Carlton. Although clearly I was not, slipping on the luxurious robe took me mentally away to a more wonderful place outside of the cares of the moment. I can't explain it, and I know that sounds so odd, but it offered me, and I am sure all the other women there, the same psychological lift. I was transformed! . . . I cannot do justice to how wonderful this kind act of giving by Ritz-Carlton made me and my sister-patients feel on the day of surgery. I just wanted to thank you for your kindness and sensitivity to our psychological well-being at an emotionally challenging time."

Sending the Message That Play Is Acceptable

In a company often thought of as staid and serious, Wow stories also serve to show that playful and creative service are celebrated within the culture. Numerous members of The Ritz-Carlton San Juan Hotel, Spa, and Casino staff were recognized for their efforts to respond to a late-coming request for dinner reservations for five and an accompanying birthday cake to be presented to the guests' son. Emily Vallejo "owned" the request, and she immediately found a way to get the dinner reservation confirmed, in an otherwise full restaurant. Emily also called a local baker to prepare the cake because she knew the turnaround time was too short to have the cake prepared in-house.

The guest mentioned in the conversation with Emily that his son, Dayson, was turning four years old and loves Spiderman; therefore, Emily sought a Spiderman design or figures to decorate the vanilla cake. Then came the significantly playful twist: Emily contacted a company to have the cake delivered by a man wearing a Spiderman costume. Maria Castano from the concierge department looked for Spiderman pictures from the Internet and created a superhero coloring book and brought balloons to the festivities. The staff related, "You should have seen Dayson's face as Spiderman approached the table. He couldn't take his eyes off him."

When Dayson blew out the candles, the whole restaurant started clapping. Dayson's mother tearfully and joyfully watched the event. Dayson was not only impressed with his visitor but was also heard to say, "Spiderman even knew my name." Emily and Maria sent the guests off with framed photos of the event, and they were praised for their playful creativity and the memorable impact it had on Dayson and his family.

Providing excellent service is a reward unto itself. Whether a staff member is working individually or in concert with a team, service gives back to the giver. At Ritz-Carlton, those acts of giving are held up as examples of how well-defined values come alive through the collective efforts of staff each and every day. Leaders celebrate and cement culture by the stories they tell and retell.

LIVING THE NEW GOLD STANDARD

- Wow moments happen in every workplace. Collect and share those stories with all employees to generate an environment of top performance.

- Annual awards presentations are valuable, but regular, frequent recognition is necessary to sustain a culture of excellence.

- Reward excellence by publicly acknowledging the person who went above and beyond, to motivate others to emulate those behaviors.

- Look for ways to catch your employees doing something well!

- Whether you rent a small plane to make someone's wedding happen on time or hand a soaked person a warm towel and hot beverage, it's the personal caring that will create lifetime customers.

- Help your employees to understand how much interpersonal power they have individually and collectively to positively affect the lives of their customers and the overall success of the business.

- Providing excellent service is a reward unto itself.

∙⊰**I** PRINCIPLE **I**⊱∙

5

Leave a Lasting
Footprint

Aspire, Achieve, Teach

Do not go where the path may lead,
go instead where there is no path
and leave a trail.

RALPH WALDO EMERSON

In the competitive world of business today, corporate leaders are looking for opportunities to maintain the relevance and sustainability of their established brands. One key strategy for achieving this outcome is to broaden product offerings to meet evolving needs of their customers. Writing in *Circulation Management* magazine, marketing researcher Kathryn Fry-Ramsdell advises, "Based on customers' perception and knowledge of your brand, there are certain types of products that they would expect you to sell. These are products that fit well with your brand. Products that . . . are natural extensions of the expertise or information you already provide. . . . Likewise, there are many products that they want and need, but for various reasons don't expect to get—or don't want to get—from your brand."

As suggested by Kathryn, in order to understand the acceptability of a brand extension, companies have to gauge the perception of their customers about new possibilities. Bob Phillips, senior vice president of business development for The Ritz-Carlton Clubs, says, "We at Ritz-Carlton started brand extension work by first talking to loyalists. We sampled business travelers, leisure guests, and those who have used the hotels for business meetings or significant life events such as weddings. We wanted to understand what our offerings meant to them." Since leadership believed that the core competencies of Ritz-Carlton were linked to service excellence and the creation of high-quality hospitality experiences, customers were asked about possible real estate ventures associated with leisure travel. According to Bob, "As we went through our research process, we found very deep emotional reactions emerging from the hotel customer. For many, Ritz-Carlton was such an important part of their lives that they eagerly wanted to reconnect with the company whenever possible. For example, they looked forward to scheduling future business meetings or vacations at the hotel properties. In essence, we were hearing that many of our guests wanted Ritz-Carlton to play an even bigger part in their lives. This let us know clearly that our ideas for fractional ownership or full ownership ventures would be well received."

Given this customer data, the Ritz-Carlton Club concept was launched in 1999, representing an expansion of the Ritz-Carlton brand from a hotel/resort company into an exclusive, luxury-tier, deeded fractional ownership real estate management firm. The Ritz-Carlton Club merged the company's personalized hotel services with the exclusive benefits of vacation property ownership. Additionally, Club owners are provided the option to vacation at other Club locations.

Bob Phillips adds, "The Ritz-Carlton Club is a natural extension of the Ritz-Carlton brand, and it allows existing and future customers to enjoy another level of the Ritz-Carlton experience. We offer the finest accommodations, beautiful locations, exemplary service, and exceptional leisure experiences for our members." Ritz-Carlton Club locations consist of residences designed for affluent travelers who prefer to have the benefits of second home ownership without the time-draining responsibilities that usually go along with owning property. For example, at The Ritz-Carlton Golf Club & Spa, Jupiter, Florida, Club members spend their vacation time just minutes away from world-class shopping; water activities including yacht charters, deep-sea fishing, and pristine beaches; several protected nature preserves and parks; and Minor League baseball. Club members enjoy exclusive dining privileges and can choose golf club membership in the Jack Nicklaus–designed Signature Golf Course and The Ritz-Carlton Spa, both on site in the development.

By enhancing the customer experience to broader levels, Ritz-Carlton heightens consumer loyalty in authentic ways. Bob explains, "We've found that the real value for our Club members, much more so than the value of real estate or the value of the services offered, is found in the intrinsic and emotional benefits of enhancing relationships within their family or within their circle of influence. We use the term 'legacy.' Ritz-Carlton Club members acknowledge that their membership anchors them to the most important parts of their lives. It's fulfilling for us to be able to do something that delivers that depth of experience."

James J. Creighton, Jr., M.D., owns memberships in Florida and in Colorado. He explains how the Club concept not only meets the lifestyle needs of his family but also exposes future generations and friends to the Ritz-Carlton standards. "We wanted a place where we could develop some traditions as a family, such as going to play golf at certain times of the year in Florida and going snow skiing in Colorado, and yet not be totally anchored to that location. We have ownership, yet flexibility. We frequently go to St. Thomas, and we feel as at home in St. Thomas as in Florida, thanks to the staff at the Ritz-Carlton Club. Wherever we go in the world, the staff members welcome us as if we owned that property. They make sure our favorite food and drink are waiting for us when we arrive, and they know our interest in particular leisure activities." James adds, "We also invite friends to stay with us and it's very special to them as well.

They enter through the gates, using the communication system, and by the time they drive up to the golf course, the caddies already know they are on property and greet them by name. A lot of Clubs don't go to that effort. What's even more amazing is when our friends come back another year, the staff remembers they've been here, call them by name, and welcome them back again. It's not just about the beautiful golf course or the ski lift right out the back door—it's about the attention."

Given that guests relish the elegance and service delivered in the Ritz-Carlton hotels and Clubs, the brand was further extended into day-to-day lifestyle offerings in the form of the Ritz-Carlton Residence concept. The Residences are privately owned properties, overseen by homeowners' organizations, and professionally managed and served by the Ladies and Gentlemen of Ritz-Carlton. The breadth of services enjoyed by these property owners includes everything from housekeeping and valet to concierge and gourmet dining, all of which are offered in a "five-star" environment. Strategically these Residences are developed adjacent to Ritz-Carlton hotel properties in highly desirable areas such as Georgetown, Toronto, Boston Common, and Grand Cayman.

John Cottrill, senior vice president of The Ritz-Carlton Clubs and Residences, shares the economic benefits of building mixed-use hotel and residence facilities: "From the standpoint of developing a hotel project, mixed-use real estate has been instrumental in getting proper financing since the developer can actually buy down the debt through the sale of real estate. When you add that to the Ritz-Carlton brand premium (significantly higher than the competitive values), it is a strong incentive for developers to create a mixed-use development."

But there are longer-term financial benefits for the company as a whole. As John explains, "When people buy a Residence, they are not only buying the hard asset, where they live, but they are buying an investment property as well. They are buying the Ritz-Carlton brand and the luxury lifestyle experience. The brand itself adds value to their investment because of the Ritz-Carlton legacy service experience." Great brand extensions not only borrow the equity from the original offerings (in this case the service excellence of Ritz-Carlton hotels) but also actually enhance the overall strength of the brand and the value the brand offers to a company's customers.

While brand consultants such as Alycia de Mesa talk about the "elasticity" of a brand (how far a company can stretch its diversity of offerings before customers reject the products), leadership at Ritz-Carlton is more focused on how brand extensions can strengthen one another. In essence, they view each offering as an opportunity to strengthen connections between their products. For example, hotel experiences can lead customers into vacation experiences at the Ritz-Carlton Club, which in turn can fuel purchases of Ritz-Carlton Residences.

Despite their successes with Clubs and Residences, Ritz-Carlton leaders continue to look for other new, yet prudent, directions to take their company. In the spirit of innovative and market-responsive brand extensions, Ritz-Carlton has worked with developers to create an even more exclusive resort concept called "The Reserve." Molasses Reef on the island of West Caicos in the Turks and Caicos Islands was the first property for this endeavor. The Reserve brand extension is designed as a singular boutique resort that elevates sophistication while adding seclusion. The Reserve represents the evolution of Ritz-Carlton offerings consistent with the "define and refine" principle discussed in Chapter 3.

In essence, the Reserve reflects the well-defined Gold Standards of service provided at all Ritz-Carlton properties, while refining the design and experiential aspects to appeal to the changing wishes of their customers. All of the Reserve properties will be located in prime settings, each with a sense of place and its own distinctive personality.

Karim Alibhai, the developer in the Molasses Reef project, says, "Our partnership with Ritz-Carlton on Molasses Reef shows the innovation of the leadership. By creating an exclusive resort option, which takes the traditional resort hotel experience to the next level, leadership has partnered with us to provide opportunities that allow for even greater individualized experiences for guests. The Reserve captures the essence of unique and personalized service in a brand extension that is a truly one-of-a-kind destination."

Ritz-Carlton President Simon Cooper shares some of the ways the Reserve properties will differentiate themselves from other Ritz-Carlton offerings: "Reserves are smaller than our typical resorts. They are low-rise buildings and specifically designed with transient leisure travelers in mind."

Leadership's focus on producing memorable and unique properties reflects their commitment to produce relevant brand extensions that meet and exceed the current desires of luxury travelers in all market segments.

STRIKING GOLD

- ► When considering new products or expansion opportunities for your brand, have you explored the perceptions of your customer base?

- ► What product or service offerings would stretch the elasticity of your brand?

- ► How can you best position your products or services to strengthen your overall brand, while driving your customers from one business offering to the next?

⋅◁ From Quality Excellence ▷⋅ to Excellence in Training

Ritz-Carlton also extended its brand and the overall reputation of the company in its response to internal and external training needs. Leadership developed two training arms—the global learning center (which is internally focused) and the Leadership Center (which is externally directed). Both educational entities exemplify how the strength of the company can be leveraged to make a meaningful difference both in the lives of its own staff and, more broadly, in the lives of individuals in other businesses. The global learning center and the Leadership Center emerge primarily from the company's pursuit of quality excellence.

Internal Training: The Global Learning Center

The global learning center's services are directed toward enhancing the lasting excellence of the Ladies and Gentlemen of Ritz-Carlton and include offerings such as the orientation process and training in areas like

- Managing difficult situations

- Understanding the difference between guests' expressed and unexpressed wishes

- Staff operational certification

- Leadership development

- Use of the Mystique customer relationship management (CRM) process (See Chapter 7 for more information about Mystique.)

- Total quality management (TQM) processes such as the Ritz-Carlton Six Steps to Quality Improvement (See Chapter 6 for additional information about these processes.)

Through the efforts of the staff in the global learning center to advance education for the Ladies and Gentlemen of Ritz-Carlton, the learning culture of the company has achieved one of the highest recognitions available, acknowledged for being the best global training company in 2007 as ranked by *Training Magazine*. In his summary about why the global learning arm of The Ritz-Carlton Leadership Center was chosen for the award, Jack Gordon, contributing editor of the magazine, remarks, "There is much to recommend Ritz-Carlton as the No. 1 company on this year's *Training* Top 125 list: the fact that it invests a whopping 10 percent of payroll on employee training; long-standing excellence in areas such as leadership development and employee orientation; customer-oriented diversity training that extends even to interaction with service animals such as seeing-eye dogs; management and training philosophies that account for an annual voluntary turnover rate of 18 percent in an industry where 100 percent rates are the norm. But what really made *Training* say 'Wow' was the way the company went about shifting its perception of its very hallmark: elegant service."

The magazine award reflects the long-term value of making the difficult transition from being a training organization to a true learning culture. To leave a legacy, companies not only must transfer information and corporate knowledge from the top down but they must also focus on developing skills in accord with the individual needs of staff, support formal and informal opportunities that are driven by staff, and create process-based approaches that weave learning systems into the enduring culture of the company.

Staff Pride and Learning

While accolades and awards are always appreciated, the legacy aspect of Ritz-Carlton training ultimately lives in the impact the global learning center's curriculum has on giving staff members the tools they need to creatively respond to customer needs and powerfully drive customer loyalty. The company's learning focus—to develop the right tools delivered at the right time through the right methods—facilitates the development of service professionalism not only across their worldwide properties but also in businesses that have inherited the knowledge of former Ritz-Carlton staff.

President Simon Cooper shows evidence of the effects of Ritz-Carlton training in the broader service world by sharing, "My wife made a reservation for a restaurant we'd heard about in eastern Maryland. I never tell anybody what I do, and she doesn't either, so she just made the reservation with the phone number. Upon entering the restaurant, we saw busboys standing at attention and the hostess was alert, friendly, and attentive. Everything about the restaurant's presentation was sharp. It was a cut above the service of most restaurants in the adjacent area. Lo and behold, the owner of the restaurant comes along and it's a gentleman who worked for us at Central Park South. What he'd done in his restaurant was what I expect every Ritz-Carlton restaurant manager or front office manager to do with his or her team. He's leveraging a legacy by teaching people how to carry themselves, what to say, how to dress. It's well beyond the written language about procedures and dress code; it's how you execute against standards of excellence."

Simon continues, "It's the whole idea that you're always ready—ready to serve. We don't train people through memos saying they shouldn't congregate at a cash register if the restaurant's empty. There's nothing worse than being one of only three or four tables in a restaurant, and all the servers are off chatting in the corner. We train people how to think about the guest's experience. That type of training helps men and women like the owner of that restaurant take their game up a notch."

Cherie Y. Webb, manager of learning at The Ritz-Carlton, Atlanta, sees the training of employees at Ritz-Carlton as a source of pride. "My job allows me to take amazingly talented people and offer them the tools they need to fully realize their service potential. When our Ladies and Gentlemen grow as service professionals, they increase the impact they have on our guests, which in turn has an effect on the guests' families. It may sound a bit silly, but when you think about knowledge as being powerful, then you realize that the responsible transfer of that power is a tool that transforms lives."

External Training:
The Ritz-Carlton Leadership Center

During the application process for the Malcolm Baldrige National Quality Award, Ritz-Carlton executives were aware that if they were ever chosen as a winner, they would be obligated to share best practices with other businesses; a requirement for being selected is sharing such information during the year in which the award is conferred. Upon winning the award for the first time in 1992, Ritz-Carlton shared best practices with companies in a fairly informal way as interest dictated.

After winning the Baldrige Award for the second time in 1999, Ritz-Carlton leadership could not let the corporate information exchange remain nothing more than an obligation. Diana Oreck, vice president of global learning and the Leadership Center, explains, "We decided to elevate this training opportunity by creating a more systematic way to teach other businesses. We achieved our objective by opening the doors of our Leadership Center in 1999. From that time onward, interest in our business practices has been high, and the Leadership Center has grown steadily. Now we have a catalog of rich offerings, and we add at least one new course per year since we have a lot of repeat customers. Many of the companies that come to us have been through a wide variety of training programs and are seeking something new, fresh, and timely. As such, we develop our new curriculum offerings to suit the needs of their businesses."

Since its inception, the Ritz-Carlton Leadership Center has served individuals from businesses worldwide, including Smith Barney, Putnam Investments, the Emory Clinic, and Umpqua Holdings Corporation. The "it's not about you" principle discussed in Chapters 7 and 8 is evidenced not only in the course offerings of the Leadership Center but also in the way those programs are delivered to attendees. Rather than create a training program based on the efficiency needs of their own business (such as streamlining processes that make delivery of training easy for the Ritz-Carlton staff), they instead planned the Leadership Center based on customer needs, designing it from the outside in. While it would have been most convenient for the Leadership Center to require all businesses to come to the headquarters of Ritz-Carlton in Chevy Chase, Maryland, and maybe even force the participants to stay at one of the four Ritz-Carlton hotels in the Washington, D.C., area, the Leadership Center staff instead delivers most of their training at the clients' locations and tailors their programs to the needs of those seeking the expertise, without any obligation to patronize a Ritz-Carlton hotel. From the standpoint of external offerings, the Leadership Center provides services that range from full-day classes for business leaders at all levels to specialized and in-depth executive education classes such as the Implementing a Customer-Centric Culture certification program developed as a strategic alliance between the Ritz-Carlton Leadership Center and New York University. The center even provides customized coaching and consulting services to a select group of applicants.

Prior to agreeing to provide intensive coaching services to a company (thus extending its own service reputation on behalf of such a company), Ritz-Carlton leadership diligently assesses the integrity and service reputation of the requesting organization. Further, Ritz-Carlton requires the unanimous support of senior leadership at the client company—particularly as it relates to that company's willingness to sustain a commitment to further enhance customer service excellence.

⋅≋⟨ Benefits of Offering Training ⟩≋⋅ through the Leadership Center

While the focus of the Leadership Center is to positively affect interested businesses, the process of teaching others has had

PRINCIPLE 5: LEAVE A LASTING FOOTPRINT

transformative benefits for Ritz-Carlton staff as well. For example, staff members from the hotels are, at times, incorporated into the training offered to outside businesses. Alexandra Valentin, director of learning at the Ritz-Carlton New York, Central Park, discusses the special nature of being selected as a presenter for the Ritz-Carlton Leadership Center: "While my main job is to offer internal training for our Ladies and Gentlemen on our property, it is a great honor to be a certified trainer for the Leadership Center because I am entrusted to share the best business practices of Ritz-Carlton with other companies. In essence, I get to help other businesses become more successful."

Getting employees involved at this level can be incredibly empowering. As Alexandra explains, "I have grown as a presenter in this role, and in the process I have helped bring in business and revenue to my own hotel through my presentations. I've also developed relationships with business leaders and have established repeat clients whom I can further help by determining which of our training offerings will best meet their needs. In a way, I serve almost in a training consultant role with them. Where else could I have that kind of influence?"

Diana Oreck, vice president of global learning and the Leadership Center, explains how hotel staff members like Alexandra are chosen as sources of "influence" for interested businesses. "We select people who can train and share their pride and knowledge of our Gold Standards. I do an average of two certifications a year. Those individuals who express an interest and are selected at the property level come here to our corporate offices and present to us. They are given a template with the core curriculum, observe one of our Leadership Center staff present the curriculum, and receive coaching as they do their presentations. At the end of the day, they either pass or fail an audition with us. You will find that our hotel-based staff members are a very dynamic group of Ladies and Gentlemen. A recent certification group of 25 applicants had staff diversely distributed from all areas of hotels including general managers, hotel managers, and even salespeople."

In addition to offering keynote speeches, frontline staff can participate in employee panel discussions for outside business leaders that offer a textural sense of the Ritz-Carlton culture. One of the participants in these panels, Tricia Chiang, a seamstress at The Ritz-Carlton, Washington, D.C., shares, "Speaking on panels adds great variety to what I do. Don't get me wrong; I love my job in the hotel, but it's an unusual change of pace to answer questions from important business people during a panel discussion. They ask questions about why I decided to work at Ritz-Carlton, how lineup is done, what my job as a seamstress is like, or if I've ever used my $2,000-per-guest credit on a given day. Sometimes I stop and realize that I am working at a very special place. I like being able to honestly answer questions, and I am amazed that so many leaders from different types of companies want to know my answers."

Training at the Leadership Center also allows participants the opportunity to see the lineup process firsthand. Kevin Walsh, senior director of customer relationship management, notes, "I always welcome the chance for the students at the Leadership Center to observe lineup. If you lead lineup, you always want to do the best job you possibly can, and when students are there, you know that you are affording them a special view of our culture in action. That makes the opportunity all the more important." From the vantage point of course participant Donna Brewer, director of learning and development at Saskatchewan Gaming Corporation, "Attending lineup and having the Ladies and Gentlemen present in panel discussions was particularly valuable to me, as it took what I was hearing in the lectures and made it real and genuine. You see that this is not philosophy as much as it is the way they do business."

Mike Figliuolo, managing director of thoughtLEADERS, LLC, attended a multiday leadership program through a joint offering of the Leadership Center and the Corporate Learning Services division of NYU's School of Continuing and Professional Studies. Being able to observe employees in action allowed him to understand "the absolute importance of daily alignment and getting everyone on the same page every day. It's impressive to see a nonnegotiable approach to daily reinforcement of the company's service values. It's done through constant communication and the regular provision of the Wow stories that model great customer service examples. You can talk abstractly about great service, but when you hear 5 or 10 stories about people who deliver it, everyone, including new employees, can get the texture of what's expected of them."

President Simon Cooper concludes that the company's staff offers some of the most powerful, heartfelt lessons about Ritz-Carlton: "A chairman of a global bank had heard from one of his team that Ritz-Carlton was able to create a world-class global culture with a small team of leaders. As a result, the bank chairman flew from London and spent the morning with my team. In the end what really impressed this bank executive was the lunch we set up with six of our Ladies and Gentlemen at Ritz-Carlton in Washington, D.C. In essence, my leadership team and I could talk about our culture, but the difference came when our Ladies and Gentlemen shared how they lived it."

The Impact of Training Received from the Leadership Center

While The Ritz-Carlton Leadership Center was created from a commitment to elevate service excellence, the viability of its programs must be measured against the results produced for those who attend. Mike Figliuolo shares his reasons for seeking training through The Ritz-Carlton Learning Center: "I attended the course to look for ways to distinguish a service business. Essentially many service companies are, at times, commodity industries. I believe that the best way to really differentiate oneself in a commodity industry is through service delivery—service being either the way the work is performed on the line or the way an issue is handled when a customer calls in with a problem. My goal was to benchmark our business and get ideas in creating customer experiences from a true leader."

Mike continues, "The training was well rounded, applicable to our day-to-day activities, and enriched with a pretty healthy dose of pragmatism. I was struck by the Ritz-Carlton's emphasis on staff empowerment, what that empowerment really looks like, and some of the mechanisms for achieving it."

For attendee Paula Enrietto, executive director at Balfour Senior Living's independent living community, The Lodge, The Ritz-Carlton Leadership Center training has resulted in efforts to incorporate Ritz-Carlton best practices within her company. Paula notes, "We have a very clear mission, but we had never really outlined in detail what our values are, and so we've begun the process of defining those values in a management training setting, engaging the managers and line staff in that process. While I went to the Leadership Center in Washington, D.C., my colleagues at the Balfour assisted living and memory care communities are also thinking about bringing some Ritz-Carlton training into their properties and have them on site."

While the original intent behind the Leadership Center was to fill the needs of those who wanted to benchmark themselves and learn from a leader in service excellence, the quality of senior leadership's commitment to the program produced a financially profitable business line. The Leadership Center is a classic example of what happens when leaders appreciate the unique value offerings of their business and place high-level executives in charge of serving a growing consumer demand. From a dollar perspective, Vice President Diana Oreck reports, "We've grown like gangbusters despite having not spent any money advertising. Zero dollars. It's all word of mouth. Not only do people in the audience fall in love with this brand but they also become enchanted by the dynamism and passion of our speakers. It's invigorating to see how something that started as a limited obligation to share best practices could be built into a strong and growing Leadership Center that is expanding its presence and influence throughout the world."

Emulation: A High Form of Flattery

The footprint and impact of the Leadership Center and other service training is more than a financial generator for Ritz-Carlton. Allan Federer, general manager of The Ritz-Carlton, Millenia Singapore, says, "This hotel is a trusted training partner with Citibank in Singapore. Through that process they have developed a modified version of our Credo Card that they call 'Client 1st.' Additionally, Citibank has a variation of our daily lineup that they refer to as a 'huddle.' Ritz-Carlton staff in our hotel train Citibank's staff, including their relationship managers, private bankers, branch greeters, tellers, and call center staff. Many of the cultural components of Citibank's credo in Singapore really are an outgrowth of the Ritz-Carlton Gold Standards." Allan adds, "The CEO of Citibank locally came to us as part of his vision to take Citibank back to its roots—from a transaction-based organization to a service-based one."

Jonathan Larsen, CEO of Citibank Singapore Limited, comments on their business partnership with Ritz-Carlton: "We feel the Citibank reputation has been built to a large extent on service, alongside of product innovation. Over the years we became more sales oriented, and we did so at the expense of the service ethos that we had created in the early to mid-1990s. We had a lot of customers who had banked with us for very many years telling us the bank wasn't what it used to be. I could see it from how long we were asking our customers to wait for telephone service. I could see it from a lot of our services that were designed to be efficient for the bank and not necessarily efficient for the customer. It was clear to me that there was a lot of opportunity to improve and we had lost some of our edge over time."

The company looked for organizations that clearly demonstrated leadership through cultural values, because, as Jonathan explains, "We believe that individual service challenges can be solved technically, but whatever temporary solution you put in place can go away pretty easily without reinforced cultural values. We were intrigued by the Credo Card and with our personal experience at the Ritz-Carlton property here in Singapore. We were aware that when we went to the property, the staff seemed to live and breathe the values outlined on the Credo Card. We talked with the leadership at the hotel, and although they had only an internal training program in place at the time, both of our organizations were eager to forge this relationship."

Businesses like Citibank Singapore can become distracted in their customer service focus and require assistance to return to their core service values. To help Citibank develop the internal training program that addressed their needs, a team of Ritz-Carlton employees visited Citibank and observed service delivery and the physical environment. Upon completion of their diagnostic review, the Ritz-Carlton team members offered a range of findings. For example, they looked at Citibank's setting through the lens of scenography, examining how the Citibank property looked and the emotional reactions that emerged from being in their physical space. Further, Ritz-Carlton staff attempted to infer what Citibank was trying to communicate by the look and feel of their environment. According to Jonathan, "They showed us things we had overlooked: a stain on the carpet outside an elevator that had obviously been there for several years; our salespeople leaving their drink bottles in the foyers of the branches; six different uniforms for our staff—things we just weren't paying attention to but that make a very fundamental difference in the impression the customer has. They just brought a totally different perspective to us."

Jonathan acknowledged that the mere presence of Ritz-Carlton staff surveying bank functions was met with initial resistance. His staff wondered, "Who are these people? Why are hotel staff assessing us?" Other individuals suggested that any benefits derived from such an assessment would be superficial at best and wouldn't justify the time or expense. Jonathan said that the skepticism dissipated as his staff tangibly saw improvements occurring from the involvement of Ritz-Carlton staff: "Over time, with the right reinforcement and support, we launched a program through which every staff member at Citibank would go to the training program at Ritz-Carlton, witness a daily lineup, and experience Ritz-Carlton values. Our employees saw the staff at Ritz-Carlton speak with extraordinary passion and commitment for the values of the organization that they clearly put into practice every day. We had seasoned people with 20 or more years with the bank who were quite cynical when we began the program and then came away saying it was the most impressive service training experience they'd ever had in their lives. It had a profound effect."

From that training, Citibank launched their own version of a Credo Card and Citibank's set of 15 values, in addition to their daily huddle. Jonathan credits the huddle with getting bank staff excited about their commitment to their customers. Jonathan observes, "In some large organizations, the staff doesn't tend to get together very frequently; we found having this daily process creates a rhythm and rapport. It's informal, it's fun, it's a fabulous way to start out the day, and it's changed our employee dynamic. Our VOE (Voice of Employee) survey scores have gone from the low 70s to the high 80s in the space of a year. We think that this process has been a key ingredient to make that happen. We are seeing the results in terms of customer scores as well. I think the program has been a great experience, and we've received tremendous value from it. We have enormous respect for Ritz-Carlton. The organization epitomizes the power of ideas combined with the power of passion and commitment to create the best experience for every customer, for every employee, and for external partners, like us."

While some business leaders might be reluctant to share best practices with other businesses, Ritz-Carlton leadership realizes that by teaching others, the service standards of the communities where they do business are elevated. By helping Citibank raise the bar for service, Ritz-Carlton employees who are Citibank customers also receive enhanced service. Information sharing becomes a mutually profitable enterprise. More important, Ritz-Carlton leadership views the exchange of ideas as a *responsibility* of success. By taking an "abundance" approach as opposed to a "scarcity" approach to knowledge and information, Ritz-Carlton amply shares and receives knowledge; in the process it broadens the scope of the footprint the company leaves.

·◦⟦ Legacy Building ⟧◦·

If you operate from the perspective that The Ritz-Carlton Hotel Company is in the business of creating experiences, it logically follows that they would expand the lasting impact they have on the business landscape by producing more services designed to uplift vacation, resort, and homeowner experiences. Further, Ritz-Carlton leadership logically continues to enhance the capabilities of those who seek their expertise by the transformative power of knowledge not only in the areas of leadership but even at the property level, as evidenced by partnerships such as the one forged between Ritz-Carlton and the Viking Range Corporation. This relationship enhances the experience for guests wishing to shadow and learn from celebrity restaurant chefs at Ritz-Carlton Culinary Centers.

President Simon Cooper best sums up the brand extension journey of the Ritz-Carlton: "We add value to people's lives through uncompromising service and an unwavering commitment to quality. As leaders, we must steer this business into opportunities that are true to those strengths, whether that is serving a hotel guest, or a Ritz-Carlton Residence owner, or teaching an employee of another business at the Leadership Center." The breadth and significance of the footprint for the Ladies and Gentlemen at Ritz-Carlton and other great businesses are measured in leadership's ability to effectively avoid landmines and dead ends and instead "steer the strengths" of their organizations into appropriate opportunities that add value in the lives of those they are entrusted to serve.

LIVING THE NEW GOLD STANDARD

- Truly engaged clients are anxious to experience expanded product and service lines from the businesses they trust and respect.

- Great brand extensions emerge from the core competencies of a company.

- Sharing knowledge is often more a strength than a liability in the collaborative world of business.

- Take service beyond necessary business transactions. Make it a part of your culture—ingrained in your organization's DNA.

- Businesses too focused on the bottom line will create a legacy only for their investors. Great businesses focus on their people, customers, and communities as well.

- Steer the strengths of your organization into avenues that add value in the lives of the clients you serve.

Sustainability and Stewardship

The great use of life is to spend it
for something that will outlast it.

WILLIAM JAMES

 The true test of an organization's success and the significance of its leadership extend well beyond Wow stories, current economic performance, or even offering products that address the immediate preferences of consumers. Increasingly, businesses are judged for the lasting nature of the footprint they leave on individuals, communities, and other businesses.

Myopic companies focus on short-term profitability instead of ecological sustainability, or they prioritize advertising over efforts to train and grow their people. The Ritz-Carlton Hotel Company was founded on a different set of values. The company's mission statement, since its inception, included the idea that "Ritz-Carlton will be known as a positive, supportive member of the community and will be sensitive to the environment." Early visionary and former president Horst Schulze explains the rationale for including this philosophy early on in the company's development. "A business is only as great as its focus. If you focus narrowly on the bottom line, you leave a legacy only for the investors. Great businesses grow their people, their communities, their customer base, and their profitability. From the day we opened our doors at Ritz-Carlton, all we wanted to be was a truly great company."

In essence, modern assessments of business can be scrutinized from the context of the Gallup CE[11] survey of customer engagement. As you will recall, Gallup seeks to determine whether individual customers are emotionally engaged with a company like Ritz-Carlton by asking if they would endorse the statement "I can't imagine a world without Ritz-Carlton." When it comes to building a lasting legacy as a member of a community, it would be hoped that customers, fellow business leaders, and nonprofit groups might offer their sense of community engagement with a statement like "This community and the world at large are strongly benefited because of a company like Ritz-Carlton." Leadership at Ritz-Carlton seeks to affect its community at multiple levels, including efforts to assist others financially, share leadership ideas, and provide training opportunities.

Keeping It Real

Many companies today are embracing the trendy nature of corporate social involvement programs and are examining whether socially responsible behavior can be monetized. Writing in *Boardroom Briefing* magazine, Dr. Deborah Talbot, a strategic consultant and former senior executive at JPMorgan Chase, makes the case for viewing corporate social responsibility (CSR) not as philanthropy but as a sound long-term financial choice: "CSR reflects a concern for . . . profits, people and place. By no means is profitability of the corporation set aside but rather supplemented, by additional considerations that go beyond financial success. Furthermore, while socially responsible action may initially reduce profits, many corporations are finding that it may also create new opportunities for adding to profits and/or reduce a greater threat of operating losses due to legal/regulatory actions or loss of favor in the marketplace."

While many leaders champion corporate social responsibility programs as a wise business investment, some cynically suggest that these programs are necessary only to create a politically correct impression in the mind of the consumer. Simon Cooper takes a more holistic approach to the importance of corporate social responsibility at Ritz-Carlton: "For us, doing the right thing and giving back to our Ladies and Gentlemen and to the communities we serve, and even making contributions for good causes in areas of the world that we don't serve, are not a business strategy; rather, they are part of our DNA. In fact, if anything, we often underplay our social contributions because we don't want them to appear self-serving."

Leaders understand that socially responsible efforts are difficult messages to communicate. If too much is said about a company's socially responsible behavior, it can quickly be perceived as propaganda. On the other hand, a dearth of information leads to criticisms that a company is not concerned with broader social issues. Sue Stephenson, vice president of Community Footprints, Ritz-Carlton's community partnership program, says, "More and more people are asking us about what we do on behalf of communities and the environment. We are careful not to rush out and communicate everything we do. For our efforts to be successful, they must be authentically committed to service and not about patting ourselves on the back. At the same time, there needs to be a way to responsibly communicate the fruits of a company's efforts without being aggrandizing."

It is critical, then, to create a well-thought-through approach to communication concerning the breadth of socially responsible offerings and to make sure that those programs emerge naturally from the core values of the business. The mission statement for the Community Footprints program reads: "At Ritz-Carlton we have built a legacy of extraordinary service. This tradition extends into our Community Footprints program and inspires us to positively impact the lives of others. Every contribution we make is an opportunity to leave an imprint in our communities. It is through this collection of imprints that we make a meaningful difference."

Vivian Deuschl, vice president of public relations for Ritz-Carlton, shares her thoughts on this issue. "We are more focused on our underlying commitment to service excellence and acknowledge how that commitment lives beyond the confines of our hotels and flourishes in communities throughout the world. Overall leadership wants to make sure that our efforts are shared in the context of an overarching and systematic approach to environmental and social concerns. If we fail to put our efforts into context, all corporate communication sounds like we are championing projects that are nothing more than 'flavor of the month.' You have to have substance behind what you're doing when you go to the media, particularly in the luxury sector." As is common among many companies today, customers, partners, and prospective employees are increasingly evaluating the substance behind the Ritz-Carlton commitment toward social causes.

Dr. Bradley Goggins, founder of the Center for Corporate Citizenship at Boston University, offers insight into the growing relationship between corporate social responsibility practices and the recruitment of new employees. Dr. Goggins notes, "It is interesting to see how corporate citizenship is becoming a different and powerful new driver for winning the talent war. . . . The millennial generation, by many reports, is looking for workplaces that will ensure continuity between their values and their careers. This generation, socialized in community service and possessing a passionate commitment to cultural environments, expects a company to walk its talk. It also expects the company to provide opportunities for employees to act on their values—resulting in the emergence of employee engagement as a strategic issue."

Prospective employees are not alone in their interest in corporate social responsibility practices. Customers are also assessing whether businesses "walk their talk" and if they achieve their stated community objectives. Researchers Sergio Pivato, Nicola Misani, and Antonio Tencati, for example, have demonstrated that corporate social performance influences consumer trust. That trust, in turn, is linked to the future purchase behavior on the part of those customers.

Since the founders of The Ritz-Carlton Hotel Company included social responsibility in their mission statement, the company has had a long history of community involvement. This sizable philanthropy, however, was primarily reactive to the requests individual hotels received from community organizations. Further, each hotel adopted its own community partners without a consistent process for deciding which projects should be supported. That changed, however, with the help of Baldrige examiners, as corporate leadership came to appreciate the importance of offering a unified and focused strategy for their community efforts.

The integration of community involvement initiatives was realized in 2002 when Ritz-Carlton developed the Community Footprints program. Prior to rolling out Community Footprints, corporate leaders looked at the types of programs that were already established at the hotel level. As might be expected, they found that hotel staff had naturally gravitated toward social projects that were consistent with the overall values of Ritz-Carlton. For example, many hotels were actively participating in environmental conservation efforts. The impetus for this involvement could be traced to the 20 Basics (see Chapter 2), which guided staff to "conserve energy, properly maintain our hotels, and protect the environment." In addition to environmental conservation, hotels had targeted their long-standing community involvement mission in the areas of hunger and poverty relief and services to address the well-being of disadvantaged children. Given established programs at the hotel level, Community Footprints systematically focused on those three areas (hunger and poverty relief, the well-being of disadvantaged children, and environmental conservation). Since these themes emerged from existing frontline efforts rather than from a corporately driven business need, the Community Footprints program was met with enthusiasm.

To further encourage initiative while maintaining integration throughout all properties, corporate leadership tasks each hotel to develop its own annual Community Footprints plan. Leadership then helps hotel staff measure progress against their locally defined objectives. Representatives at the corporate level raise the profile of Community Footprints through internal messaging and by sharpening the strategic focus placed on the program. By dedicating human and capital resources and coordinating engagement across all Ritz-Carlton properties, efficiencies of scale are achieved and the impact of philanthropic efforts is maximized.

As a result of measuring the impact of these programs, Ritz-Carlton is able to quantify the value of volunteer hours and product donations made to nonprofit organizations, as well as direct monetary contributions. For example, in 2007, The Ritz-Carlton Hotel Company contributed approximately $7.4 million in products, services, and donations, and the Ladies and Gentlemen logged over 40,000 hours of charitable work. Sue Stephenson, vice president of Community Footprints, understands how the structured focus of the Community Footprints program helps guide difficult choices involved in community partnerships. "There are so many wonderful causes that tug at the heart. At our hotel in Naples, for example, we probably receive 50 requests a week for in-kind donations from charitable organizations. The priorities we have set in the Community Footprints program help our hotel staff focus on delivering maximum impact.

"The Naples hotel is the prime founding sponsor of the Naples Winter Wine Festival. We donate the food and all of the labor for the three-day event. In seven years the festival has raised over $45 million to the benefit of 29 children's charities in

Collier County. That type of support turns out to be more effective than scattering our product and service donations more haphazardly."

During the preopening phase of a hotel, the Community Footprints program assists in forging a relationship between the hotel staff and a local organization whose mission falls into the three target assistance areas. One such example occurred during the 2008 opening of The Ritz-Carlton, Denver. Audrey Strong, director of public relations, shares, "Our employees broke a two-hour time period record at The Food Bank of the Rockies as they assembled boxes of nonperishable food items for the Community Supplemental Food Program. That program helps low-income pregnant or breast-feeding women, new mothers, children, and the elderly. In the course of those two hours, 1,250 boxes were assembled by Ritz-Carlton volunteers at a pace of 10 boxes per minute. Employees who volunteered that day also made a cash donation that facilitated the purchase of 236 meals for Colorado's needy."

On the other side of the globe in China, the preopening team at The Ritz-Carlton, Guangzhou, conducted the hotel's first Community Footprints event a full six months before the hotel was set to open. Guangzhou Social Welfare Institution for children celebrated Children's Day with Ritz-Carlton staff and management present to provide every child a T-shirt, a holiday gift, and warm personal attention. By encouraging volunteer activity, even in a hotel's preopening phase, leadership sends a message to staff that volunteerism is a fundamental aspect of the company. Sue Stephenson believes this signals that "we're not just a hotel with very wealthy guests. We are part of the community. Our Ladies and Gentlemen understand that we are very serious about giving back to these local organizations that touch their lives."

The hotel's mission makes it clear that this type of involvement shouldn't stop once the hotel is up and running. There are regular procedures in place to ensure continuous contributions and participation by employees throughout the company, including active committees at the local level. Becky Gill, area director of quality and member of her hotel's guidance team, reflects on her involvement in planning community interactions: "Each year we meet to look at our partnership efforts. We have goals to drive regular volunteer participation from across the hotel with our community partner, the Atlanta Food Bank. During our planning process, we realized that our success depended on every hotel division taking ownership of its participation in food bank activities. As such, the teams in these departments have structured opportunities to go to the food bank and strengthen their overall group function through the shared volunteer activity. We have also arranged regularly scheduled participation times so any of our Ladies and Gentlemen can attend." Whether at the corporate or property level, the social responsibility program is not left to chance. These leaders understand that the success of corporate social responsibility is achieved by enacting the same strategic and operational practices necessary for a business's overall profitability.

STRIKING GOLD

- Have you clearly defined a systematic approach to corporate social responsibility with specified themes for giving?

- How does your social responsibility program align with your goals for community support, employee recruitment, and customer relationship management?

- What measures do you have in place to assess the impact of your social giving?

◦⟦ Giving Serves All ⟧◦

By their nature, social giving programs are designed to enrich the lives of individuals who are often not the identified customer market for a business. Since these programs do not have an obvious link to the current bottom line and are unlikely to fuel future growth, a 2007 survey conducted by the professional staffing company Hudson shows that "less than half of companies have a formal corporate [social] responsibility program." Of those businesses that have developed CSR initiatives, Hudson finds that 70 percent organize group volunteer activities, while only 20 percent compensate their employees for volunteering (through salary or paid time off).

Given that companies with CSR programs are still in the minority, Bill Bolling, founder and executive director of Atlanta Food Bank, offers a perspective on the misguided nature of failing to organize and support corporate social giving: "I think companies oftentimes are just thinking about the quarter that they're in. This is true for leaders trying to deliver returns for stockholders and for the small tire recapping place down the street. I have seen repeated examples where companies take a short-term view when it comes to caring for employees, delivering health care benefits, or making sure the community is fed. Ultimately, these nearsighted approaches undermine local economies and are very detrimental to those communities."

Bill adds, "I find when some companies aren't doing well, they'll say they don't have time to volunteer. Often leaders at those same companies say the same thing when they are doing well. Fortunately, great leaders look to the long term for their people and the sustainable relationships their companies forge."

The Atlanta Food Bank is an example of how employee involvement in volunteerism serves not only long-term community needs but also the needs of the volunteering business. The Atlanta Food Bank, founded in 1979, is part of a national network of over 200 food banks throughout the United States called "America's Second Harvest." The primary mission of the food bank is to collect surplus and unmarketable food and distribute it to community-based organizations. To achieve this end, the Atlanta Food Bank has taken an entrepreneurial approach to program development, melding the food bank's core competencies in warehousing and distribution while developing new product lines so they will be certain there will be a reliable network of companies to provide needed contributions.

For instance, Bill says, "'Atlanta's Table' is a prepared-food program, where we work with the hospitality industry—restaurants, caterers, hotels like Ritz-Carlton—where the partners donate their surplus of prepared food. Basically the idea is that if you're the chef and run the restaurant, the last thing you want to do is throw away food. You want to sell it if you can, but you don't want to throw it away at the end of the day. So we've created safe, judicious ways to handle that food, and get it to those most in need." The Ritz-Carlton involvement in the Atlanta Food Bank extends beyond donation of food items and includes representation on the advisory board for the Atlanta's Table program, support for the Atlanta Food Bank fund-raising efforts, and regular volunteer participation in community gardening and food distribution processes.

From the Food Bank's perspective, Bill shares, "Our relationship with Ritz-Carlton hotels here in Atlanta goes back to 1997, when I went to the hotel management and asked if they could provide customer service training to the staff of the food bank. That was a great benefit for us. Additionally, we have special events where we might have food-tasting fund-raisers or an evening with noteworthy chefs. Ritz-Carlton always steps up and not only brings a chef but brings the food. It really heightens our own event to have them there. But one of the company's ongoing involvements is food sorting, where the Ladies and Gentlemen regularly help us select food for distribution. I can only tell you that their service professionalism, work ethic, and commitment to excellence shine in their productivity and passion toward that effort."

While the investment by Ritz-Carlton in the Atlanta Food Bank aids hungry families and children throughout the Atlanta area, great benefits are also experienced by the staff of the hotels.

Becky Gill, a participant in food drives on behalf of the Atlanta Food Bank, relates, "I love the opportunity to contribute. It's gratifying to facilitate that process of getting donated food items and helping get food to where it needs to be. It's also fun to see how many pounds of food our team has sorted at the end of the day. Besides the outcome, I love the camaraderie my team experiences when we go there. While the tasks are repetitive, it allows us time to talk with one another outside of work and to pull together for a common goal." The sense of pride and the team-building skills of corporate volunteerism are a part of the overall benefits that are derived from these activities and that go back to the Ritz-Carlton staff. On a broader scale, these volunteer activities reinforce the culture of Ritz-Carlton and create a foundation of collegial support.

By structuring opportunities, leaders encourage their staff to look beyond personal gain and toward the broader well-being of their community. For example, staff members at The Ritz-Carlton, Grand Cayman, were recipients of the Community Footprints Property of the Year for cleaning and making repairs to the Grand Cayman Family Crisis Center, as well as volunteering at a number of other nonprofits in the area. Additionally, staff participated in many environmental projects including beach cleanup, glass recycling, and rainwater collection.

This external focus helps employees also look out for the greater good of coworkers and the economic needs of the business. To that end, staff members at Ritz-Carlton have a rich history of serving their fellow Ladies and Gentlemen and others caught in the throes of natural disaster. Paul Westbrook, senior vice president of product and brand management, has been witness to some extraordinary circumstances. "Post–Hurricane Katrina, in New Orleans, we offered every employee the opportunity to relocate with his or her family and have a job at another Ritz-Carlton hotel. Clearly there was a cost associated with that decision. But it was the right thing to do. People had been displaced; many employees lost their homes. There was no immediate opportunity for them to regain housing. We knew the hotel would be closed for a significant period of time. Some business leaders would need to know the return on an investment before they would support such a decision. Ultimately, we knew that doing the right thing for our people is what produces our uniquely engaged workforce. Our company has always been focused on the right work environment. By creating that environment for the Ladies and Gentlemen, they deliver great service to the customers." President Simon Cooper goes on to note that many staff members seized the opportunity for relocation; managers, for example, "were relocated around the system. We also had a reunion for them in Miami about a month later. National Basketball Association star, Shaquille O'Neal, spent an hour with our Ladies and Gentlemen. Our hotel owners reached out, especially Mercer Reynolds, owner of The Ritz-Carlton, Reynolds Plantation, who also offered free housing to a number of employees."

The spirit of assistance in crisis transfers to the actions of the Ladies and Gentlemen, as articulated in a letter written to the *Miami Herald* by Beatrice Hines. She was a guest at The Ritz-Carlton, Golf & Spa Resort, Rose Hall, Jamaica, when Hurricane Dean hit the island. Beatrice wrote, "First Class to all the Ladies and Gentlemen who ensured that all guests and the children from Blossom Gardens Orphanage were safe and comfortable throughout the night. You all did an amazing job in preparing the hotel for the hurricane and then worked very hard to bring the property back to life by clearing debris and refreshing our guest rooms. The day immediately after the hurricane, the guests started enjoying their vacation again, as if nothing had happened, and it is all because of your efforts and hard work in enlivening the Credo."

The Ritz-Carlton, Rose Hall, "adopted" the Blossom Garden Orphanage in 2001. Since that time, the Community Footprints activities established by the employees at that location have included hosting quarterly "fun days for the children" with food and games. Additionally, the resort's engineering crew volunteers their time to provide repairs to the orphanage. The resort also donates bed linens, cribs, clothes, books, and other educational materials. Ellen Terry, regional director of sales at the International Sales Office, relates, "Hurricane Ivan was one of the worst hurricanes to ever hit Jamaica. Our Ladies and Gentlemen at The Ritz-Carlton, Rose Hall, moved all of the children and staff from a local orphanage because there was no power or water service in Montego Bay. The hotel staff provided shelter, food, water, and clothing for these children as well as their caregivers for many days. The guests in-house became involved with caring for the children." In essence, the care offered to orphans in Jamaica by Ritz-Carlton staff resulted in life-impacting experiences for the staff and guests.

As was the case during the Jamaican hurricane effort, hotel guests frequently become engaged in outreach and support. Micah Dean worked the front desk at The Ritz-Carlton, New Orleans, during Hurricane Katrina. He shares, "It was not like a normal Ritz-Carlton experience, of course. We had no idea how long we would be there, so breakfast would be one banana, one muffin, and one cup of water, and that was it. Everybody had to be selfless. I worked an overnight shift at the front desk, and around 2 or 3 a.m., an 84-year-old guest called me and told me she had kidney pain. We called the nearest hospital, but their first floor was under water so we could not get her treated there. Abbott Laboratories had been having a conference with us, so I called a guest listed as a doctor. I woke him up from his sleep, and he gladly came from his room to help the woman."

That type of noble service Micah witnessed during Hurricane Katrina, from both guests and his fellow staff members is indelibly etched in his memory. "I will always remember the efforts of our Ladies and Gentlemen. To get our guests to safety, we took them on a journey of about three blocks using laundry carts—the kind with a metal frame and vinyl around the frame. We had the guests' luggage placed inside of those, and we put the guests on top. We pushed the carts across Canal Street to the highest part of the asphalt, where the streetcar runs. We walked down Canal Street to the JW Marriott. I'm about six-foot-two, and the water was about midthigh on me. That was the depth on Canal Street, which was nothing in comparison to eight-foot depths in other areas. So we went to the Marriott, and the buses picked us up from there." When asked if he felt a sense of pride in helping others during that time, Micah replied, "It was just people helping people. It wasn't about work; it wasn't about who people were. It was just our Ladies and Gentlemen at their best doing what we were born and trained to do. We all had to band together because without each other, we wouldn't make it through. They were our guests and they needed us."

This spirit to "band together" is strengthened by leadership's emphasis on corporate volunteerism. Sue Stephenson tells the story of 30 employees who came in from Jamaica and Turkey to work the summer season at one of the Ritz-Carlton hotels. She elaborates: "At the end of their employment period, we wanted to do something to recognize them. Should we throw a picnic to thank them and enjoy the social benefits of that? Angella Reid, the general manager of The Ritz-Carlton, Coconut Grove, Miami, Florida, said no—the hotel was going to participate in a Habitat for Humanity project in their honor. While the employees may have enjoyed the picnic, all the employees felt rewarded by the positive community benefits and the exceptional stories that came out of that event. That Habitat for Humanity project created such a memory for the people who participated."

In addition to appreciating the community-based benefits of volunteerism, cutting-edge leaders weigh the risk of volunteerism against the "return value of that giving." Walter P. Pidgeon, author of *The Universal Benefits of Volunteering: A Practical Workbook for Nonprofit Organizations, Volunteers, and Corporations,* defines "return value" by noting, "The benefit that volunteering provides has traditionally been thought of as the good works given by the individual to the nonprofit organization and the community. While this is and should remain the main reason for volunteering, there is another reward that is created—namely, that return value that the individual receives from the process. Return value has not been discussed a great deal, but most individuals who volunteer understand that they receive value in return for their volunteering, including the 'great feeling' that is received from helping others." In addition to the positive emotions that come with volunteerism, the return value of corporate efforts include team building, cohesion, employee pride, and the development of specific skills such as project management abilities.

Always Looking for the Opportunity to Do Good

Ritz-Carlton leadership is vigilant in looking for ways to engage staff, guests, and even business partners in their community outreach efforts. Not only are employees encouraged to participate in social causes in lieu of compensation or recognition parties but so are the key business partners and vendors at Ritz-Carlton.

At a function designed to strengthen these relationships with key account representatives held at The Ritz-Carlton, Amelia Island, Florida, senior leaders throughout the organization and premier travel agents (those who refer significant business to Ritz-Carlton hotels worldwide) assisted in packing school and medical supplies for children in the Democratic Republic of Congo while learning about efforts to protect an endangered species.

The event supported children in the northeastern region of the Congo where the endangered okapi (a zebra-striped mammal in the giraffe family) is being protected as part of the Okapi Wildlife Reserve management plan. Gilman International Conservation and the White Oak Conservation Center have built schools in the Congo and support those who guard the okapi from poachers. Steve Shurter, director of conservation at White

Oak Conservation Center and international programs director for Gilman International Conservation, is appreciative of the dedicated corporate alliance. "Our partnership with Ritz-Carlton has been very beneficial to us. By bringing select people to our location, Ritz-Carlton increases awareness of the conservation issues we champion, and at the same time it helps us tangibly serve the needs of families in the Congo. This project involving their key account representatives packaging medical and school supplies addresses our practical need while allowing us the opportunity to inform. I sense the event was also meaningful to the participants."

John Meehan, hotel manager of The Ritz-Carlton, South Beach, has seen that community outreach events with key business partners provide a multitude of benefits. "All of our best referral sources are here, so it's an opportunity to forge relationships through face-to-face contact. The added bonus is that any time we can get people involved in accomplishing meaningful goals, those relationships are strengthened all the further. If we had stayed in meetings all day, we wouldn't have the same depth of personal attachment."

Rather than being put off by the prospect of offering their work efforts at a key business partner event, Marty Covert of Covert Operations, a meeting planner specializing in the needs of luxury and high-end business travelers and meetings, has taken advantage of opportunities to partner with Ritz-Carlton to make a difference. "I'm part of the Association Advisory Board for the company, and I have not only participated in these community events but have learned a lot about the charitable efforts of Ritz-Carlton. Recently, a client of mine was looking for a team-building exercise for an event, and based on my experience at Ritz-Carlton, I suggested that their group participate in a community activity during their meeting to achieve both team building and a sense of accomplishment in the process." By offering the experience of community involvement at meetings with business partners, the leadership team at Ritz-Carlton inspires their allies in the meetings and travel industry to also influence the social engagement of their clients. But more than that, they strengthen valuable business relationships in an authentic and unforgettable way.

Executives at Ritz-Carlton work to help those conducting meetings in their hotels to make connections with community-based organizations, to add social responsibility aspects to a meeting or conference. Sue Stephenson explains, "These programs are still evolving. You can enjoy a luxury meeting experience, and you can also participate in an activity that lets you give back in some way. We're working with people out in the field, and there is huge enthusiasm for creating these opportunities. But we must always be respectful as we strike the balance of giving our guests the opportunity to be involved while protecting the dignity of those they serve in the community."

There are additional ways for individuals to make contributions that respect those served through the Community Footprints program. One is by creating a Community Footprints Fund to accept direct contributions and a portion of the revenues from the sale of select merchandise, such as the Ritz Coffee Candle, which is sold in their hotel stores. Another is an initiative called "Meaningful Meetings," which allows groups booking a certain number of room nights at any Ritz-Carlton hotel or resort in the United States, Canada, or the Caribbean to have 10 percent of the total room revenue donated in equal portions to a charity of their choice and to causes supported by Community Footprints.

Bruce Himelstein, senior vice president of sales and marketing, explains how this initiative came about: "We know many groups that elect to stay at a Ritz-Carlton are supporters of charitable organizations, and we believe the Meaningful Meetings program satisfies their commitment to give something to a worthy cause, while at the same time knowing their meeting will receive the attention to detail we are known for when it comes to caring for the needs of our group clientele." From the onset of

Meaningful Meetings, the sales staff at Ritz-Carlton has heard from meeting planners who have identified the concept as being the deciding factor in booking an event at their respective properties.

In order to walk the social responsibility talk, leadership conducts meetings throughout Ritz-Carlton that involve social activities. Every corporate meeting has a Community Footprints element; past projects have included creating playgrounds, constructing landscaping, painting murals at a Boys and Girls Club, and engaging in a restoration project on Ellis Island.

STRIKING GOLD

- How far is your company willing to go in support of corporate volunteerism and social involvement? Will you reach the point of organizing and scheduling volunteer activities or actually pay staff to participate in community-enriching events?

- What return value does your staff receive from their social responsibility efforts?

- How can you invite your company's stakeholders (customers, vendors, strategic partners) to participate in volunteer activities with your staff?

It's Not Always That Easy

While Ritz-Carlton has seen growing success in integrating volunteerism and community giving programs, it has also faced considerable challenges when integrating environmental considerations into the guest experience. It is not unusual, for example, for a guest room to be staged before the guest arrives. This may involve having the room lit appropriately and even having a guest's preferred music playing. Luxury-seeking guests might not be accustomed to being afforded the option of having their linens left unchanged during their stay. Asking guests to partner with them in environmental conservation while at the same time not suggesting anything that decreases the perceived value of the stay is a balance that Ritz-Carlton leadership weighs carefully. Simon Cooper comments, "We continue to craft our messages in these regards. We have pilot projects naturally occurring in locations such as our California properties. We want to make sure we don't impute guilt on guests who are paying for a luxury experience but at the same time we want to create openings for our guests to help us steward precious resources."

In an effort to strike this balance, several Ritz-Carlton hotels, including those at Half Moon Bay, Tyson's Corner, Reynolds Plantation, Sarasota, and Beijing Financial Street, are experimenting with different ways to communicate to guests about the hotels' focus on conserving natural resources without impacting the luxury experience. Specifically, each hotel is looking at different avenues (for example, signage, information in the room, or a conversation at check-in) that give the guests an option to select a less-frequent linen and towel change service if they desire or that emphasize ways for the guests to participate in the recycling or reduced use of environmentally sensitive products. Rather than rushing to a nonviable solution, leadership is methodically looking for the most effective and respectful approach.

Bill Bolling of the Atlanta Food Bank observes that Ritz-Carlton leadership is known for thoughtful consideration of complicated issues: "It's not as much a negative as it is a cultural thing. When Ritz-Carlton goes about doing something, it doesn't do it quickly. It does it thoroughly. It's one of the things we've learned about partnering with them. I actually support and respect that because in the long run when we decide what it is that works, I fully assume we're going to be successful."

Sue Stephenson offers examples of how Ritz-Carlton looks at ways to have a positive environmental impact. "One of our approaches has been to partner with organizations that have environmental conservation expertise such as Jean-Michel Cousteau's Ocean Futures Society. Additionally, we work within our company by forming teams led by our hotel general managers. Those groups have evolved to 'Ritz-Carlton Environmental Action Conservation Teams' that focus on energy and water conservation, as well as waste management issues like recycling. Depending on where the property is located, these groups will also focus on natural habitat or wildlife conservation, particularly in our resorts. We also have a team called the 'Sustainable Development Committee' that reports to our senior executive committee. That group drives initiatives that potentially touch our customer. We continue to embark on additional customer research to determine how engaged our customers want to be with our environmental efforts." (Please see the sidebar "The Ambassadors of the Environment Program.")

The Ambassadors of the Environment Program

The Ambassadors of the Environment program developed by Jean-Michel Cousteau offers daily activities for various age groups at The Ritz-Carlton, Grand Cayman. Daily courses turn the Cayman Islands' ecological resources into a natural classroom and living laboratory. Families participate in eco-adventures such as these:

Have You Ever Seen a Blue Iguana? Grand Cayman is home to the endemic and endangered Cayman Blue Iguana, found nowhere else in the world. Participants learn about the Cayman Blue Iguana and the international efforts to save them. Additionally, participants visit the blue iguanas at the breeding program at Queen Elizabeth II Botanic Park.

Eco-Discovery. Participants draw upon engaging and educational audio/visual resources created by Jean-Michel

Cousteau's team. These resources provide opportunities to explore aspects of reefs and mangroves impossible to see during a typical stay on Grand Cayman.

Each of the activities presented through the Ambassadors of the Environment program is designed to create a deep appreciation and respect for nature. Additionally, lessons are offered to guests to enhance their understanding of how they can live in a more environmentally responsible way upon returning to their homes.

To date, most of the Ritz-Carlton environmental efforts occur outside the purview of the guest. These include such things as retrofitting laundry areas to use the last rinse in the laundry cycle as part of the next load's first wash cycle and reducing water consumption by recycling dishwater to irrigate golf courses. However, Ritz-Carlton also takes proactive environmental measures in the development of new properties. An example is the company's decreasing dependency on chemical use in landscaping and its investment in sustainable design for projects such as Molasses Reef, which is located at the far west end of the Turks and Caicos archipelago and has been uninhabited for almost a hundred years. For the privilege of living within a small ecoconscious community, each owner will share in the responsibility of living mindfully and sustainably, stewarding this natural treasure for future generations. Karim Alibhai, founder of the Gencom Group, the Molasses Reef developer, cites, "While extra care and cost were involved based on our ecological approach to Molasses Reef, the guest will experience the richest of surroundings. We could have compromised the environment for things like ease of access, but we held the environment and long-term sustainability as an overarching consideration for the project." Similar design innovations can be found in the first-of-its-kind project at The Ritz-Carlton, San Francisco. Paul Savarino, the director of engineering, notes, "In a nutshell, we're cogenerating a quarter of our hotel's electricity through compressed natural-gas–fired microturbines. In the process we offset a portion of our utility costs by generating electricity, but the big payback is the tremendous amount of heat that comes from the four turbines. That heat is captured by an absorption chiller. The chiller takes hot air from the turbines and turns it into chilled water, which takes care of the hotel's cooling systems. It ends up that we're saving about $12,000 to $15,000 per month that we would have normally paid if we hadn't purchased this system. From an environmental perspective, we are saving the amount of electricity used by about 250 homes on a normal day."

In some instances, the environmentally conscious practices of Ritz-Carlton staff result in opportunities for guests to have a very active and positive impact on the ecosystem. For example, before the arrival of Hurricane Dean to the Yucatán Peninsula, a number of guests were waiting to be evacuated as sea turtles made their ill-timed arrival to nest on the hotel's beach. Once the guests were secured, staff members from different areas of the hotel retrieved turtle eggs from 193 nests to protect them from the threatening storm. These staff members worked for hours to ensure the survival of a species that is in danger of extinction. As a result, they rescued 23,056 eggs and witnessed baby turtles hatching before their eyes. The experience led to ongoing efforts on behalf of the sea turtle and the development of a "Turtle Camp" for guests.

Luis de Dios Marin, a loss prevention officer who works the night shift at the hotel, patrols the beach and is responsible for the nesting process. Luis says, "I previously worked at another resort down the beach, but when I heard about Turtle Camp at the Ritz-Carlton, I knew I had to work here. At the other hotel, we were responsible for protecting the eggs and the turtles from the guests; here, the guests are educated and actively participate in helping the turtles." Luis continues, "Some guests 'adopt' the eggs they rescue, and we send pictures to the adoptive parents when the eggs hatch." Turtles that hatch in the night can find their way to the water, but turtles that hatch in the day have to be placed back in the sea later that evening. Guests request to be awakened in the night to help Luis and other staff members release those baby turtles into the water. The educational Turtle Camp program at The Ritz-Carlton, Cancún, affords an extraordinary ecological experience that hotel guests can't find elsewhere.

Beyond Turtle Camp, Community Footprints has formally developed "Give Back Getaways," which are facilitated half-day local community experiences that involve Ritz-Carlton staff members and hotel guests working together in a Community Footprints humanitarian or environmental activity. While Give Back Getaways activities vary by location, The Portman Ritz-Carlton, Shanghai, offers work on the restoration of heritage houses with programs benefiting underprivileged children in the ancient water town of Wuzhen in the south of the Yangtze River.

Through careful planning, environmentally conscious investments in new construction, retrofitting existing properties, and seizing naturally occurring opportunities, the leadership at Ritz-Carlton continues to demonstrate good stewardship of the environment while not compromising—and even enhancing— the luxury experience of their guests.

⋅≺] The Essential Legacy [≻⋅

Great businesses strengthen communities often by their mere presence. Ed Staros, one of the founders of The Ritz-Carlton Hotel Company, has seen this phenomenon firsthand: "I am truly proud to have worked with a group of visionaries who have played a role in literally creating communities like Naples, Florida. At a time when the interstate highway system was connecting the east and west coasts of Florida, and with a new airport in the area, we purchased 25 acres of swampland and opened a Ritz-Carlton on one of the world's most beautifully pristine beaches. Even though there were a lot of naysayers who predicted we'd be out of business in short order given that we were trying to open a $100 million hotel in a city with 20,000 permanent residences, we made it. In fact, we built a business by catering to the board meetings of Fortune 500 executives. Not only is the $17 million land purchase worth millions more today but in addition, we were catalytic to the growth of that vital beachfront community and the lifting of property values overall."

Past president and cofounder of The Ritz-Carlton Hotel Company Horst Schulze was also involved in the site procurements: "We knew we were going to create hotels that were committed to excellence. I am not sure that we fully understood the impact those hotels would have on creating communities. I laugh when I think about the land I personally could have purchased near our new properties if only I had been that smart."

Communities with Ritz-Carlton hotels not only benefit in increased property values but also in the pride, job creation, and improved standard of living they afford their employees. Jennifer Oberstein, area director of public relations at The Ritz-Carlton Hotels of New York and Boston, speaks specifically to the issue of community pride associated with the opening of The Ritz-Carlton New York, Battery Park, hotel on January 9, 2002: "We were the first new building to open in Lower Manhattan after the September 11, 2001, terrorist attacks on the World Trade Center. It was an incredibly emotional day, at a difficult time. The opening drew a crowd that more than filled our ballroom. Since Mayor Bloomberg's inauguration, this was the first time he and Mayor Giuliani appeared together. They both spoke at the event and cut our ribbon along with Joe Torre, then general manager of the New York Yankees, who was our first guest. That opening was symbolic; it was uplifting; it was a time to say that we're here and we remember, but we will move forward."

Businesses like Ritz-Carlton do move communities forward in many ways, including through the lasting impact of job creation. President Simon Cooper shares, "Sometimes it's daunting to think about your responsibility as an employer. I like to look at the geographical diversity of our locations. While we are in major cities, we also have hotels that are in more remote locations. In some cases, we entered a community as the largest employer and functionally changed the landscape of jobs that were available in that area. In Grand Cayman, 7 or 8 percent of the gross domestic product of the island is the Ritz-Carlton alone. That's a huge responsibility that you take on. Whether you like it or not, you're going to have a permanent impact on anything you touch on that island. You just hope that all of the impacts are good.

"Half Moon Bay entered a market where many of the jobs were for seasonal farm work. If you look at The Ritz-Carlton, Reynolds Plantation, in Georgia, you will see a community where many of the factories had been closed down and where the largest employer was the prison system." Simon continues, "I know we create great jobs. But when you go to those locations, you know something else is happening beyond the careers of our Ladies and Gentlemen. Particularly in more remote locations, solid employment actually creates families. It's a life for our people. It's a life for their children. In Bali, for example, I am incredibly proud to go out in those communities and see the changes that have occurred in the lives of families as a result of Ladies and Gentlemen choosing to work for Ritz-Carlton. It could have been some other company, but in that case, it happens to be us. For that, I am grateful."

When values-based companies make positive investments in communities, the gratitude is often reciprocated by those they employ and the people in the communities they serve. Elena Mullican, director of catering sales at The Ritz-Carlton, Atlanta, and The Ritz-Carlton, Buckhead, developed etiquette courses for children ages 8 to 12 and for teenagers 13 to 17. She voluntarily offers these courses to children of economically disadvantaged backgrounds through the "Bridges from School to Work" program. Elena champions the efforts. "The classes have been a huge success because I focus on the etiquette portion of the Ritz-Carlton service standards. We talk about the Three Steps of Service, and I utilize our service standards to deal with introducing yourself to someone, interviewing skills, cell phone etiquette, fine dining basics, conversation skills, and the importance of thank-you notes and follow-up. It's amazingly rewarding to see that what we covered makes the young people feel special and that they walk away with usable tools as they enter the workplace."

As employers help their people develop workplace skills, the same employees frequently transform the service standards of the business itself. Ronald Thomas, an Employee of the Year at Ritz-Carlton, frequent recipient of Five Star quarterly service awards, and honoree for a JW Marriott Award of Excellence, shares how the service culture helped transform him as an individual. "I was homeless. I was addicted to drugs and alcohol. After being shot and hitting bottom, I went into drug rehabilitation. As part of the treatment, I participated in a job training program and had to go on job interviews. One of the interviews was at Ritz-Carlton, and they hired me. I was stunned, and it's still hard to believe."

Ronald's natural talents were developed across hotel functions including grounds keeping, lobby attendant, and housekeeping. By trusting in and developing Ronald, Ritz-Carlton was reciprocally driven to greater excellence in their community involvement. Ronald shares, "I'm in charge of the community involvement at my hotel, as far as the homeless are concerned. I'm in the community doing a lot of work with homeless people, and I find areas where the Ladies and Gentlemen of Ritz-Carlton can help. We started doing picnics for the homeless out of the trunks of our cars. A couple of the staff and I would buy soda, chips, bread, and items to barbeque. We'd load our trunks with chicken and charcoal and take the grills downtown. We did this for a year or two, and then I went to the hotel and asked them if they would buy the food. Now we have monthly picnics for the homeless. Ritz-Carlton donates the food, and our volunteers cook and serve it. We do a major Thanksgiving meal at a church each year and serve between 1,000 to 1,500 homeless that day alone. I can't stress the importance enough, though, that this doesn't happen just once a year. This continues—starving continues—all year long. We do something big every month. We also take sheets, linens, and other items every month to the shelters . . . sometimes two or three times a month."

True leadership involves not only serving owners and guests but developing staff members who can teach the managers how to increase the permanent impact of the business. Ronald sums up what is possible from a true community-based company: "Because of my affiliation with Ritz-Carlton, I'm able to help more people. I couldn't afford all this food on my own. I couldn't touch as many lives. One young man who works at the restaurant in our hotel is helping me coach basketball downtown, and others come down to the gym to help. I used to see things go in the dumpster—pillows and linens—and I said, hey, there are people who can use that! One Thanksgiving, the culinary department prepared food for a large group that cancelled. Management was going to try to use the food to feed our employees, but I talked to the chef, and he said as long as the food hadn't been served, it wasn't considered leftovers. So we loaded the food into a van and took it down to the Mission. If there weren't a Ritz-Carlton, where would I personally be? If there weren't a Ritz-Carlton, where would the community be?"

Ronald's questions pose a lingering challenge for all business leaders. What are the opportunities awaiting you to uplift the lives of those inside and outside your business? What is your lasting footprint?

LIVING THE NEW GOLD STANDARD

- Community engagement efforts by businesses might not provide measurable dividends to investors, but great leaders consider this engagement as a long-term benefit for their people and an essential ingredient to creating sustainable relationships in the areas where they do business.

- The success of any corporate social responsibility program is achieved by enacting the same strategic and operational practices necessary for a business's overall profitability.

- Invite your staff, clients, business partners, and vendors to be involved alongside you in outreach efforts. Not only does it help the community but it also forges more meaningful personal connections.

- When employers encourage and help their people have impact in their communities, the same employees frequently transform the service standards of the business itself.

- When your business decisions are made thoughtfully, slowly, and thoroughly, it will be fully expected by your clients that your future endeavors will be successful.

- Great businesses strengthen communities often by their mere presence. Be mindful of keeping all your internal and external clients involved with your business so that they can help you create a greater community footprint.

- Communities in which there are Ritz-Carlton hotels not only benefit in increased property values but in job creation and the standard of living they afford their employees. Seek ways to add value to the communities you serve.

Conclusion:
A Lasting Impression

Achievement is largely the product of steadily raising
one's levels of aspiration and expectation.

JACK NICKLAUS

 Knowledge alone is not power. Power comes only when knowledge is transferred through action. So what are the action steps you will take to set the bar for world-class excellence and quality in your industry? The first ingredient of the success of Ritz-Carlton is already present in you. Ritz-Carlton leadership is constantly seeking out businesses to benchmark, just as you have chosen to take the time to study them. Ritz-Carlton leadership has, in essence, produced a company of inquiry—one that is always looking for the best metrics to ensure that their employees find their work meaningful, that their customers are engaged, and that their business continues to stay relevant as they aspire to fulfill the lasting needs of all those they serve.

A process of inquiry is essential to excellence. Service in the Ritz-Carlton culture is little more than delivering a product the customer wants without defects, delivering the product when and how the customer wants it, and providing the product with genuine care and concern for that customer. While these three aspects of service are fairly simple and timeless, the complexity of this seemingly uncomplicated formula requires constant listening and disciplined execution.

To these ends, Ritz-Carlton leadership constantly asks questions like, "Are these the products the customers want today? What are the products they will want tomorrow? What products attract customers to our competitors? What can we do to ensure our processes are devoid of defects to create the perfect guest experience? How do we help our staff members as they seek to deliver genuine care to a guest? Given the inevitable imperfections of people and processes, how do we help staff members swiftly fix breakdowns in a compassionate manner?"

As the data from these inquiries stream in, Ritz-Carlton leadership responds to the information received in very specific ways. First and foremost, they acknowledge and share the data collected. Unlike business leaders who have asked for but never act on the information that has been received, leadership at Ritz-Carlton thanks those who offer input and then distributes that input in an understandable manner. They "refine" their offerings and practices by creating a manageable set of objectives that are anchored to the company's core values, measure progress against those objectives, and remain open to further refining targets, if that is indicated by ongoing inquiry. So would your business pass the Ritz-Carlton white-glove test?

- What processes do you have in place to regularly and sincerely seek an understanding of both the satisfaction and engagement of your staff, customers, and other stakeholders?

- How do you appreciate, acknowledge, and report the information you receive in a way that helps key players understand and participate in fulfilling future business objectives?

☞ Are the objectives you are setting clear, manageable, and congruent with the core values of your company?

☞ Are you measuring progress against your objectives?

☞ Is the data from measurement provided in an understandable way so that everyone can see how their effort is affecting progress?

☞ Are you wedded to your objectives, even in the face of new trends emerging from ongoing data collection?

In the spirit of Ritz-Carlton, no matter how well you are doing on these issues and no matter how solidly you have created your business's foundation, there is surely room for improvement. John Timmerman, vice president of quality and program management, states: "We're not satisfied with just doing things better. The experience should have been perfect in the first place. While I know that perfection can be elusive, we need to shoot for it or else will settle for 90 or 95 percent. We're not going to be a world-class organization if we start to think that way."

☞ Seeking the Lasting ☞

While The Ritz-Carlton Hotel Company embraces an inquisitive, customer-centric culture, it is still defined by strong immutable traditions. Essential aspects of the company's success are clearly articulated, and even with changes in senior leadership, the core aspects of the company's culture remain. When founder and former president of The Ritz-Carlton Horst Schulze left the company, Simon Cooper, his replacement and the current president, realized, "I needed to be the chef who didn't change the menu. I had to honor the culture of this company and gently advance its financial sustainability through relevant offerings distributed in places where our guests need to find us."

The key elements of the Ritz-Carlton service culture are easily found on the Credo Card that each Lady or Gentleman carries and in daily lineups that reinforce the culture by discussions of values and purpose and by the sharing of examples of legendary service. Just as Citibank in Singapore has relied on the Ritz-Carlton Credo Card and lineup process as a springboard to create cultural enhancement, so too can you consider ways to take these Ritz-Carlton success generators and put them to work for you. Specifically, you may wish to consider whether

1. Your mission statement has been condensed in a manner like the Ritz-Carlton Credo that makes it clear and actionable for everyone in the organization.

2. You seize all available opportunities for regular conversations about the company's mission and values.

3. You align your corporate values with the financial objectives of your business and clearly show how living the values results in business success.

4. You create an environment of positive corporate storytelling that allows for people to see how they can deliver Wow experiences.

5. You view business as a two-way relationship through which leaders make and uphold promises to staff members, in as much as staff members are expected to live up to the expectations of leaders.

The degree to which your business addresses each of these considerations on a day-to-day basis will be the degree to which the culture of your workplace fosters an environment that allows individuals to shine.

Selection, Orientation, and Empowerment

To truly understand how Ritz-Carlton views the role of their Ladies and Gentlemen in propelling the success of their business, one need only hear the words of Horst Schulze: "We

...ed a truth at Ritz-Carlton that Adam Smith concluded some three hundred years before us—namely, that an employee cannot relate to orders and directions but can relate to motivation and objectives in his or her own area. But what do many managers do? They hire people and go about giving them supervision, orders, and directions. They don't allow their people to live up to their potential or give them elbow room to create their work processes. They don't allow them to be creative human beings; they put their people in a box and say 'Here you go.' That's Taylorism—a production principle—where you limit what a person can do with the function you want them to have."

When asked to address this philosophy in the context of people's failing to live up to the trust placed in them, Horst responds, "Of course, I trust people to think and create, and sometimes they violate my trust and fail. But do you want to manage to avoid failure or manage to succeed? The situation failed, but if that manages me, that means I am making an excuse to become the true power. These are nothing but management excuses to have power and be in control. That only works for a while."

"Managing to succeed" at Ritz-Carlton involves a methodical and patient selection process, a culturally rich orientation, immediate skills training and certification, a swift employee reengagement process (effectively achieved through Day 21), daily lineups, annual acknowledgment of an employee's service, and entrusting the Ladies and Gentlemen with individualized service and experience enrichment. How does your business meet these standards?

- Having the patience to avoid the "I will take anyone" syndrome, where the immediate crisis of understaffing leads to hiring compromises?

- Involving your current employees in the interview process?

]⊶ Having senior management present at every new employee orientation?

]⊶ Requiring that all employees go through orientation prior to showing up for the first day of work?

]⊶ Using orientation as a way to celebrate the employee's decision to choose your business and to imprint the rich history and values of your company?

]⊶ Offering training and certification so that your employees are capable of performing their function prior to allowing them to serve customers?

]⊶ Affording new hires a chance to give honest feedback about the breakdowns and disillusionment they may have encountered during their first weeks of work and correcting those shortcomings and reengaging them in the mission?

]⊶ Allowing employees a voice in the processes, quality improvements, and changes that affect them?

]⊶ Celebrating the accomplishments of your people as well as their anniversaries with your business?

⊰[A Fond Farewell]⊶

In light of all the best practices followed by Ritz-Carlton, it is important to note that the company has its share of shortcomings and vulnerabilities. Clearly, they face significant challenges maintaining their service excellence and overall business relevance. This will be particularly true over the next several years given that Ritz-Carlton is scheduled to manage 100 properties by the year 2011, thus causing leadership to select, acculturate, and maintain excellence with an additional 45,000 Ladies and Gentlemen and 7,200 new managers. Additionally, given worldwide economic challenges, Ritz-Carlton leaders must resist the urge to overreach their core market, an error that has affected other premier hoteliers. Horst Schulze suggests, "There was a time that other hotel companies were the leaders in the luxury hotel business. What happened? Why did they lose that position? They all made the same mistake. They reached down to the next tier of hotel traveler and began losing their share of their highest-paying clientele. They made compromises in their product to attract a wider market segment and lost the very people who not only influence the travel decisions of their companies but actually have the authority to dictate them."

The real challenge for Ritz-Carlton will be to remain nimble enough to take a legacy brand and accept the risks required to place it squarely in the sights of future generations. Despite these vulnerabilities, this hotel company has a striking advantage. The leadership understands the timeless value of quality and the art of professional service. Furthermore, they still humbly try to reach a yet-higher standard. Ed Staros, cofounder of The Ritz-Carlton Hotel Company, puts it well: "I was blessed by being chosen to be one of the original team members to put this company together. The excitement of it all comes from focusing on how good 'good' can be. That's what drives me to come to work every day. In fact, I am still trying to experience excellence at a higher level. We are good, but we have so much more we can do. We have not created that ultimate experience. It's still out there. It's that magic carrot we keep trying to approach. If you can come to work every single day focusing on how much better you can be today than you were yesterday, you will draw nearer to that carrot. You might never touch it, but you'll get one step closer."

It is that constant quest for excellence that not only transforms the guest experience but also transforms everyone who comes in contact with the company and its people. In the words of Simon Cooper, "I wasn't a bad person before I came to work here, but I am better for having been in an environment where standards of excellence are upheld and people are valued and respected. When a company pulls together for service excellence, everyone along its journey is elevated."

It is my hope that this part of your journey with Ritz-Carlton affords the same long-term benefits for you and your business as you go forward to achieve the New Gold Standard.

Notes

Chapter 1. The Ritz-Carlton Experience

Information about César Ritz and the history of The Ritz-Carlton Hotel Company, L.L.C., was obtained from various Internet sources, including www.referenceforbusiness.com, "The Ritz-Carlton Hotel Company, L.L.C., Company Profile, Information, Business Description, History, and Background Information on The Ritz-Carlton Hotel Company, L.L.C.

Other sources included Stephen Watts, *The Ritz* (The Bodley Head Ltd., Great Britain, 1963), and Adrian Waller, *No Ordinary Hotel: The Ritz-Carlton's First Seventy-Five Years* (University of Toronto Press, 1989).

Information about recognition awards at the Ritz-Carlton was obtained at www.ritzcarlton.com and from Vivian Deuschl, vice president of public relations.

Chapter 2. Set the Foundation: Communicating Core Identity and Culture

27–28 The biography of Horst Schulze presented in the sidebar was obtained directly from Mr. Schulze.

Chapter 3. Be Relevant

49 "'Antennae should be trained to register changing market conditions, e.g., customer feedback, sales force intelligence, monitoring word of mouth. And all staff [should be] alerted to [the importance of] customer experience and their own performance in delivering it'": Jennifer Kirby, "Part three: Evolving an adaptive strategy," mycustomer.com, November 1, 2007.

50 "'The problem with something like Levitz isn't so much the consumer perception of the name or even the merchandise mix. The problem is that over many, many years, the demographics have moved and their stores haven't'": Jerry Epperson, as quoted in *Furniture Today* article by Clint Engle, November 19, 2007.

52 "'Stay relevant. That's the name of the game, no matter what industry you're in'": Thomas A. Stewart, "Forethought Conversation: Northwestern Mutual's Ed Zore on staying relevant to customers; A conversation with Ed Zore," *Harvard Business Review,* December 2007.

52 "'You can see if you're relevant by how you are performing. . . . Another measure is: Are we gaining or losing ground [on the competition]? . . . We also gauge relevance by listening to our customers. . . . To stay relevant, you've got to keep increasing the value you deliver to customers'": Stewart, "Forethought Conversation."

54 "'Most big companies tend to keep their brands the same all over the world. . . . [They think] if it's Pizza Hut here, it's Pizza Hut everywhere'": Cindy Dyer, senior manager of consumer strategy and insight at Frito-Lay, Inc., and former marketer for Pizza Hut, Inc, as quoted in *The Talent Blog (http://blogs.aquent.com)* in an article by Anne Stuart, November 2007.

54 "'If you are Pizza Hut, it has to be pizza for each market. But you can't just export it and have it be that everywhere you go'": Dyer, *The Talent Blog.*

55 "'The concept is that you put something—a treat—in the crust edge. But it's different from place to place. In the United States, the crust edge is stuffed with cheese. In Asia, they put meat in the crust. In Mexico, they stuff it with cream cheese and jalapeño peppers'": Dyer, *The Talent Blog.*

55 "'Find out what's culturally acceptable from a marketing perspective, what's motivating to the customer'": Dyer, *The Talent Blog.*

Chapter 4. Select—Don't Hire

86 "'The main reason newly hired outside executives have such an abysmal failure rate (40 percent according to one study) is poor acculturation: They don't adapt well to the new company's ways of doing things. In fact, some three-quarters of 53 senior HR managers I surveyed cited poor cultural fit as the driver for onboarding failures'": Michael Watkins, "Help Newly Hired Executives Adapt Quickly," *Harvard Business Review,* June 1, 2007.

Notes

Chapter 5. It's a Matter of Trust

94 "'True leadership is a process of building a trust environment within which leaders and followers feel free to participate toward accomplishment of mutually valued goals using agreed-upon processes'": Gilbert Fairholm, *Leadership and the Culture of Trust* (Praeger Publishers, an imprint of Greenwood Publishing Group, Westport, Conn., 1994).

100 "According to Jim, staff members 'place an increasing premium on the amount and quality of development they receive when deciding to remain in an organization. This is a key fact to remember given how critical it is today to retain top talent'": Jim Bolt, "How Real Leaders Identify and Develop Talent: Part 2," *Fast Company*, May 17, 2007.

103–104 "'At a time when leadership books and seminars are flooding the markets, our country finds itself with confused leadership expectations. The countless number of leadership training resources now available provides great opportunity for us to understand the essential components of long-term, effective leadership. And yet, our newspapers and newscasts remind us daily not of our leaders' effectiveness but rather of their failures. It is important that we expect leaders to be role models and to lead us in producing significant results. The standards and values that they live by set the bar for the others in the organization'": John Hawkins, "The Imperfect World of Excellent Leaders," Leadership Edge, Inc., www.leadershiplifestyle.com, August 1999.

108 "'What's missing in business today is a commitment to honesty. It seems that much of the time, the truth is inconvenient. Business leaders buy into the notion that their team members should be sheltered from certain business issues. In fact, the most powerful teams are led by leaders with a passion for getting to what's true about a person or a situation, and then acting upon it'": Charrise McCrorey, "Honest Leadership," Emergence Business Coaching, www.emergencebiz.com, January 3, 2008.

Chapter 6. Build a Business Focused on Others

137 "According to J.D. Power, 'Ritz-Carlton ranks highest for a second consecutive year. . . . Ritz-Carlton performs particularly well in six of the eight factors: guest room, hotel facilities, staff, food and beverage, check-in/check-out, and hotel services'": J.D. Power Asia Pacific Press Release, Tokyo, "J.D. Power Asia Pacific Reports: Associa Hotels & Resorts, Dormy Inn, Richmond Hotels, Royal Park Hotels

and The Ritz-Carlton Rank Highest in Customer Satisfaction among Hotels in Japan," January 25, 2008.

Chapter 8.
Wow: The Ultimate Guest Experience

166 "'This is pretty scary news for businesses in all arenas. Even if you have a perfect track record of accuracy, meeting delivery deadlines, product quality, and service with a smile, your customers won't be loyal to you. Apparently, we've moved beyond the era of 'delighting' customers and are now in an era where much more is expected. Beyond adequate service, consumers today want to be thrilled, to feel a rush of extraordinary satisfaction by getting much more value, attention, or enjoyment than they expected'": Jeanette McMurtry, "Creating Memorable Experiences More Critical Than Delivering Excellent Service," *Advertising and Marketing Review*, www.ad-mkt-review.com, September 2007.

171–172 "'Human nature being what it is, organizations often run into trouble at the boundary between business units or between departments. The trouble is that most tasks which need to get done in order to actually service the customer or produce a product require communication to happen across these boundaries'": Operational Dynamics Web site www.operationaldynamics.com, "Improve cross-departmental communication."

173 "'Our everyday lives are typically involved with serving others. If you are an employee, you are most likely serving your supervisor and customers. If you are a homemaker, you are probably serving the needs of your family. If you are a business traveler, your journeys are strenuous enough with long daily meetings in a new city each day, as well as being away from the comforts of family and home. We all work hard in whatever field of endeavor we have chosen, and so it is vital to reward ourselves whenever we have the opportunity. I have found luxury travel to be a well-deserved reward for hard work'": Joel Widzer, *The Penny Pincher's Passport to Luxury Travel: The Art of Cultivating Preferred Customer Status* (Publishers Group West, Berkeley, Calif., 2004).

175 "Research conducted by professors Laurette Dubé and Leo Renaghan . . . validates the universal importance of 'attentiveness' among hotel staff.": Laurette Dubé and Leo Renaghan, "Building Customer Loyalty—Guests" Perspectives on the Lodging Industry's Functional Best Practices (Part 1)," *Cornell Hotel and Restaurant Administration Quarterly*, October 1999.

176–177 "'Consumers are becoming more privacy and security savvy. They are increasingly reluctant to share personal information. Most will only share once they see a clear benefit, and then many still only share reluctantly'": Melody Vargas, "The Value of Privacy," Part 2 in a Series on "Loyalty Retailing," About.com: Retail Industry.

Chapter 9. Turn Wow into Action

191 "The author of *The Leader's Guide to Storytelling: Mastering the Art and Discipline of Business Narrative,* Denning suggests that 'although good business cases are developed through the use of numbers, they are typically approved on the basis of a story—that is, a narrative that links a set of events in some kind of causal sequence. Storytelling can translate those dry and abstract numbers into compelling pictures of a leader's goals'": Stephen Denning, *The Leader's Guide to Storytelling: Mastering the Art and Discipline of Business Narrative,* (Jossey-Bass, An Imprint of Wiley, San Francisco, Calif., 2005).

191 "Similarly, Noel M. Tichy indicates in *The Leadership Engine: How Winning Companies Build Leaders at Every Level* that 'the best way to get humans to venture into unknown terrain is to make that terrain familiar and desirable by taking them there first in their imaginations'": Noel M. Tichy with Eli B. Cohen, *The Leadership Engine: How Winning Companies Build Leaders at Every Level* (HarperCollins, New York, 1997).

Chapter 10. Aspire, Achieve, Teach

207 "Based on customers' perception and knowledge of your brand, there are certain types of products that they would expect you to sell. These are products that fit well with your brand. Products that . . . are natural extensions of the expertise or information you already provide. . . . Likewise, there are many products that they want and need, but for various reasons don't expect to get—or don't want to get—from your brand'": Kathryn Fry-Ramsdell, "Researching Your Way to Winning Brand Extensions," *Circulation Management,* November 2000.

211 "While brand consultants such as Alycia de Mesa talk about the 'elasticity' of a brand (how far a company can stretch its diversity of offerings before customers reject the products), leadership at the Ritz-Carlton is more focused on how brand extensions can strengthen one another": Alycia de Mesa, "How Far Can a Brand Stretch?" brandchannel.com, February 23, 2004.

214 "There is much to recommend Ritz-Carlton as the No. 1 company on this year's *Training* Top 125 list: the fact that it invests a whopping

10 percent of payroll on employee training; longstanding excellence in areas such as leadership development and employee orientation; customer-oriented diversity training that extends even to interaction with service animals such as seeing-eye dogs; management and training philosophies that account for an annual voluntary turnover rate of 18 percent in an industry where 100 percent rates are the norm. But what really made *Training* say, 'Wow' was the way the company went about shifting its perception of its very hallmark: elegant service'": Jack Gordon, "Ritz-Carlton: Redefining Elegance (No. 1 of the Training Top 125)," Manage Smarter, the online home of *Training*, www.trainingmag.com, March 1, 2007.

Chapter 11. Sustainability and Stewardship

229 "'CSR reflects a concern for . . . profits, people and place. By no means is profitability of the corporation set aside but rather supplemented by additional considerations that go beyond financial success. Furthermore, while socially responsible action may initially reduce profits, many corporations are finding that it may also create new opportunities for adding to profits and/or reduce a greater threat of operating losses due to legal/regulatory actions or loss of favor in the marketplace'": Dr. Deborah Talbot, "From Shareholders to Stakeholders: The Corporate Board's Newest Challenge," *Boardroom Briefing*, a publication of *Directors & Boards* magazine, Winter 2006.

231 "'It is interesting to see how corporate citizenship is becoming a different and powerful new driver for winning the talent war. . . . The millennial generation, by many reports, is looking for workplaces that will ensure continuity between their values and their careers. This generation, socialized in community service and possessing a passionate commitment to cultural environments, expects a company to walk its talk. It also expects the company to provide opportunities for employees to act on their values—resulting in the emergence of employee engagement as a strategic issue'": Dr. Bradley Goggins, "Corporate Citizenship and the War for Talent," Center for Corporate Citizenship at Boston University, Web site www.bcccc.net, October 2007.

232 "Researchers Sergio Pivato, Nicola Misani, and Antonio Tencati, for example, have demonstrated that corporate social performance influences consumer trust": Sergio Pivato, Nicola Misani, and Antonio Tencati, "The impact of corporate social responsibility on consumer trust: the case of organic food," *Business Ethics: A European Review*, www.blackwell-synergy.com, vol. 17, issue no. 1, January 2008.

Notes

236 "Since these programs . . . a 2007 survey conducted by the professional staffing company Hudson, shows that 'less than half of companies have a formal corporate [social] responsibility program": Hudson, "Employees Value Corporate Social Responsibility, Just Not for Making Job Decisions,'" *Critical Thinking* Web site, www.hudson.com, Hudson CSR Workplace Survey conducted August 4–5, 2007.

241–242 "'The benefit that volunteering provides has traditionally been thought of as the good works given by the individual to the nonprofit organization and the community. While this is and should remain the main reason for volunteering, there is another reward that is created—namely, that return value that the individual receives from the process. Return value has not been discussed a great deal but most individuals who volunteer understand that they receive value in return for their volunteering, including the "great feeling" that is received from helping others'": Walter P. Pidgeon, *The Universal Benefits of Volunteering: A Practical Workbook for Nonprofit Organizations, Volunteers, and Corporations* (Wiley, Hoboken, N.J., 1998).

Sources

Much of the content of this book emerged from interviews with Ritz-Carlton corporate and hotel senior leaders, as well as owners and corporate visionaries, including

Allan Federer, general manager of The Ritz-Carlton, Millenia Singapore

Bhavana Boggs, vice president and senior counsel

Bob Kharazmi, senior vice president of international operations

Bob Phillips, senior vice president of business development, The Ritz-Carlton Clubs

Brian Gullbrants, vice president of operations

Bruce Himelstein, senior vice president of sales and marketing

Debi Howard, manager of corporate guest relations

Derek Flint, general manager of The Ritz-Carlton, Beijing, Financial Street

Dermod Dwyer, executive chairman of Treasury Holdings

Diana Oreck, vice president of global learning and the Leadership Center

Ed Mady, vice president and area general manager of The Ritz-Carlton, San Francisco

Ed Staros, vice president and managing director of The Ritz-Carlton Resorts of Naples

Erwin Schinnerl, general manager of The Ritz-Carlton, Boston Common

Francisca Martinez, vice president of talent management

Hermann Elger, general manager of The Ritz-Carlton, Cancún

Hervé Humler, president of international operations

Sources

Horst Schulze, past president and cofounder of Ritz-Carlton and founder of The West Paces Hotel Group, LLC

Jean Cohen, vice president and general manager of The Ritz-Carlton, Grand Cayman

John Cottrill, senior vice president of The Ritz-Carlton Clubs and Residences

John Timmerman, vice president of quality and program management

Julia Gajcak, vice president of communications and marketing

Karim Alibhai, founder and manager of the Gencom Group

Katerina Panayiotou, manager of internal communication

Kathy Smith, senior vice president of human resources

Ken Rehmann, executive vice president of operations

Kevin Walsh, senior director of customer relationship management

Laurie Wooden, vice president of new business development and corporate strategy

Mandy Holloway, senior director of global learning

Mark DeCocinis, regional vice president of Asia Pacific

Mark Ferland, general manager of The Ritz-Carlton, Orlando, Grande Lakes

Michael King, general manager of The Ritz-Carlton, Denver

Myra deGersdorff, general manager of The Ritz-Carlton, New Orleans

Paul Westbrook, senior vice president of product and brand management

Peter Mainguy, general manager of The Ritz-Carlton, Dubai

Ricco de Blank, general manager of The Ritz-Carlton, Tokyo

Roberto Van Geenen, general manager of The Ritz-Carlton, Dallas

Simon F. Cooper, president and chief operating officer

Sue Stephenson, vice president of Community Footprints

Susan Strayer, director of talent management

Tom Donovan, general manager of The Ritz-Carlton, Kapalua

Tony Mira, general manager of The Ritz-Carlton, Dearborn

Victor Clavell, vice president and area general manager of Hotel Arts, Barcelona,

Vivian Deuschl, vice president of public relations

Additionally, the following individuals from all levels of the organization made themselves available to provide information necessary to make *The New Gold Standard* possible:

Abbey Millett, Adam Hassan, Ajith De Silva, Alexandra Valentin, Andrea Aichinger, Andy Sun, Antje Geister, Apple Wang, Audrey Strong, Aziz Yasin, Becky Gill, Beth Ridenour, Betty Lewis, Bjoern

Sources

Hartmann, Bob McDonald, Bonnie Crail, Brian Doyle, Char Schroeder, Charles J. Gilbert, Cheng Chi Keung, Cherie Y. Webb, Christoph Moje, Cleria Ferreira, Daniel Mangione, Darin Duvernay, Dean Fearing, Donald Stamets, Elena Mullican, Elizabeth Rodriguez, Ellen Terry, Emily Vallejo, Emmie Lancaster, Emnet Andu, Esezi Kolagbodi, Evelyn Yo, Flavia Bonilla, Fred Boutouba, Gary Weaver, Harold Rodriguez, Ho Ching Yin Ada, Hope Nudelman, Jackie Peake, Javier A. Olivos, Jennifer Oberstein, John Meehan, Joselyn Hernandez, Julia Zhu, Julie Lytle, Kathleen Coady, Kathryn Medico, Kelly Tiernan, Kelly Wood, Kent Kruse, Kevin Baker, Kevin Richeson, Kevin Sbraga, Laura M. Downes, Laura Gutierrez, Laura Perez Diaz, Lauren McCloud, Lauren Mitchell, Loren Solomon, Layla Eid, Liza Kubic, Luis de Dios Marin, Marguerite Dowd, Maria Alvarez, Maria Castano, Maria-Luisa Dittrich, Maria Thompson, Mark D. Nadonza, Marlene Szczodrowski, Marsha Barns, Marty Premtaj, Maurice Pearson, Melissa Young, Micah Dean, Michael Clemons, Miguel Saldivia, Mildred Sjostrand, Molly Clark, Myra Folwell, Nicolas Dousson, Nina Romanelli, Paul A. Boguski, Paul Savarino, Philip Fingerle, Ralph Galloway, Raouf Drissi, Raveendran Thundil, Rebecca Dickow, Rich Felton, Ronald Thomas, Rose Huddleston, Rubén Paredes, Saad Khatib, Sandra Ryder, Sarah Santanella, Scott Doran, Steven Schaefer, Suzanne Holbrook, Tricia Chiang, Wan Kin Fung, William Gilbreath, William P. Perry, Jr., Yolanda Guzman,

Additional Resources

The Ritz-Carlton Hotel Company, L.L.C.
4445 Willard Avenue, Suite 800
Chevy Chase, MD 20815, United States
301-547-4700
Reservations: 800-241-3333
www.ritzcarlton.com

The Ritz-Carlton Leadership Center
301-547-4806
corporate.ritzcarlton.com/en/LeadershipCenter

The Ritz-Carlton Club
877-201-4290
407-770-5882
www.ritzcarltonclub.com

Sources

The Ritz-Carlton Residences
6649 Westwood Boulevard, Suite 500
Orlando, FL 32821
866-467-0110
www.ritzcarltonrealestate.com/residences/default.jsp

The Michelli Experience
300 Garden of the Gods, No. 203
Colorado Springs, CO
888-711-4900
www.themichelliexperience.com

The New Gold Standard Web site
www.yournewgoldstandard.com

Gallup
901 F Street, NW
Washington, DC 20004
877-242-5587
or
202-715-3030
www.gallup.com

Talent Plus
One Talent Plus Way
Lincoln, Nebraska 68506-5987
800-VARSITY
402-489-2000
www.talentplus.com

Team One
1960 East Grand Avenue
El Segundo, CA 90245
310-615-2000
www.teamone-usa.com

Index

Index

Index

Index

Index

Index

Index

Index

About the Author

Dr. Joseph Michelli is an organizational consultant and the chief experience officer of *The Michelli Experience*. He has dedicated his career to studying successful businesses, both large and small. Prior to *The New Gold Standard*, Dr. Michelli authored the *Wall Street Journal, Business Week,* and *USA Today* best seller *The Starbucks Experience: 5 Principles for Turning Ordinary into Extraordinary*. Additionally, he coauthored *When Fish Fly: Lessons for Creating a Vital and Energized Workplace* with John Yokoyama, the owner of the World Famous Pike Place Fish Market in Seattle.

Dr. Michelli transfers his knowledge of exceptional business practices through his keynote speeches and workshops. These informative and entertaining presentations, which are provided by Dr. Michelli and his associates, focus on the skills necessary to

- Create meaningful customer experiences

- Drive employee and customer engagement

- Enhance a commitment to service excellence

- Create quality improvement processes

- Increase employee morale

In addition to dynamic keynote presentations offered globally, *The Michelli Experience* offers

- Consultation on the development of optimal customer and employee experiences

- Service excellence training

- Enhancement of staff empowerment

- Leadership team development services

- Group facilitation and team-building strategies

- Creation of customer and employee engagement measurement processes

- Customized management and frontline training programs

Dr. Michelli is eager to help you bring *The New Gold Standard* fully to life in your business. He can be reached through contact information on his Web site, www.themichelliexperience. com, or by calling either (719) 473-2414 or (888) 711-4900 (toll free within the United States).

Visit yournewgoldstandard.com for interviews with the president, founders, and corporate executives from The Ritz-Carlton Hotel Company; resources; podcasts; and an interactive blog.